The Controversy

Books in the Critical Concern series:

The Controversy

Roots of the Creation-Evolution Conflict

DONALD E. CHITTICK

MULTNOMAH PRESS
PORTLAND, OREGON 97266

Unless otherwise indicated, Scripture quotations are from the Holy Bible: New International Version, © 1978 by the International Bible Society. Used by permission of Zondervan Bible Publishers.

Scripture quotations marked Phillips are from The New Testament in Modern English, Revised Edition, © 1958, 1960, 1972 by J. B. Phillips. Used by permission of Macmillan Publishing Company.

Scripture quotations marked NKJV are from The Holy Bible, New King James Version, © 1982 by Thomas Nelson, Inc.

Cover design and illustration by Britt Taylor Collins

THE CONTROVERSY
© 1984 by Donald E. Chittick
Published by Multnomah Press
Portland, Oregon 97266

Printed in the United States of America

Library of Congress Cataloging in Publication Data

Chittick, Donald E.
   The controversy : roots of the creation-evolution conflict.

   Bibliography: p. 271
   Includes index.
   1. Creation.   2. Evolution.   3. Bible and science.
I. Title
BS651.C46   1984   231.7'65   84-22670
ISBN 0-88070-178-1 (pbk.)

87 88 89 90 91 92 93 – 10 9 8 7 6 5 4 3 2

To my wife Donna, for her encouragement, patience, and aid
To our daughter Annie for her prayers and support
To our son Peter now home with our Lord
To all my other family and friends who have encouraged
and helped in innumerable ways.

Contents

Acknowledgments

The author wishes to express special appreciation to all those who have encouraged and helped him in completing this work:

For typing . . . my wife Donna, Mrs. Paula Abbott, Mrs. Toni Sunseri
For loaning a word processor . . . Phil Friesen
For first reading entire manuscript . . . Mrs. Dorothy Wood, Bob Bauer, Jack Smith

Multnomah Press . . . Encouraging me to undertake the project.

Introduction

As a topic, creation-evolution is interesting in its own right. But there are additional reasons why a modern Christian must be informed in this area. We Christians live in a culture that does not share our convictions. In order to effectively reach people with the gospel, it is essential to have some knowledge of the Bible and science and associated issues. From many years of public lecturing on creation and evolution to a variety of audiences as well as in the classroom and from personal interchange, I have observed that people are often uninformed and perplexed about the creation-evolution issue. When presenting and sharing biblical truths, Christians are often asked about Bible and science topics. Scripture instructs us to be prepared with answers.

We are engaged in spiritual warfare. There is a battle for the minds and souls of men and women. We dare not yield territory to the enemy by being unprepared. For this reason, it is important to have at least a basic knowledge of Bible and science issues. I am not alone in this conviction.

> For if we are to reach men and women with the gospel, we must do so in the context of their real-life experience. Among other things, this means that we must take account of our present scientific culture if we are effectively to evangelize.[1]

It needs to be emphasized too that one does not need to be a scientist to have some effective answers. It is true in many cases that research into basic scientific questions and searching out answers is best done by Christians who are scientists. Once those answers have been provided, however, they are then available for use from books and other printed materials, audio tapes, visual aids, and other media. The nonscientist can certainly be aware of some of these resource materials and of the basic issues covered by them.

One's view of origins has important implications. It explains who man is, his place in the universe, and his relationship to it. It also affects the very meaning of life itself. And for the Christian, the creation and evolution question has far-reaching consequences for biblical interpretation.

Many Christians, while realizing that creation is an important doctrine, may still not know just why it is important or be aware of its many ramifications. This is especially true for many Christian young people. From their study of the Bible, they learn that creation is an important doctrine. However, especially in public schools, they often encounter a philosophy antagonistic to creation. This conflict causes confusion and distress particularly when they do not get the help they need from the Christian community. I hope this book will eliminate some of this confusion by showing why the issue is important and by demonstrating how the roots of the creation-evolution issue arise from a conflict of world views. Some areas in which the conflict is most intense will be discussed. Also examples will be given to illustrate how scientific data interpreted within a creation framework provide satisfying answers. However, a detailed treatment of creation science is not my purpose here. Such treatments can be found in other sources. The emphasis here will be on the roots and nature of the creation-evolution conflict.

We will approach our study from two perspectives. The first part of the book will discuss the creation-evolution issue itself. We will discover that at its root, the issue is one of philosophy and not of science. The second part discusses some specific scientific data relating to creation and evolution. Our purpose there is not to provide an exhaustive or detailed explanation of data from a creation point of view, but simply to demonstrate how data can be interpreted from that viewpoint.

Finally, suggestions will also be given for defending oneself against the world-philosophical system and for presenting scriptural truths in a loving way. Some comments will be directed especially toward those involved in public education.

Introduction, Notes

1. Prof. E. H. Andrews, *God, Science & Evolution* (Welwyn, Hertfordshire, England: Evangelical Press, 1980), 29.

Chapter 1

Roots of Modern Science

*H*istorically, most of the highly productive early modern scientists (e.g., Boyle, Newton, Pascal, Faraday, Pasteur) believed in creation. This was still true of most scientists even as recently as 150 years ago. In our day, however, this is no longer the case. A majority of present-day scientists believe in evolution. What caused the change? Why was there a move from belief in creation to belief in evolution?

It is surprising how many people think that scientific discoveries caused the shift in belief. This is not the case. A close examination of history and the creation-evolution issue reveals this shift in belief was associated with a change in world view rather than new scientific discoveries. A brief historical review will help us clarify this point.

The Basis of Modern Science

The rise of modern science began only a few hundred years ago. Numerous historians and scholars have noted the fact that this rise was associated with Christianity.[1] Historian Robert G. Frank, Jr., for example, recognizes this association in his review of a book on the subject:

> [G]enerations of historians of science have been in-
> trigued by the possibility of a relation between two
> pivotal sets of events in the history of early modern
> Europe: the transformations that go under the names
> of the "Protestant Reformation" and the "Scientific
> Revolution." . . .
>
>   . . . Was the one's succeeding the other merely a
> chronological accident? Or was there a causal re-
> lationship between the two? . . . [the author's] gen-
> eral argument: the predominant forms of scientific
> activity during England's Puritan decades can be
> shown to be a direct outgrowth of a Puritan ideology.
> The argument is a stunningly convincing one.[2]

Why did modern science start from a culture with a Christian base? The reasons are not difficult to determine. A proper
philosophical base for investigating the universe was needed
and the Christian doctrine of creation provided that base. The
Creator established laws for people and laws for the natural
world. A created universe was expected to have design, order,
and purpose. Man, using his created rational mind, could study
this ordered universe in a rational way and seek to discover its
laws; and modern science is based on the assumption of scientific law. In addition, moral laws given by the Creator established the ethical base for science. Scientists must be honest and
truthful.

By contrast, if the universe were not created, it must have
come to its present state by the impersonal interaction of the material of the universe itself. No intelligence would have been involved. With such a philosophy, there would be no reason to expect such a universe to operate in a rational way. Man's mind
would also be a product of the same chance universe. It should
not be capable of rationally studying anything. Hence, a
materialist philosophy of this sort would tend to discourage one
from becoming a scientist.

In his book *Escape From Reason*, Francis Schaeffer notes
the view of the well-known scientist J. Robert Oppenheimer to
emphasize this point:

What we have to realize is that early modern science was started by those who lived in the consensus and setting of Christianity. A man like J. Robert Oppenheimer, for example, who was not a Christian, nevertheless understood this. He has said that Christianity was needed to give birth to modern science. ["On Science and Culture", *Encounter,* October 1962] Christianity was necessary for the beginning of modern science for the simple reason that Christianity created a climate of thought which put men in a position to investigate the form of the universe. . . .

The early scientists also shared the outlook of Christianity in believing that there is a reasonable God, who has created a reasonable universe, and thus man, by use of his reason, could find out the universe's form.[3]

Thus Christianity, with its doctrine of creation, provided a firm philosophical foundation for scientifically investigating the universe. This explains why so many of the early scientists were Christians. It also explains why science did not develop in the Eastern countries with their materialist philosophies and pantheistic religions. They simply did not have the proper philosophical base. In fact, modern science would probably not have arisen at all had it not been for the Christian base.

Creation is the foundation on which modern science began. As creationists, the early scientists could approach their study of nature with enthusiasm. They could expect positive results from their study of science because they believed the natural world to be one of law and order, and they believed that using their rational minds they could search for that order and find those laws. Not only did the early scientists expect to find the laws of nature, they ran up a very impressive record of discovering those laws. It is instructive and exciting to study the biographies and the accomplishments of some of the early modern scientists.[4]

Names of productive early scientists easily come to mind. We can think of Johannes Kepler (1571-1630) astronomy, Blaise Pascal (1623-1662) barometer, Robert Boyle (1627-1691) gas laws, Michael Faraday (1791-1867) electric generator, and Louis Pasteur (1822-1895) vaccination and immunization. These scientists are among those whose discoveries are still recognized as major attainments in science. They also upheld and respected the Scriptures. Some skeptics might argue that there is not necessarily a cause and effect relationship between the cultural acceptance of creation and the rise of modern science. They would argue that it may only be coincidence. The undeniable fact remains, however, that science only originated in a culture that had accepted the Christian doctrine of creation.

Even more convincing is the fact that these early scientists themselves stated in their writings that their enthusiasm for science was a direct result of their belief in creation. They were motivated by the belief that the universe, the world, and life came into being by direct acts of the Creator and that by studying and learning about the universe, they could reflect glory back to the Creator and be productive as scientists. Early modern scientists believed that the universe had a supernatural origin, rather than a naturalistic one.

The Shift toward Naturalism

In our day, however, the situation is quite different from that of the early days of science. Now most scientists (but by no means all) believe in some form of evolution. They no longer believe that life arose by direct supernatural acts of a Creator. Now naturalistic philosophy reigns. What were the causes of this change?

As we already noted, it was not the discovery of new scientific information. "If we ask why scientists rejected creationism in the 19th century in favor of evolution, then *part* of the answer must be that they rejected super-natural explanations of phenomena that appeared to be susceptible to naturalistic explanations, and to that extent adoption of evolutionary theory accompanied a decline in the strength of religious belief.[5]

The change came about as a result of a shift in the philosophy used by scientists, a shift toward antisupernaturalism. The idea of direct acts of creation was rejected in favor of an explanation of origins from a naturalistic point of view using only the laws of chemistry and physics. Nothing supernatural was involved in the new explanation. This trend was also accompanied by a general decline in "religious" faith.

Charles Darwin and Religion

Charles Darwin himself experienced such a religious decline.

> There are some who think that Darwin accepted the theory of evolution only after many, many years of studying the subject. This, however, is not the case. As his religious faith ebbed his faith in evolution developed. It came in to fill up the void that was being left by his rejection of creation.[6]

It wasn't that evolution was such an attractive theory, one that provided a better interpretation of scientific fact. *Rather it was all that was left to fill the void created by his rejection of the alternative of special creation.*

Darwin's move away from creation was not just a passive rejection of one philosophy and acceptance of a new one. Instead, he actively tried to fight the creation view and those who held it. This fact has been observed by those who have studied his work. Dov Ospovat, in his review of the book *Charles Darwin and the Problem of Creation*, notes that the author "shows that theological considerations played a major role in the biological science of Darwin's day, including Darwin's, and from this he argues that the reason there is so much theology in the *Origin* is that theological issues were still live ones for Darwin and, more important, that special creation was a 'living and powerful idea' among his professional colleagues, one that required him to attack it with whatever weapons would be effective, including ridicule."[7]

Although Darwin's name is associated with the

popularization of evolution, he was not the first one nor the only one of his time to reject supernatural creation. A general move away from supernatural creation had begun many years earlier in the culture at large, with theologians and philosophers leading the way. Some leading theologians were more ready to accept evolution than were scientists. Scientists themselves were somewhat slow to accept evolution since scientific facts did not seem to support it (as even Darwin himself noted). Evidence from the fossil record was particularly lacking, a fact which bothered Darwin greatly. He was also troubled by the abundant evidence of design in nature, the eye being a prime example.

The facts of science were not what led to a rejection of creation and acceptance of evolution. Rather, what led to that rejection was a change in philosophy or theology; it was a change from one world view to an opposing one. Those who have studied the Darwinian Revolution, such as well-known scientist and evolutionist Ernst Mayr, have noted and emphasized this point: "A scientific revolution is supposedly characterized by the replacement of an old explanatory model by an incompatible new one. In the case of the theory of evolution, the concept of an instantaneously created world was replaced by that of a slowly evolving world, with man being part of the evolutionary stream."[8] Although I do not agree with all his points, Mayr has summarized well the nature of the Darwinian Revolution—a revolution rooted in a philosophical shift that has continued right up to the present day.

Many people in our day, however, are unaware that evolution was adopted for philosophical rather than scientific reasons. Darwinism was readily accepted because a shift had taken place in people's thinking. There was a desire for a naturalistic explanation for origins that would avoid supernatural creation—and Darwinism filled the bill. Evolution is a belief system, and the philosophical climate was right for its acceptance. Creation implies responsibility to a creator, a responsibility people wished to avoid.

When they first learn of the philosophical bias behind the shift to Darwinism, Christians, particularly younger Christians who have had university training, display an interesting reaction. Their university training almost always pressures them into accepting evolution. Even after hearing me lecture on creation and evolution for several class sessions in which scientific evidence is provided in support of creation, they have a difficult time believing that evolution is not a scientifically proven fact. When I point out to them that science gathers facts and then interprets those facts by means of a theory based on assumptions, and that human factors such as philosophical bias are involved as well, they still often believe that evolution is the only reasonable choice. They do not understand that the clash between evolution and creation is between one belief system and another. They have been propagandized into thinking evolution is a scientific fact.

When this is pointed out to them, they still wonder, "Granted that evolution replaced creation, but didn't it happen because of scientific discoveries? Didn't the facts of science force people to accept evolution? Hasn't evolution been proven scientifically? And anyway, what's all the fuss about? You can believe in evolution and still be religious." The continual presentation of evolution as fact has taken its toll on their thinking.

The students' questions quoted above are common, not only among scientific laymen but even among scientists. In order to find and appreciate answers to them, we will need to take a closer look first at thought systems and how they are used, and then at some scientific evidence.

22   **Roots of Modern Science**

Chapter 1, Notes

1. R. Hooykaas, *Religion And The Rise Of Modern Science* (Grand Rapids, Wm. B. Eerdmans Publishing Co., 1972).

2. Robert G. Frank, Jr., review of *The Great Instauration* by Charles Webster, *Science*, 28 January 1977, 385-86.

3. Francis A. Schaeffer, *Escape From Reason* (Downers Grove, Ill.: Inter-Varsity Press, 1968), 30-31.

4. August J. Kling, "Scientists Who Believed," *Good News Broadcaster*, January 1981, 11-13; Henry M. Morris, "Bible-Believing Scientists of the Past," *Impact* #103, January 1982, i-iv.

5. Stephen G. Brush, "Creationism/Evolution: The Case AGAINST 'Equal Time,'" *The Science Teacher*, April 1981, 33.

6. Robert Clark and James D. Bales, *Why Scientists Accept Evolution* (Grand Rapids: Baker Book House, 1966), 35.

7. Dov Ospovat, review of *Charles Darwin and the Problem of Creation* by Neal C. Gillespie, *Science*, 1 February 1980, 520.

8. Ernst Mayr, "The Nature of the Darwinian Revolution," *Science*, 2 June 1972, 987.

Chapter 2

Fact, Faith, and Logic: An Organized Approach

While trying to fit together the numerous individual facts relating to creation and evolution, scientists and others use an overall plan to help organize the thinking process. There certainly are many bits and pieces of data, many facts to deal with. The situation could be compared to a jigsaw puzzle with a large number of pieces, each piece representing a scientific fact. Putting an actual jigsaw puzzle of a thousand or more pieces together could be a very difficult task. However, most would try to simplify the process somewhat by using an organized approach. One might pick all the pieces of the same color and place them in one area; another person might assemble all the border pieces first. This systematic approach makes fitting the individual pieces into an overall pattern a much simpler task than just randomly picking pieces which might happen to fit together.

Christians would do well to know and understand that scientists, like others, use such overall thought plans to help put the pieces of the puzzle together. God made our minds to work in organized ways or thought patterns. Every day innumerable facts crowd in upon us. We would be overwhelmed if we had no systematic way of handling this vast amount of information.

23

The pattern our mind uses is known as a thought system. The following diagram explains how a thought system works.

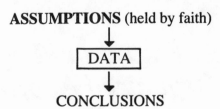

A thought system consists of assumptions, data, and conclusions. Logical thought is the means by which we draw conclusions from the facts after starting with certain assumptions.

Since no one knows it all, his assumptions are held by faith. This is as true for the study of science as for any other discipline. Nonscientists often do not realize scientists use faith. As a result, there are many misconceptions about conclusions scientists draw from scientific data. All scientific explanations are based on faith because faith is the grounds on which the original assumptions are held.

Assumptions in Science

An eminent scientist, the late Dr. Vannevar Bush, recognized that people hold many mistaken ideas about the thought systems scientists use. In an effort to correct some of these, he wrote an article to try to eliminate "the misconception that scientists can establish a complete set of facts and relations about the universe, all neatly proved, and that on this firm basis men can securely establish their personal philosophy, their personal religion, free from doubt or error. . . . Science never proves anything, in an absolute sense. It works by process of induction, and of deduction. . . . Deduction uses the rules of logic to proceed from a set of assumptions to their consequences."[1] Others have emphasized this point.[2]

Different Assumptions, Different Conclusions

Scientists, then, like others, use thought systems in order to organize and make sense of data. Beginning with their assumptions and using logic, they draw conclusions from the data. And their assumptions are held by faith. This means that even using the same data, different assumptions will lead to different conclusions. The following diagram will help to illustrate this point.

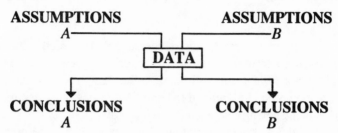

ASSUMPTIONS
A

ASSUMPTIONS
B

DATA

CONCLUSIONS
A

CONCLUSIONS
B

If we start with assumption A and look at the data (and make no mistakes in our thinking), we will end with a corresponding set of conclusions (A). Someone else, starting with different assumptions B and looking at the same data, will draw a correspondingly different set of conclusions (B). In general, conclusions A drawn from the data will be as different from conclusions B drawn from the *same data* as are the initial assumptions A and B.

There are many illustrations of this, even in everyday life. People can see the same data, hear the same words, and still draw very different conclusions. The story is told, for example, of a discussion between a Texas rancher and a farmer from another state. The Texan owned an extremely large ranch, while the farmer had only a modest farm. The Texan was bragging about the size of his state, and how everything there was done on a grand scale. He was especially boasting about how very large his ranch was. He said to the farmer, "You know, I got up this morning at sunrise and started driving across my ranch and by noon I was only halfway across my land." Nodding sympathetically, the farmer replied, "Once I had a *car* like that, too." Both were using the same data (the rancher's words) but drew entirely different conclusions.

Different assumptions lead to different conclusions from the same facts. It is an error to think that everyone starts with the same set of assumptions. Of course it is possible, using the same assumptions, to draw different conclusions from the same data if we make an error in logic. But if our logic is correct and our conclusions are still different, our starting assumptions must also be different.

Wind and Leaves

In helping college science students grasp the fact that even in science assumptions are used for interpreting data, I would often play a little game with them. While emphasizing that it was just a game, I pretended to be serious. I began by asking, "What is the scientific reason that wind blows?"

"Well," a student would usually respond, "at some point on earth the weather pattern is such that the air pressure there is low. Somewhere else on earth, by contrast, the air pressure is high. Air tends to move from the place of high pressure toward the spot of low pressure. This movement of air is called wind. Therefore, the wind blows because there are places of high and low air pressure causing the air to move."

I would then ask, "How many of you believe that high and low air pressure is the correct explanation for wind? If you believe this explanation, please raise your hand." Usually everyone raised his hand. They were recording their belief about what made the wind blow. They had committed themselves and were personally involved with the game at this point.

After seeing their response, I would reply with mock surprise in my voice, "You believe that the wind blows because of high and low air pressure? That's wrong! Do you know what makes the wind blow? It's the leaves wiggling on the trees." The class would respond with a look that said, "Surely you don't expect us to believe that!" I would then say, "I can tell by your reaction that you don't believe me. You don't believe that leaves wiggling on trees make the wind blow, but you are wrong. I have facts to back up my side. Have you ever seen the wind blow without leaves wiggling on the trees?" That statement caught them by surprise. I was using facts to back up my position, and they were unaccustomed to the idea that the same data could be interpreted with different assumptions.

At this point, I would invite them to prove me wrong. It was my hope that they would fall into the trap of citing a few more facts, thinking they could force me into a different belief system. The trap was nearly always successful.

Usually, some bold student would say, "In the winter there aren't any leaves on the trees, and the wind still blows." He thought he had trapped me with this fact. He, along with the rest of the class, thought I would not be able to respond and would have to change my belief system.

To their surprise I would respond, "That's exactly right. In winter there aren't any leaves on the trees and the wind still blows. I accept that fact. *But* when it's winter here, somewhere else on earth it's summer and trees there have leaves on them. Thus, where the wind got started, there were trees with leaves wiggling." I pressed my point further. "You people only believe this *old* idea about high and low air pressure causing wind because you don't know *modern* science. Did you know that our most recent investigations in science prove that I'm right? When our astronauts landed on the moon, they found no wind there. Do you know why?"

The students responded in chorus, "There are no trees on the moon."

Students get a chuckle out of this little game, but it illustrates that the same scientific data can be interpreted with different assumptions. On a more serious level, in the case of creation and evolution, the same situation applies. The same scientific data are available to those who believe in creation and those who believe in evolution. However, different assumptions are used for interpreting the data. What are these assumptions and how are they used?

Two Basic Assumptions

In considering the question of origins, there are two options which, in my view at least, encompass the whole range of possibilities open to thinking man. Those two great assumptions are: (1) a Creator acted; (2) a Creator did not act. Acts of a

Creator are supernatural acts or divine fiats, and so this view is sometimes known as fiat creation or special creation. In the second view, with its presupposition that a Creator did not act, nothing supernatural was involved for either the origin of the universe or the origin of life. No divine fiats took place. No intelligence was involved. Only natural processes occurred, describable entirely using only principles of chemistry and physics.

(Some may wonder if there isn't a third option—theistic evolution. Theistic evolution covers a broad range of ideas. Generally it takes the position that evolution happened but postulates that a Creator or intelligence was somehow involved at a particular *point* in the process or at *points* during the process. Theistic evolution is not an acceptable alternative in my mind and I will discuss this point later.)

Dr. Robert Jastrow, well-known geologist, astronomer, and physicist, claims to be an agnostic with views similar to those of Darwin.[3] His analysis of the question of the origin of life is instructive:

> Perhaps the appearance of life on the Earth is a miracle. Scientists are reluctant to accept that view, but their choices are limited. *Either* life was created on the Earth by the will of a being outside the grasp of scientific understanding, *or* it evolved on our planet spontaneously, through chemical reactions occurring in nonliving matter lying on the surface of the planet.
>
> The first theory places the question of the origin of life beyond the reach of scientific inquiry. It is a statement of faith in the power of a Supreme Being not subject to the laws of science.
>
> The second theory is also an act of faith. The act of faith consists in assuming that the scientific view of the origin of life is correct, without having concrete evidence to support that belief. [emphases his][4]

There are two points to be noted from what Dr. Jastrow is saying. First, one has only two options for assumptions about origins: (1) a Creator acted, or (2) a Creator did not act. Jastrow is not the only evolutionary scientist who feels this way.[5]

One should also note that since Dr. Jastrow does not accept the creation view, he also defines evolution as "the scientific view." However evolution is not *the* scientific view. To a scientist who believes in creation, creation is "the scientific view." Thus even the definition of what is the scientific view is determined by one's bias about origins.

The second point to be noted from what Jastrow says is that whichever view or assumption system one chooses, he does so by faith. A scientist, whether he is a creationist or an evolutionist, must use faith. He has faith in his beginning assumption. Beginning with faith does not make one's position weak. All human beings are subject to that same limitation: since they do not know everything, they must use faith in their assumptions. Thus all scientific explanations involve faith in the assumptions on which the explanations are based. Regarding creation and evolution, the assumptions and thought system one uses are a matter of personal choice.

An Old Conflict

The conflict between natural and supernatural views (or evolution and creation) is not new, however. It did not begin with Charles Darwin. The conflict was discussed by early thinkers even before the time of Christ.[6] The earthly life of Jesus also provides many illustrations. People used the same two approaches in his day. Jesus did many remarkable acts during his life and ministry. These acts were witnessed by many, many people, and there was much discussion about the things that he said and did, because they were so out of the ordinary. It is interesting, however, to note the response of the observers. In John 7:12, for example, we read, "Among the crowds there was widespread whispering about him. Some said, 'He is a good man.' Others replied, 'No, he deceives the people.'" Some observed Christ's miracles with the assumption that God was acting, and that something supernatural was involved. Therefore, they concluded that these acts were miracles.

Others, seeing the same factual information, watching the same acts, also agreed that something was happening. But since they held an antisupernatural set of assumptions or bias, they had to conclude that it was deception. In plain language, what Jesus was doing was a bunch of neat tricks. They could observe, for example, water being turned into wine. They saw that the wine came from water pots used for washing, and they tasted the wine. But they interpreted it not as an act of God but as a trick.

They might also watch Jesus walking on the water. Some would conclude that it was a miracle; others, that it was another trick, a pretty convincing trick, perhaps, but nevertheless a trick. They might wonder how he was able to make it appear that he was walking on water, but they would try to seek some kind of natural explanation, since they assumed nothing supernatural was involved. To them it was not a miracle; it was deception.

Another interesting example is recorded for us in John 12:28-29. "'Father, glorify your name!' Then a voice came from heaven, 'I have glorified it, and will glorify it again.' The crowd that was there and heard it said it had thundered; others said an angel had spoken to him." In this instance a specific event is listed. After Jesus prayed, sound was heard from the heavens. Those who made the assumption that a Creator can act perceived a communication in the form of words. On the other hand, those who made the assumption that nothing supernatural was involved concluded that the noise was thunder. They drew a naturalistic conclusion and tried to find a naturalistic explanation for the noise. (Although they might explain the noise as thunder, I have often wondered what explanation they would give for thunder sounding like words.) The two groups of people had the same facts available to them. They agreed that something happened—a noise came from the heavens. Their conclusions about it, however, were quite different and depended on the assumptions they held.

There are many other illustrations which could be given. My point, however, is that the conflict between natural and supernatural is an old one. It continues to our present day.

Recognizing the Philosophical Roots

Different words and phrases may be used for describing these two thought systems. But they still refer to the two great assumptions or presuppositions used. Each of the two fundamental assumptions forms the basis of a total world view. All of life and reality is interpreted within one or the other assumption system. The following table will be helpful in summarizing the contrast between these two world views.

THOUGHT SYSTEMS

Creator Acted		Creator Didn't Act
Supernatural origins	vs.	Naturalistic origins
Design	vs.	Chance
Miracle	vs.	Properties of matter (chemistry and physics)
Event	vs.	Natural process
Creation	vs.	Evolution

Creation and evolution are conflicting philosophies. They each constitute a belief system about the past. For a long while, this point did not receive much emphasis in discussions of creation and evolution. Lack of widespread recognition that at its roots the debate between creation and evolution is philosophical has no doubt contributed in large measure to the misunderstanding which has arisen over this issue. From time to time, a few very perceptive individuals have, however, pointed this out. Martin Luther, for example, recognized and emphatically discussed the point.[7]

In a discussion on the origin of life, the well-known scientist George Wald, an evolutionary biologist, makes an interesting observation about present day biologists.

> . . . many scientists a century ago chose to regard the belief in spontaneous generation as a "philosophical necessity." It is a symptom of the philosophical poverty of our time that this necessity

is no longer appreciated. Most modern biologists, having reviewed with satisfaction the downfall of the spontaneous generation hypothesis, yet unwilling to accept the alternative belief in special creation, are left with nothing.[8]

Much of the confusion over creation and evolution would be cleared away if the philosophical foundations behind the two views were more openly discussed. Fortunately the situation may be improving. Judging from recent scientific literature and letters to editors in scientific publications, there are indications that the philosophical roots of the creation-evolution controversy are being recognized. For example, after an article derogatory toward the creation position appeared as an editorial in a science magazine, a subsequent editorial made the following observation.

> The scientist enters into a study with certain preconceived notions and interprets the results of the study with the same preconceived notions. True objectivity simply does not exist in the scientific world. A creationist and an evolutionist can agree on the data, the physically observable phenomena (whether it be the distribution of radioisotopes in a given geological structure or the bone formations of a living animal or fossil). They will then proceed to interpret that data according to their own presuppositions ('God created this' or 'It all happened by accident'). Both employ the same data, but reach strikingly different conclusions.[9]

We must pray that recognition of the part played by presuppositions will become more widely recognized.

Logic Is Not Perfect

As we have noted, creation and evolution are both explanatory systems. They both begin with assumptions and try to explain the data from those assumptions. Deductive logic is used to draw conclusions and meaning from the data. But logic itself is not a perfect tool.

> Deduction uses the rules of logic to proceed from a set of assumptions to their consequences. But we have troubles here. Logic itself is by no means a perfect tool and, even if it were, it could do no more than transfer the question of the validity of a deduced relationship to the question of the validity of the premises on which it is based. And these premises are merely statements that are assumed to be valid for the purposes of the argument: simple statements, so simple that they cannot be expressed in terms of statements which are more simple.[10]

Conclusions logically drawn from factual data are no more valid than the assumptions on which they are based. Thus creation and evolution can be no more true than the supernatural or anti-supernatural assumptions on which they are based.

Stepping Out of the System

Logic is also not infallible. This became even more clear when in the 1930s Kurt Gödel showed that no closed system could be proved free of contradictions without stepping outside the system.[11] An absolute reference point is needed. The Gödel theorem is a very important development in logic, and it is too bad that this theorem and its ramifications are not more widely presented and appreciated. Gödel's theorem hit logic so hard that some tended to write it off as a linguistic trick. "In the 1930s, Kurt Gödel shook the world of mathematics by showing that there are statements in every logical system whose truth or falsehood simply cannot be determined by staying within the system."[12] The implications of Gödel's theorem were far-reaching and many did not like them. They thought the theorem did not apply to situations that really mattered. Further discoveries have shown, however, that it does apply to situations that matter.[13]

Mathematics is supposed to be the most logical of the sciences. If Gödel's theorem applies here, it would also apply elsewhere where logic is used. This is why his theorem is so important. It shows it is not possible to determine the truth or falsity of any logical system (as, for example, creation or evolution) without stepping outside that system. An absolute reference point is needed.

An Absolute Reference Point

Evolution is a philosophic system, and creation is a philosophic system. But how can we know which system is true? To answer this question, it is necessary to have an absolute reference point. If we had an absolute reference point, a premise or assumption which was known to be absolutely true, then we could use logic to reason from that point to check evolution or creation as a system.

This situation can be compared to an eighth grade math class. Two students may have worked through a fairly complex problem. Each of two students read the problem, carried out mathematical calculations, and arrived at an answer. Both students had the same data, the same problem. They also had the same training and the same skill in using mathematical logic. However, their answers were different. Each student thinks his answer is correct. How can they know which answer is right? It would not do to check with another student, because the other student is as limited as the first two. His answer might agree with one or the other of the first two students' answers, but that would not necessarily prove anything. Both may have made the same mistake. What they need is an absolute reference point, a point on which there could be no argument because that point would be known to be true. In our example, this might be the answer book. Each student could check his answer with the answer book and find out which was correct.

Of course, this illustration is only an analogy, and most often analogies fall short when compared to the real situation. But it can help us understand the problem in using logic. Human beings are finite beings. We do not have all knowledge and all wisdom. We cannot serve as an absolute reference point for truth. No one knows it all. Thus, anyone using human logic alone cannot be absolutely certain that his conclusions are true. He certainly should not try to force his views on others.

Finite man is not absolute. He cannot serve as the absolute reference point. He cannot say on his own that any logical system is completely true. The only way possible to know that a system is true is to place our faith in an absolute from outside the system. Jesus Christ came from outside the system and is the absolute reference point.

This is exactly what the Bible has already told us. Hebrews 11:6: "And without faith it is impossible to please God, because anyone who comes to him must believe that he exists and that he rewards those who earnestly seek him." This verse teaches two things. First, absolutes begin with God. Faith in God is the basis for all logical certainty. Second, God rewards those who genuinely seek Him. The search may be difficult and one may have to work very hard, but his search will be rewarded.

However, God does not force His truth on anyone. Man is free to rule God out and to begin his own autonomous logic system. He can invent his own autonomous assumptions and use logic to draw conclusions, but he cannot, by doing this, know that his conclusions are ultimately true. Ultimate truth—absolute truth—begins with God and His Word. Truth is what God says it is.

God is outside man's system. He is the absolute reference point. The Bible-believing Christian can have confidence not only that truth exists, but that he has an absolute reference point, one by which to truly know. This does not mean that a Christian will know exhaustively, but he can know truly. Our Lord gave us the definition of truth in His prayer recorded in John 17:17. "Sanctify them by the truth; your word is truth."

Chapter 2, Notes

1. Vannevar Bush, "Science Pauses," *Fortune,* May 1965, 116, 119, 167.

2. John Beckwith and Larry Miller, "Behind the Mask of Objective Science," *The Sciences* (November/December 1976), 16-17.

3. Robert Jastrow, "Evolution: Selection for Perfection," *Science Digest,* December 1981, 87.

4. Robert Jastrow, "God's Creation," *Science Digest,* Special Spring Issue, 1980, 68.

5. George Wald, "The Origin of Life," *Scientific American,* August 1954, 46.

6. Paul A. Bartz, *Luther and Evolution* (Minneapolis: Bible-Science Assn., 1977), 11-28.

7. Bartz, *Luther and Evolution.*

8. Wald, "Origin of Life," 46.

9. Donald F. Calbreath, "The Challenge of Creationism: Another Point of View," *American Laboratory,* November 1980, 10.

10. Bush, "Science Pauses," 167.

11. Ernest Nagel and James R. Newman, *Gödel's Proof* (New York: New York University Press, 1958).

12. Gina Kolata, "Does Gödel's Theorem Matter to Mathematics?" *Science,* 19 November 1982, 779.

13. Ibid. pp. 779-780. Ralph E. Ancil, "The Limits of Human Thought and the Creation Model" *Creation Research Society Quarterly* (June 1983): 30-39.

Chapter 3

Evidence and Experts

We consider now two basic parts to science. First, science *observes* the present universe, the material universe as it is *now*. For example, the observation might be simply recording the number and types of trees in a given area. In addition to using unaided senses, observations might also be made with the aid of instruments. A biologist, using a microscope, might examine the finely detailed cellular structure in a leaf, or an astronomer might use a telescope to observe the stars. It must be emphasized again that these observations are made on the universe as it exists in its present condition. Scientists cannot directly observe the past.

Second, science is more than just a collection of observations about the universe. In addition to collecting observational facts about the present universe, and perhaps cataloging those facts, scientists also attempt to fit those facts into some kind of pattern to make meaning out of them. When a scientist makes enough of a certain type of observation so that a pattern becomes apparent, a hypothesis is formulated. A hypothesis seeks to make meaning out of the observational facts or data. It is used for interpreting facts when relatively few observations are involved. With continued observations (if these new observations fit the same pattern) the hypothesis is elevated to the status of theory. Theory may be thought of as a more mature hypothesis. With still more observations fitting the same pattern, and when the number of observations has become quite large, theory is advanced to the status of scientific law.

There is a definite progression from hypothesis up through theory to law. A scientific law is a summary statement concerning a very large number of observations all fitting the same pattern.

Hence *a theory in science may cover a wide range of degrees of verification.* With very few observations for support it is barely out of the hypothesis stage. Theories which have been verified many, many times are elevated to the status of scientific law. We are reminded, for example, of the law of gravity. An object such as a ball which is released above the earth will fall toward the earth. This type of experiment has been repeated so many times with the same result that we have a law known as the law of gravity.

An example will aid in illustrating this point. Let us suppose that we have in front of us a black box about the size of a large brief case. Coming through one side of the box are two metal shafts, each with a wheel attached. As we face the box, we note that the wheel on the left has a small crank attached to it so that the wheel can be rotated easily by hand.

Although we cannot see inside the box because it is completely enclosed, we proceed to make a series of scientific observations. Initially we make only the following three observations. First, when we rotate the left-hand wheel with the crank, we note that the right-hand wheel also turns. Second, when we rotate the left-hand wheel more rapidly, we note that the right-hand wheel also rotates more rapidly. Third, when we stop rotating the left-hand wheel, we note that the right-hand wheel also stops rotating. Having made these three observations on the box, we ask ourselves, "Is there any pattern to these observations?" Note that we do not know the history of the box. We have no information regarding where the box came from or what it contains. All we have are three observations on the box as it exists in the present.

Let us further suppose that three "scientists" have also made these observations. Each scientist has a different background. The first scientist is Mike Mechanic, who works with machinery every day for a living. The second scientist is Clyde Clockmaker, who puts gears and springs and weights together to make grandfather clocks. The third scientist is Patricia Petstore Owner who has all kinds of animals and birds in her pet store.

These three scientists have all agreed on the scientific observations made on the black box. The question before them now is, Do the observations made thus far seem to fit any kind of pattern? Can any pattern be discerned from the data? There does indeed seem to be a pattern. It seems that whatever the left-hand wheel does, the right-hand wheel does also.

What can account for this pattern? How can we explain this behavior? This is where the second part of science, that of attempting to make meaning out of the data by interpreting it and forming a hypothesis, comes into play. Often in science, more than one hypothesis can be formed to explain the same data. To explain their data thus far, our three scientists want to form a hypothesis about the contents of the box. Hypothesis, we remember, begins with assumptions, then looks at the data, and finally uses logic to draw conclusions from the data.

Mr. Mechanic assumes that inside the box is a pulley on each of the shafts. He also assumes that the two pulleys are connected by means of a belt, much like that used on some electric sewing machines. With these assumptions and the data at hand, he concludes that whenever the left wheel is turned, the right one will turn also. If the left wheel is turned faster, the right wheel will turn faster. If the left wheel is stopped, the right wheel will also be stopped. With this hypothesis, he says that he can explain all of the data.

Mr. Clockmaker, however, suggests a different hypothesis. He thinks Mr. Mechanic is wrong. Mr. Clockmaker assumes that inside the box is a set of gears which connects one shaft to the other shaft. He concludes that whenever the left wheel is turned, the gears transfer the motion to the right wheel. He claims that he can explain all the data with his hypothesis.

Miss Petstore Owner thinks both men are wrong, and she has a different hypothesis. She assumes that the box contains a very ticklish pet squirrel, with its tail resting on the left-hand shaft inside the box. The front feet of the squirel rest on a small squirrel-cage-type wheel attached to the right-hand shaft. With these assumptions, she concludes that when the left-hand wheel is turned, the motion of the shaft tickles the tail of the squirrel and makes it laugh. As the squirrel laughs, its up-and-down motion causes the animal's front feet to rub against the wheel attached to the right-hand shaft. Thus when the left-hand wheel is turned and the squirrel laughs, the right-hand wheel also turns. When the left-hand wheel ceases to move, and the squirrel is no longer tickled, the animal stops laughing and its front feet stop moving the right-hand wheel.

We thus have three different hypotheses, each beginning with different assumptions, each attempting to explain observational data. Each scientist thinks the other scientists' hypotheses are wrong. Mr. Mechanic, being an active "research scientist," is anxious to try further experiments and make further observations to increase the amount of data available. He feels his assumptions about a rubber belt connecting two pulleys inside that box must be correct. If he is able to explain further observations with this assumption, he can advance his hypothesis to the status of theory. At least, being first with new research data will catch the other two scientists off guard and they will have a hard time catching up to explain his new data.

Mr. Mechanic experiments by placing his ear close to the box while turning the left-hand wheel. He makes two observations. First, when the left-hand wheel is being turned, he hears a muffled sound from inside the box. Second, he observes that there is a periodic click coming from inside the box. With this new data he claims that his hypothesis can explain what is happening. The muffled sound coming from inside the box is caused by the rubber belt moving against the pulleys. Also, since the rubber belt is probably formed by joining two ends of a length of rubber tubing with a metal clip, every time the metal clip strikes one of the pulleys, it makes a clicking sound. His theory, he claims, can explain the data and is therefore correct.

Mr. Clockmaker, however, still thinks he is right. He claims that the muffled noise coming from inside the box is produced by gear teeth meshing with one another. Mr. Mechanic asks, "How then do you explain my new discovery of the clicking noise? Your theory must be wrong." Mr. Clockmaker responds by saying that perhaps one of the teeth on a gear is missing. Every time the missing tooth comes around it makes a clicking noise. So he feels his theory is still correct.

Miss Petshop Owner says to the men, "I think you're both wrong. The noise coming from inside the box is of course the squirrel's feet, striking the squirrel cage inside the box. Also one side of the cage has a loose piece of metal on it, and every time the squirrel's feet touch the loose metal, it makes a clicking noise. "Furthermore," she adds, "I am doing some research which seems to prove you're both wrong. My theory of a ticklish squirrel in the box is really the correct one. Note that when I begin turning the left wheel at a fairly rapid rate of rotation, the right wheel also turns at a fairly rapid rate of rotation. After a while, however, when I continue turning at a constant rate, the motion of the right-hand wheel gradually becomes slower and slower." She continues, "This can only be explained if there is a squirrel inside the box. For even though he is being tickled, the squirrel will gradually get tired, run out of breath, and so will make his motions more and more slowly. Since after turning the left wheel rapidly for a while, the right wheel slowed down as we observed, my theory is correct."

Mr. Mechanic scoffs at this. "No, what is happening is that the belt is wearing out inside the box and it begins to slip more and more and more as it passes over the pulleys."

Mr. Clockmaker, on the other hand, concedes that his theory can no longer explain the facts. Gear teeth simply don't slip past one another. He sides with Mr. Mechanic. "It is unscientific" he says, "to think that anything besides machinery can be inside the box." He insists that a mechanistic explanation is the only one acceptable for a scientist. Both men scoff at Miss Petshop Owner because she insists that something besides machinery is in the box. They claim she is being religious by believing myths about ticklish squirrels.

The Limitations of Science

What is really inside the box? Which explanation is true, a mechanistic or a non-mechanistic one? In this case the experts disagree. Which one are we to believe? We do not have sufficient data to prove it one way or the other, and we are not omniscient. We have not seen inside the box. We do not have an absolute reference point.

Some scientists believe in creation. Other scientists believe in evolution. When experts disagree, how is one to decide which position is correct?

> A plea for greater responsibility on the part of scientists when they engage in scientific debate in the public forum poses serious practical, even epistemological questions. How can one know, when two scientists disagree on a scientific matter, whether it is because the issue is really beyond the proficiency of science or because one scientist has investigated the matter more thoroughly than the other?[1]

Weinberg brings up the interesting case in which scientists take opposite sides on an issue. It is an illustration of the situation in which "experts" disagree. In those situations in which both sides cannot be right, how does one get at the truth? Even in those cases where both sides may have the same experimental data and the same factual evidence, and even when they may agree that the factual evidence is correct, they might still disagree on the interpretation of that data.

Unfortunately, quite often the difference is resolved not by seeking the truth, but by political methods. Whichever side has the most political clout ends up winning the debate. In other words, force rules the direction that is taken. Might makes right. This of course is exactly what traditional Darwinism has taught. Survival of the fittest translated into plain, everyday language means might makes right. Truth suffers.

The problem of knowing and seeking the truth is not limited just to laymen in science. It occurs also among those of us who are scientists. Scientists are normally specialists in only one or, at the most, a few areas of science and are laymen outside those areas. A geologist, for example, may be a layman with respect to astronomy, or a biologist may be a layman with respect to archaeology. Therefore they also must evaluate what experts say in areas of science outside their own fields.

Even those of us who are considered experts in a particular field are painfully aware that we don't know it all. Experts have limitations, too. Also, one does not have to look very far to find examples of cases and situations in which experts disagree. Only God's Word can be trusted to give us absolute truth, and if experts disagree with it we may be confident the experts are wrong.

As an illustration, consider a series of hypothetical discussions between various levels of "experts." A first grader who believes in creation might be talking with a second grade student who claims to be smarter and who holds antisupernatural assumptions. Obviously, the first grader is at an intellectual disadvantage with the second grade "expert." The first grader might say, "I believe in creation because it is in the Bible." And the second grader says, "Well, I'm smarter than you. I know more than you do and I don't believe in creation. I believe in evolution. When you get as smart as I am, you will have to give up your belief in creation."

We can imagine a similar discussion between, say, a fourth grader and a fifth grader, or between a high school student and a college student, or between a twenty-year-old and a forty-year-old. No matter how far along the line you go, you can always find someone older and supposedly smarter who believes differently. It is nearly always possible to find someone who is more "expert" who will not accept the Christian world view.

Should we therefore wait until we are the oldest person on earth or the most educated person on earth to make up our mind whether we should be a creationist or an evolutionist? The obvious answer is no. God has created the world and our minds so that we use thought systems for interpreting the world around us. Each person, regardless of how old or how educated, stands equal before God. Each person is responsible for the world view he holds. Each person is responsible for interpreting the data. No one else has a right to do that for him. Each person adopts a world view based on faith. If he accepts creation, he does so by faith. If he rejects creation, he does so by faith.

Creation has not been scientifically or logically disproved. It is only disbelieved. Arlie Hoover writes, "When I recently read a passage from Pascal it lunged dramatically into the center of my thinking. Pascal reasoned that if God had wished to overcome the stubbornness of the most hardened of unbelievers he could have done it by revealing himself so openly that the truth of His existence would be inescapable. But, Pascal continued:

> It is not in this manner that he chose to appear in the gentleness of his coming; because since so many men had become unworthy of his clemency, he wished them to suffer the privation of the good that they did not want. It would not have been right therefore for him to appear in a way that was plainly divine and absolutely bound to convince all mankind; but it was not right either that he should come in a manner so hidden that he could not be recognized by those who sought him sincerely. He chose to make himself perfectly knowable to them; and thus, wishing to appear openly to those who seek him with all their heart, he tempered the knowledge of himself, with the result that he has given signs of himself which are visible to those who seek him, and not to those who do not seek him (Pensees, #309)."[2]

Thus a young student needs to remember that he has as much right to believe as the oldest man on earth. Even though those around him may be applying tremendous pressure for a different interpretation, and even though the student may not yet be an expert, he can still be a good student while he remembers that ultimate truth does not come from "experts." Ultimate truth comes from The Expert.

How then is one to determine the truth of a certain matter? Science alone cannot do this for us. Science is practiced by scientists and this means that human factors must also be taken into account.

Human Factors in Science

The human factor in science has all too frequently been overlooked or ignored. However, a few scientific philosophers have begun to address this issue. The philosopher Paul Feyerabend of Berkeley and Thomas Kuhn are two such thinkers who have stirred up quite a reaction by calling attention to the misconception that human factors are not involved in the formation and acceptance of theories.

What is still probably the most generally held view of science, among both scientists and the public, is one that was shaped during the 1930s and 1940s by the school of positivist philosophers known as the Vienna Circle.

According to this view, science is a strictly logical process. Scientists propose theories on the basis of inductive logic, and confirm or refute them by experimental test of predictions deductively derived from the theory. When old theories fail, new theories are proposed and adopted because of their greater explanatory power, and science thus progresses inexorably closer to the truth.

Logical empiricism, as this view is known, deliberately ignores the historical context of science as well as the psychological factors which many people would consider important in science, such as intuition, imagination, and receptivity to new ideas.[3]

Human factors are very influential in science. They affect the way a scientist makes assumptions, and even the assumptions he chooses to hold. Human factors are involved in the theories a researcher makes and holds. Each scientist has his own biases. Even the way he goes about looking for scientific data or the type of experiments he sets up are related to human factors, including biases.

The Myth of Objectivity

Even scientists themselves are sometimes trapped into believing the myth that only objectivity enters into science. The history of science, however, certainly indicates otherwise. One can find many examples in which a particular theory was actively propounded and defended—in some cases even against the evidence. Scientists who have spent a lifetime defending a particular point of view are not likely to give it up without some emotional reaction.

It may be difficult for those of us who are scientists to see ourselves this way. Sometimes we have to have this human factor pointed out to us by those outside our own particular specialty. One forum for this is in the letters-to-the-editor section of scientific periodicals. Those letters are often instructive and sometimes even entertaining, especially after the publication of a controversial topic.

Men from Mars

Because scientists are human, they are not totally objective. They don't become something different from other human beings just because they are scientists or because they enter a laboratory. While discussing a rather heated debate about a controversial topic in astronomy, one author brings up this point.

> The most dispassionate cosmologists like to imagine that they have created their theories solely by objective analysis of the data, their minds passive as a

monk in a cell sifting the information that arrives through the senses. The physiologists and psychologists disagree. They tell us that the brain theorizes almost as quickly as it perceives. The eye, they say, is part of the brain and delivers not television pictures to be observed by a resident homunculus, but processed information, much of it in the form of hypotheses about what it is seeing. And in the dialogue between the eye and the rest of the brain, what we see can become what we expect to see. A field mouse is transformed into a snake to the hiker who fears snakes. Ghosts and flying saucers favor with visits those who most expect them. Mars has produced canals and the sun has spawned moons for observers who imagined these to be their attributes.[4]

Those of us who are a little older can well remember the debate about canals on Mars which some astronomers thought they saw. Other scientists took exception to this point of view. It was a famous discussion and the news media helped popularize it and even sensationalize it. Some astronomers believed their telescopic observations of Mars indicated straight lines on the planet, and they interpreted these as canals. This led these scientists to hypothesize that intelligent beings must have designed the canals, perhaps for carrying irrigation water. If this were so there must be some type of intelligent life on Mars—Martians. The public, of course, was fascinated by this debate. In recent years, however, information sent back by the Mars probes largely laid to rest the idea of Martians.

The point is that scientists were involved in this debate. How was a layman to know which was true when the "experts" were taking opposite sides? I am not trying to put science down; I make these comments in answer to the question, Is science a reliable guide to ultimate truth? My comments are meant only to show that scientists are not always totally objective even in their most intense efforts in science.

This is especially true in such a highly emotional issue as creation and evolution. In this case, the problem is intensified because the past cannot be brought into the laboratory. Scientists have limited data. It is not possible to put the past into a test tube and repeat the experiment. Scientists can only study the universe as it exists at present. From such data they make extrapolations into what may have happened in the past to arrive at the present condition. Hypotheses about past events are very vulnerable to influence by human factors.

A Self-Correcting Enterprise?

It is often stated by those who may wish to minimize the influence of human factors in science that science is a self-correcting enterprise. They admit human factors may play a part in science, but maintain that since science is self-correcting, these factors are not significant to any great degree. In the case of what has been termed neo-science, it may largely be true that science is self-correcting. Neo-science is a study of the present universe. Experiments can be repeated and data checked for accuracy. If someone contends that a particular result is incorrect, further experiments can be carried out and the results checked by repetition of the experiment.

In the case of paleoscience, however, repetition of what happened in the past is not possible. One of the basic methods of science, repeatability, cannot be applied to earth history. We cannot do fossil breeding experiments, for example. We cannot put history into a test tube and experiment with it. History happened only once. We cannot go back and observe someone putting gears or belts or a squirrel into the box, as it were.

> Evolution, if it actually took place, would now be a matter of history, and history cannot be repeated in the laboratory. By the experimental method, for example, one cannot prove that Pasteur ever worked an experiment. What experiment carried on in the laboratory today could prove that Pasteur ever lived, much less prove that he worked certain experiments? It would, of course, be possible to show this by historical testimony, and to show in experiments today

that such experiments are possible. But even so one would still have to establish by historical testimony whether they were possible to Pasteur's day and whether he actually worked experiments.[5]

This puts severe limits on any scientific discussions of the past, a fact that has great significance for the idea of creation and evolution.

It is therefore much more difficult for paleoscience to be self-correcting, and human factors are at least as operative in paleoscience as they are in neoscience.

Even if we were to put chemicals together in the laboratory to make a rock, for example, and even if the rock were identical to a rock found in nature, this would still not mean that natural rocks were made by this process. At best it would only show that rocks could be formed by the method. There may be other ways to achieve the same result.

And yet it is in the area of paleoscience that much of the disagreement between creation and evolution occurs. Paleoscience cannot really be studied by methods which are generally termed "scientific." This limitation has been noted by scholars who are evolutionists as well as by creationists. In discussing principles of reconstructing evolutionary history, one scientist, an evolutionist, comments, "How can history be scientific if we cannot directly observe a past process: (i) If we can observe present processes at work, then we should accumulate and extrapolate their results to render the past."[6] The past cannot be scientifically studied except by extrapolation of observations taken in the present. Extrapolation from the present into the past is a very risky venture.

Paleoscience is a challenging study, both for creation and for evolution.

In paleoscience one faces the awesome task of trying to explain the final state of affairs without direct observations of the initial conditions or of the processes acting in the interval between the initial conditions and the final state.[7]

Repeatability is not a characteristic of paleoscience and is one of the main reasons that it hardly ever proceeds out of the hypothesis stage. Any theory regarding paleoscience is an infant theory at best. The opportunity simply isn't available to go back and recheck what has actually happened in history.

Scientific theories are very useful, however, for helping us interpret factual data. They help us to make meaning out of the facts to which we have access. Although theories have their uses, they are also subject to abuses. Abuse of scientific theory is largely the result of human factors entering into science. An excellent discussion of both the uses and abuses of scientific theory has been presented by E. H. Andrews[8] who notes the following five abuses of scientific theory: dogmatism, extrapolation, exaggeration, subjectivism, and exploitation. It is important that we consider each of these abuses in turn, for they are among the reasons so many people are prodded into believing in evolution.

The first abuse, dogmatism, occurs when theory is equated to or confused with fact. Theory is an interpretation of factual observations and not the facts themselves. One of the ways this problem can occur is when summaries of factual information are presented without the factual information itself being available. This is a problem not only for the layman, but also for other scientists as well. In those cases in which the underlying facts from observations are not presented, one has little choice but to go along with the statements made about the facts. This makes it very difficult to separate interpretations of facts from the facts themselves.

Nowadays evolution is nearly always presented as reality. Educational textbooks present evolution as fact. Television series such as Carl Sagan's *Cosmos* and popular writings in news media present evolution as fact. "In any case evolution can be considered a complex fact rather than a theory."[9] "What is in dispute among scientists is not the existence of the fact, but the mechanism through which evolution works."[10] These and similar statements are frequently encountered. They imply that one may argue about the mode or method of evolution, but not the fact of evolution.

One scientist making a bitter attack against creation and creation scientists writes, "Evolution is a fact as much as the idea that the earth is shaped like a ball."[11] Articles on evolution appearing in popular news media also take this view.

> Evolution of life over a very long period of time is a fact, if we are to believe evidence gathered during the last two centuries from geology, paleontology (the study of fossils), molecular biology and many other scientific disciplines. Despite the many believers in divine creation who dispute this (including about half the adult population of the United States, according to one opinion poll), the probability that evolution has occurred approaches certainty in scientific terms. We can be as sure about this as we are sure that ancient civilizations once existed on earth but no longer function.[12]

This quote is an example of the abuse of scientific theory. It is dogmatism because theory is equated to or confused with fact.

A second abuse of scientific theory is extrapolation. This abuse occurs when a theory is extended to areas in which it is not known to apply, as the following illustration shows. On one college campus, there was quite a controversy about noise in the library. Some students felt that, as an aid to study, the library should be maintained with a quiet atmosphere. They felt loud talking and whispering should not be allowed. Other students felt the opposite way. The issue was discussed back and forth in the student newspaper with both points of view expressed. Eventually one student decided to do some research on the topic. He had had enough of opinions being passed back and forth and wanted to get some factual data to back up his position. To gather his data, he interviewed personally a number of students, asking them their feelings about studying in a noisy or quiet atmosphere. By an overwhelming majority, the students interviewed said they did not mind studying in a noisy atmosphere. These results were then published in the student newspaper, with the conclusion that it was not necessary to make the library a quiet place. Not being quite convinced of the accuracy of this conclusion, I did a little checking into the matter. It turned out that students indeed had been interviewed about their preference for study atmosphere. What did not appear in the newspaper, however, was the fact that the interviews had been conducted with students in the student union building. Student union buildings are not noted for being quiet places. Students who chose to study in the student union building were those who did not mind a noisy atmosphere. Students who preferred a quiet atmosphere would choose a place like the library for study. Data were not gathered from students studying in the library, however. The report was therefore guilty of extrapolation. Data gathered in the student union building had been extrapolated to the library. Extrapolation was made into an area where the data did not apply.

A third abuse of theory is exaggeration. As we mentioned earlier, theories can have a wide range of certitude. They can vary all the way from hypotheses right on up to law of nature. Theory can have a wide range of degrees of verification. Exaggeration is the abuse that occurs when theory is accorded a higher degree of verification or development than is justified by data.

A fourth abuse of scientific theory is subjectivism. This abuse displays the human factor perhaps more than any other. Sometimes a theory will be defended even when new observational facts turn up which seem to be contrary to the new theory. New facts contrary to the theory will be explained away as errors of observation or inapplicable for some other reason. Sometimes facts which support a theory will be accepted and reported while those which do not support the theory will be left out or considered erroneous and not reported.

A fifth abuse, exploitation, occurs when scientific theory is used as an excuse to support or justify activities in the political, social, educational, or economic areas. An example might be to use the theory of relativity from physics to justify moral relativism.

The listed abuses of scientific theory frequently occur in

creation-evolution discussions. We will have occasion to recall them at various places in the ensuing discussion.

The Nature of Science

Now let's examine two additional features of science. First is what may be termed *basic science*. It is science for science's sake. It is the accumulation of knowledge about the material world around us. Basic science includes not only the gathering of factual information, but also its interpretation into some kind of meaningful overall framework.

A second category of science is what I term *applied science*. It uses the fundamental knowledge gained from basic science and applies it in such areas as engineering, health sciences, and a host of other useful activities. With these distinctions in mind, let's trace the development of modern science.

Science, a Search for Truth

As we have already noted, the founders of modern science operated from a theistic base. They felt their discoveries about the material world around them should be interpreted in a God-honoring way and that they were learning truth not only about creation, but also about the Creator. In a sense, they viewed their discoveries of the natural laws of the universe as thinking God's thoughts after Him. Because they came from a theistic base and believed in a created universe, they were convinced they were discovering truth about that universe. To them, science was a search for truth.

Michael Faraday is a good illustration of this. He was not only a truly great scientist, but a thoroughly committed Christian. He made many important discoveries in the area of electricity and magnetism, discoveries which led directly to the electric motor and the electric generator. Faraday also discovered the basic laws of electrochemistry. These laws are the basis on which all electric batteries operate, and are still known as Faraday's laws in his honor.

> Science to Faraday meant truth. "And he can *smell* the truth!" claimed one of his co-workers.

Experiments were necessary to convince him of the truth. No matter what experiment he read about, he himself had to carry it out before he was convinced.[13]

The early scientists placed great emphasis on truth. They were discovering truth about the universe. To them, a scientific explanation was a true explanation, one which reflected reality. Armed thus with a biblical theology of science and a natural curiosity combined with their high regard for truth, the early scientists were led to some very fundamental and important discoveries. They not only carried out basic research to learn the fundamental laws of the material universe, but they carried out applied science as well to learn how their new knowledge could be used in a practical way. Their discoveries were quickly applied to such exciting new inventions as the telephone, the telegraph, radio, transportation, and complex machinery leading to the industrial age.

The Rise of Scientism

The success of scientists in discovering new truths about the material world and in applying them in areas that affect everyday life was great. So great in fact was the success of science that a drift in thinking occurred toward science as the ultimate guide to truth. Science itself was credited rather than its biblical philosophical base. There appeared a tendency to transfer authority for ultimate truth away from the Bible and toward science.

This gave rise to *scientism,* or the worship of science. Scientism is the tendency to attribute to man and his efforts in science what rightly belongs only to God. It credits the created (nature) with what rightly belongs only to the Creator. The Bible tells us that man has always had this tendency. "These men deliberately forfeited the truth of God and accepted a lie, paying homage and giving service to the creature instead of to the Creator, Who alone is worthy to be worshiped for ever and ever, amen" (Romans 1:25, Phillips).

Scientism is also exemplified by the inscription appearing on the National Academy of Sciences building: "To science, pilot of industry, conqueror of disease, multiplier of the harvest, explorer of the universe, revealer of nature's laws, eternal guide to truth." It is evident from this inscription that man and his activities in science are taking credit for what rightfully belongs only to God. *Scientism is really idolatry.* Like many other forms of idolatry, it is an all-too-easy trap to fall into. Idolatry is a transfer of authority from the Bible as a source of truth to man and his activities. When this happens in science, scientism is the result.

Popularization of Science

Nevertheless modern science with its roots springing from Christianity and a belief in creation became extremely successful. Many new and important inventions were the result, and these affected the lives of people in their day-to-day activities. It resulted in great respect for the power of science. Consequently, science began to be popularized. It became fashionable for one to be associated with science. There are many examples that can be given. Social studies as a course name was changed to social science; home economics became domestic science.

Popularization of science can be a good thing. People need to know about and appreciate it, and as a scientist I am pleased when people want to know about science. In order to be a good citizen in our culture, one must seek scientific literacy for a number of reasons. Important issues requiring scientific literacy often come before the voters: Fluoridation of municipal water supplies; building atomic power plants; genetic engineering, to mention only a few examples. Many jobs also depend on science and advanced technology. Even modern everyday gadgets—including children's toys—require a certain knowledge of science.

Because science plays such a large part in day-to-day living, everyone needs to know a little something about science in order to communicate intelligently. Thus, I am certainly not implying that knowledge of science is bad. What is bad, however, are abuses of the popularization of science and abuses of scientific theory. Science must not become an idol.

Abusing the Popularization of Science

Some scientists have expressed concern about a general lack of scientific literacy and also about the abuses of the popularization of science.

> The dangers of the popularisation of science show up best in phrases such as "Science has shown . . ." or "Scientists believe . . ." or "Scientists have proved . . ." Whenever I read or hear those phrases I am immediately on the defensive, because I am reasonably sure that they will preface some statement which I, as a scientist, find unacceptable or distorted.
>
> Such expressions often constitute a kind of mental processing, calculated to improve the acceptability of some idea which is not really sound. They are used as a kind of insurance against any criticism of what is about to be said. If you can introduce a remark with "Science has shown . . ." or "Scientists believe . . .", then it appears that you can say almost anything and get away with it![14]

This is a perceptive observation. When encountering statements such as "Science has shown . . .", one must not forget to retain the habit of asking, "Yes, but is the statement true?"

It is also essential to remember to separate fact from interpretation of fact. Omitting this differentiation causes much confusion. Newspaper and magazine articles, TV programs, and other media pieces often draw conclusions about an issue and present these conclusions without making the raw factual data available. When this happens, confusion can result. The average person has difficulty separating the interpretation of the facts from the facts themselves. Even if one recognizes that only conclusions are being presented, often the original facts are not reported so that it is not possible to evaluate the validity of the conclusions.

A further problem associated with the popularization of science is the tendency of the media toward sensationalism. Scientists frequently make statements in a context of qualifying details. When such a statement is presented without listing these attendant assumptions and qualifying details, problems can result. The scientist may find himself quoted as saying something he had no intention of saying. For example, we might encounter the headline "Scientist Envisions Water As Auto Fuel." Taken at face value, this statement sounds as though the gas stations of the future might pump water instead of gasoline. But what the scientist actually said was that water can be broken down, using electricity, into hydrogen and oxygen. The hydrogen, which burns well, could then be saved and stored for use as a fuel. Water as is, however, certainly will not burn. Leaving out the qualifying details can surely give a wrong impression.

Redefining Science

We have mentioned that although science began from a creation base, a change in philosophy occurred. The move was away from creation and toward a naturalistic explanation for origins. Supernaturalism was replaced by antisupernaturalism. Darwinism became popular and evolution became the favored explanation. Associated with this philosophical shift was also a new definition of the word science. This new definition was implicit if not explicit. To the early modern scientists, a scientific definition was synonymous with a true explanation; after Darwin, however, a new connotation with an entirely different meaning began to be used. In the new definition of the term, a scientific explanation was, by definition, a naturalistic one (science = naturalism). Its main emphasis was on avoidance of the supernatural as an explanation. In the new definition, science was an enterprise which attempted to explain the material universe, both past and present, in naturalistic terms. The truth of an explanation was not as important as avoiding the miraculous.

As this new definition of science began to be adopted, it was used to browbeat creationists. Creation came under special attack because it was not in agreement with the newly accepted philosophy of naturalism. Those attacking creation would frequently give a bad or incorrect representation of the creation explanation and then label it unscientific. Many examples of this can be obtained from scientific literature, theological writings, and science textbooks. For example, in what appears to be a slam at the creation explanation, one science textbook explains,

> A theory that is not fruitful is a "bad" theory because it does not lead to further knowledge. For example, the theory that the earth was specially created as is is a "bad" theory, not because it is not true, but because it does not lead one towards a better understanding of nature. Such a theory is barren, for it gives a final explanation to all things, that they are as they are because they were created that way. A believer in such a theory has no incentive to investigate nature except to describe it, for he already has all of the answers as to why things are as they are.
>
> Difficult for the layman to understand is that the scientists' criterion for *a "good" theory does not depend upon whether it is true or not*. He measures it only by its consequences—". . . consequences in terms of other ideas and other experiments. Thus conceived, science is not a quest for certainty; it is rather a quest which is successful only to the degree that it is continuous" (James Conant, *Science and Understanding*, Yale University Press, 1951, pp. 25-26).[15] [emphasis mine]

Notice the incorrect conclusion drawn about creation. The author says that a creationist "has no incentive to investigate nature." The exact opposite is true. The doctrine of creation is what the early scientists believed and it was the source of their motivation. Creation also is highly motivating to modern scientists who are creationists.

Based on the methodology of the early modern scientists who were mostly Christians, science began to achieve notable success. There was a subsequent popularization of science and it occurred at the same time that naturalistic philosophy was gaining ground. This caused confusion. The result was that the new definition of science was reinforced. Naturalistic science stole the credit for the success of science and the new successful technology it engendered.

Those who opposed a mechanistic explanation for origins were thus labeled as unscientific or even antiscientific, and were classed as ignorant and uneducated. Originally the view of origins among scientists was creation; now creation was relabeled a religious explanation. Creation science was now labeled religion and naturalistic science was simply called science. Thus there developed a conflict between "science" and "religion." Religion was portrayed as being against or inhibiting science. The underlying philosophical bases for the new definition and accusations were largely ignored. It was a subtle and vicious attack on historic Christianity and on true science as well.

The Limitations of Science

Scientists have limited data. We can only observe and perform scientific experiments on the universe as it exists at the present.

On the broad scale all the way from hypothesis through theory to scientific law, where then does evolution appear? Evolution is hardly more than a hypothesis. The fact that it is not possible to go back and repeat history and make scientific observations on it means that evolution will never be able to be more than a hypothesis. There is insufficient data to elevate it to even the status of theory, much less a law. As far as observations on the present universe go, the same is true for creation. We cannot go back and observe the creation events. Creation and evolution are both under the same handicap at this point. Neither can be studied in the laboratory today. Both are on the same footing as far as scientific observation goes. Creation, however, has at least one distinct major advantage over evolution. Creation is supported by historical testimony of the Creator. The Creator *was* present at creation, and he has communicated to us in the Bible true information about creation and about the universe.

Chapter 3, Notes

1. Alvin M. Weinberg, "Science in the Public Forum: Keeping It Honest," *Science,* 30 January 1976, 341.

2. Arlie J. Hoover, "Why History? A Defense of God's Revelatory Medium," *Christianity Today,* 28 July 1972, 6-7.

3. Nicholas Wade, "Thomas S. Kuhn: Revolutionary Theorist of Science," *Science,* 8 July 1977, 143.

4. Timothy Ferris, "The Spectral Messenger," *Science 81,* October, 66.

5. Robert T. Clark and James D. Bales, *Why Scientists Accept Evolution* (Grand Rapids: Baker Book House, 1966), 95.

6. Stephen Jay Gould, "Darwinism and the Expansion of Evolutionary Theory," *Science,* 23 April 1982, 386.

7. Charles A. Clough and Louis E. Fredricks, "Creationist Science: A Challenge from Professor Young," *Creation Research Society Quarterly* (June 1978): 49.

8. Prof. E. H. Andrews, *Is Evolution Scientific?* (Welwyn, Herts., England: Evangelical Press, 1977), 14-16.

9. A. Montagu, *New York Times,* 17 March 1981, A16.

10. Barry R. Gross, "Letters," *Science,* 15 May 1981, 738.

11. Niles Eldredge, *The Monkey Business* (New York: Washington Square Press, 1982), 31-32.

12. Francis Hitching, "Was Darwin Wrong?" *Life,* April 1982, 48.

13. Lois Hoadley Dick, "Unforgettable Michael Faraday," *These Times,* November 1982, 6.

14. Andrews, *Is Evolution Scientific?,* 5.

15. Verne H. Booth, *Physical Science* (New York: Macmillan Publishing Co., 1962), 147-48.

Chapter 4

Evidence vs. Evolution

*C*reation is the idea that the universe and life came into existence by direct acts of a Creator. It is a supernatural explanation for origins. Evolution, on the other hand, is the idea that the universe and life came into existence by the operation of natural processes. Evolution tries to explain origins in a naturalistic way. Although much of the discussion on evolution centers in the field of biology, it is not limited to that field. Evolutionists also talk about cosmic evolution, stellar evolution, planetary evolution, and so on. Even the big bang model of origins was invented as a naturalistic explanation for origins.

It is a mistake to think that those who hold to a big bang model are starting with a supernatural origin for the big bang. At a recent meeting of the American Association for the Advancement of Science, this topic was specifically addressed.

> Big bang cosmology, for instance, is cited as evidence for the concept of divine creation. Milton K. Munitz of the City University of New York addressed this question and explained the difference between the physicist's concept and the fundamentalist's concept of the beginning of the universe.

"Any interpretation of the notion of an absolute beginning of the universe as consisting in an alleged event impervious to further scientific investigations," he said, "simply misreads the logic of the situation." It's a philosophical or logical mistake, he says, "to look to those evolutionary scientific cosmologies that involve the concept of a beginning of the universe as support for a sophisticated traditional doctrine of creation."[1]

Some Christians have wondered whether the big bang might be the creation event described in Genesis. However, it is wrong to confuse the postulated big bang with creation. It is a philosophical mistake because the big bang explanation was invented as a philosophical alternative to creation. It did not come from a study of Scripture. The big bang is a mechanistic or naturalistic explanation. It is an antisupernatural explanation of origins.

Notice also in the quote above that "physicists" are pitted against "fundamentalists." This is an example of how the naturalistic evolutionists propagandize for their view. It is a gross error to label the issue as between physicists and fundamentalists. Physicists are those who are specialists in physics. Some of these specialists are evolutionists and some are creationists. Does the fact that a physicist believes in creation make him cease to be a physicist?

As we have noted, creation and evolution are opposing philosophies. One is supernatural; the other is natural. They are both interpretive schemes for explaining scientific facts. Furthermore, they are philosophical opposites. They are antithetical. If one is true, the other is false. They cannot both be true at the same time. If origins came about entirely naturalistically, nothing supernatural was involved. On the other hand, if origins involved supernatural acts, then it cannot be entirely naturalistic. Both views are based on faith. Evolution is based on faith in the idea that nothing supernatural was involved. Creation is based on faith in acts of a Creator.

Which of these two approaches is true? Which one describes reality? Which explanation fits the facts? In seeking to answer that question, we want to look at some of the details both of evolution and of creation as well as some scientific evidence.

The Bible of course presents creation. For one who accepts God's Word, creation is no problem. But what do the scientific facts really show? Do they overwhelmingly support evolution? Let's take a good look at a few of them.

The Fossil Record

Darwin suggested that all of the various forms of life we see on earth today descended from more primitive ancestors by slow gradual change over millions of years of time. Only natural processes were involved. Modern evolutionists also believe this, whether they are old-style Darwinists or some newer type of evolutionist. For example, one of the newer views of evolution is known as punctuated equilibrium. It assumes extensive changes in animals or plants may have taken place in one period fairly rapidly, followed by long periods of time without much change. It also assumes this pattern was repeated over and over. These evolutionists would not agree with slow, gradual, continuous change, but they still agree that all life forms evolved from more primitive ones over long periods of time. The difference is only whether the changes were continuous or occurred in sudden jumps. Darwinism taught that gradual changes occurred in plants and animals and these were matched against the environment. Only the fittest would survive. And so it was predicted there would be a gradual change of animals from one type into another.

If the Darwinian process really took place, remains of plants and animals (fossils) should show a gradual and continual change from one type of animal or plant into another. One of the things that worried Darwin in his day, as well as modern evolutionists, was that the fossil record did not supply these intermediate life forms.

Darwin did not base his ideas on observation of scientific data. He did not begin with data. He began with a belief system and then looked for data to support his beliefs. Not only did he *not* see evidence of a slow, gradual change from his observation of the fossil record of the past, but he believed change of one species into another in living forms could not even be observed within the single lifetime of a scientist. In other words, evolution could not be observed in the present. Actual observation of evolutionary change was therefore not possible. A modern-day proponent of evolution states, "Darwin portrayed evolution as a stately and orderly process, working at a speed so slow that no person could hope to observe it in a lifetime. Ancestors and descendants, Darwin argued, must be connected by 'infinitely numerous transitional links' forming 'the finest graduated steps.' Only an immense span of time had permitted such a sluggish process to achieve so much."[2] In Darwin's day, however, the fossil record did not support slow gradual change. The countless in-between plant and animal forms that must have been preserved in the fossil record if Darwinism were correct were simply not there. The facts of the fossil record were against Darwinism.

How did Darwin get around the obvious discrepancy between his theory and factual observation? He did it by inventing additional postulates in an attempt to prop up his theory to fit the actual evidence. He postulated that the fossil record was incomplete. Rather than admit his theory was wrong, he blamed the fossil record for being imperfect.

For more than one hundred years since Darwin's day scientists have continued to study the fossil record intensely. How has the situation changed? Of all the countless fossil remains which have been discovered and studied, in-between forms are still missing from the record. Even today, scientists still use the same excuse that Darwin used: the fossil record is incomplete; we just haven't found the in-between species yet. Stephen Gould, a strong proponent of evolution and strongly anticreationist, observes this:

> The extreme rarity of transitional forms in the fossil
> record persists as the trade secret of paleontology.
> The evolutionary trees that adorn our textbooks have

data only at the tips and nodes of their branches; the rest is inference, however reasonable, not the evidence of fossils.

Darwin's argument still persists as the favored escape of most paleontologists from the embarrassment of a record that seems to show so little of evolution. In exposing its cultural and methodological roots, I wish in no way to impugn the potential validity of gradualism (for all general views have similar roots). I wish only to point out that it was never "seen" in the rocks.[3]

Observational evidence simply does not support the idea of slow gradual change.[4] This fact is even admitted by evolutionists as we have just noted.

A direct look at the fossil record would lead one to conclude that animals reproduced after their kind as Genesis states. They did not change from one kind into another. The evidence now, as in Darwin's day, is in agreement with the Genesis record of direct creation. Animals and plants continue to reproduce after their kind. In fact, the conflict between paleontology (study of fossils) and Darwinism is so strong that some scientists are beginning to believe that the in-between forms will never be found. One scientist observes, "It is not even possible to make a caricature of evolution out of paleobiological facts. The fossil material is now so complete that the lack of transitional series cannot be explained by the scarcity of the material. The deficiencies are real, they will never be filled."[5]

The evidence simply does not support slow gradual change. To believe and advocate a theory in spite of evidence is an abuse of scientific theory known as subjectivism. It is a serious abuse and a block on the path toward finding truth.

Evidence from Genetics

Not finding support for evolution from collections of fossils in museums of natural history or in the field, supporters of evolution then turned their attention to the biology laboratory.

Animals and plants are made up of living cells which perform many different functions. Each cell in a living organism has a set of instructions or code which carries information for all the functions to be carried out by the cell. During reproduction, this code is copied and passed on from one generation to the next. The offspring inherit the genetic code of the parents. This is why offspring look like their parents. Once in a rare while, though, a copying error is made. The copying error is, of course, in the genetic material and will be inherited during subsequent generations. Copying errors are known as mutations. Mutations are almost always harmful. They result in a sick or weakened plant or a deformed, sick animal. In order for evolution to work, new genetic material must come into being. Mutations can be a source of new genetic material. Observations show, however, that by overwhelming odds these mutations or mistakes are harmful to the resulting organism. Modern followers of Darwin (neo-Darwinists) nevertheless hypothesize that very rarely a beneficial mutation may occur. They further believe that these beneficial mutations will spread throughout a population so that natural selection can take over to assure the survival of this trait. Gradually, over millions and millions of years, enough favorable mutations should collect to result in a new species. According to this hypothesis, genetics can provide the mechanism to support Darwin's original thesis.

How well does actual evidence in the science of genetics support evolution? Here again, it does not.

It is fair to say that this explanation of evolution (called the synthetic theory, because it combines Darwinism, Mendelian inheritance, and the mathematics of populations change) has utterly dominated biological science for the last 50 years. The teaching of evolution in virtually all colleges in the Western world means the teaching of population genetics. With such apparent unanimity in the textbooks and the classrooms, it comes as something of a surprise to discover that, to increasing numbers of scientists, the synthetic theory is as full of holes as the fossil record itself.[6]

Careful observation of plants and animals in nature, and experiments in the laboratory with artificial breeding of animals and plants seem to show quite clearly that the genetic system is one of maintenance. The status quo is preserved. There are definite limits to change. Species remain species.

Large numbers of mutations have been generated artificially in the laboratory by atomic radiation, by chemicals, and other means. This has afforded an opportunity to experimentally check the belief that mutations lead to new species.

One organism which has been studied very extensively is the fruit fly. Many generations of fruit flies have been raised in the laboratory. They have been artificially mutated time after time. And yet fruit flies refuse to become anything but fruit flies.[7] Observation in the laboratory simply does not support Darwinism or neo-Darwinism. Evidence agrees exactly with the statements in Genesis that plants and animals were created to reproduce after their kind.

The Origin of Life

Genetics poses an additional problem for the evolutionary hypothesis. How did the genetic code arise in the first place? The genetic code is associated with complex molecules known as DNA and RNA (deoxyribonucleic acid and ribonucleic acid). To function, these molecules need a living cell. However, a living cell, to function, needs the DNA and RNA genetic apparatus. It's sort of like the chicken and the egg question ("Which came first, the chicken or the egg?"). Evolutionists admit this is a real problem for their hypothesis, yet they will not concede to creation.

The resistance of many evolutionists to accepting the alternative explanation of special creation has amazed me. One evolutionary writer, while recognizing the problem of the origin of the genetic code, makes the following comment:

Did the code and the means of translating it appear simultaneously in evolution? It seems almost incredible that any such coincidence could have occurred, given the extraordinary complexities of both sides and the requirement that they be coordinated accurately for survival. By a preDarwinian (or a skeptic of evolution after Darwin) this puzzle would surely have been interpreted as the most powerful sort of evidence for special creation. In our day another, but still far from demonstrated (or possibly demonstrable), view seems the only logical one: that a primitive and generalized mode of replication of genetic material arose in evolution either before the existence of these critical enzymes or coordinately with proteins which gradually took on crude and generalized enzymelike functions.[8]

This is a truly amazing statement. The evidence clearly points to creation, but it is not accepted. Instead, the author prefers a position of materialistic origins even though he admits it may not be demonstrable from factual evidence. It shows his position is a belief system based not only on faith, but even blind faith, because it has no factual support and is even contrary to evidence.

Evolution as a hypothesis for the origin of life is totally devoid of factual observations for its support. It is a leap of faith into the dark after creation is rejected.

Another well-known scientist who has spoken out on this point is Robert Jastrow, who is an agnostic. (He has attached the modern definition to the word *science* in the quote below. Recall that this definition states that scientific explanation does not mean a true explanation, just one that does not involve creation. As a scientist and creationist, I would not agree to Jastrow's definition of the word "scientific." It is important, however, to realize that one's view of origins relates to how the term "scientific" is used. A creation scientist uses the term in a sense different from that of an evolutionary scientist.)

According to the scientific story of Genesis, it happened this way: Now and then in the primordial seas of the earth, collisions occurred between neighboring molecules; in some of these collisions, two small molecules stuck together to form a larger one; then another small molecule collided and stuck; and then another. Eventually, after countless millions of chance encounters, a molecule was formed that had the magical ability to divide into two copies of itself. This was the start of parenthood; it was the start of life.

From generation to generation, parent molecules produced daughters; their numbers multiplied; today, their descendents are on the earth; they are the molecules called DNA, which lie in the center of every living cell. . . .

What concrete evidence supports this remarkable theory of the origin of life? There is none.[9]

Jastrow continues by explaining that not only is there no concrete evidence to support the hypothesis of the evolutionary origin of life, but none will likely ever be found. In the evolutionary belief system, life arose so long ago that any evidence of its origin would probably have been erased even if it did exist at one time. Molecules halfway between life and nonlife would probably have decayed by now. Hence evidence of the transition from nonlife to life should not be present now.

Thus an evolutionist must invent additional postulates to explain the lack of evidence for the evolutionary origin of first life. What is the difference whether we say the supposed evidence was there and disappeared somehow or was never there in the first place?

The evolutionary hypothesis for the origin of life is without observational evidence for its support in either the fossil record or from the biology laboratory. If life arose by an evolutionary process, it must have subsequently developed by stages. Evidence in the fossil record does not support this idea.

Furthermore, evidence from genetics indicates that life forms reproduce after their kind and these kinds do not merge one into another. Evolutionary hypothesis is not only *not* supported by evidence; it is actually contrary to the evidence. To support a theory even when it is contrary to fact is an abuse of scientific theory. It is subjectivism.

Evidence of Design

In addition to all this evidence against evolution, there is much positive observational evidence that strongly points to design and purpose in nature. Evidence of design and purpose point to creation. Even Darwin recognized this. He admits that it caused him much mental distress. Modern evolutionists also recognize that there is evidence which seems to point to design and purpose, but they will not admit that there is a designer or purpose. Instead, they refer to situations indicating design as "anomalies" of evolution. The eye provides an example of an organ having a structure which seems to indicate design.

> The eye appears to have been designed; no designer of telescopes could have done better. How could this marvelous instrument have evolved by chance, through a succession of random events? Many people in Darwin's day agreed with theologian William Paley, who commented, "There cannot be a design without a designer."[10]

With new discoveries since Darwin's day, evidence for design is even stronger now than it was then. The eye, however, remains a prime example. If one were to come across an optical instrument such as a telescope or a camera, one would immediately conclude that it had been designed. Evolutionists, however, in looking at an eye, which has many of the same features and even more perfection than most cameras, conclude that there is no designer.

> But most scientists today do not share Darwin's doubts; they are convinced that his theory of evolu-

tion removes the need for a guiding hand in the Universe. The great evolutionist George Gaylord Simpson expressed a nearly universal opinion among scientists when he wrote that evolution "achieves the aspect of purpose without the intervention of a purposer, and has produced a vast plan without the action of a planner."[11]

To reject evidence of design when it is so clearly evident is again an example of the abuse of scientific theory known as subjectivism. The evidence is clear; there is no excuse for missing it. As Romans 1:20 explains, "For since the creation of the world God's invisible qualities—his eternal power and divine nature—have been clearly seen, being understood from what has been made, so that men are without excuse."

Science is not studied in a vacuum. It is always carried out in a philosophical framework. Evolution and creation are two such competing frameworks. Although many people today hold to an evolutionary philosophical framework and study science in that context, in my opinion it provides an inferior and limited view of reality. Evolution is not adequate for the big questions. It is not in agreement with the universe as we find it. It is not in agreement with facts and reality.

If evolution is not true, what do we put in its place? It is one thing to throw stones at a theory or world view, but it is another to offer something better. Creation science does offer a fully acceptable and satisfying alternative. Creation science begins with wholly biblical presuppositions and interprets data from all of reality, including science, within that framework. Why then is there such resistance to acceptance of creation? We shall examine this question next.

Chapter 4, Notes

1. "Evolution at the AAAS," *Science News*, 10 January 1981, 19.

2. Stephen Jay Gould, "Evolution's Erratic Pace," *Natural History*, May 1977, 12.

3. Ibid., 14.

4. Duane T. Gish, *Evolution? The Fossils Say No!* (San Diego: Creation-Life 1979).

5. Professor N. Heribert-Nilsson, quoted by Francis Hitching in "Was Darwin Wrong?" *Life*, April 1982, 49.

6. Hitching, "Was Darwin Wrong?" 50.

7. Ibid.

8. Caryl P. Haskins, "Advances and Challenges in Science in 1970," *American Scientist* (May-June 1971): 305.

9. Robert Jastrow, "Genesis Revealed," *Science Digest*, Special Winter Issue, 1979, 40.

10. Robert Jastrow, "Evolution: Selection for Perfection," *Science Digest*, December 1981, 86.

11. Ibid., 87.

Chapter 5

Source of Conflict: The Bible on Science

*F*or the Christian, Scripture is the guide to truth. Therefore it is important to find out what the Bible itself teaches about the two main topics of interest in Bible and science discussions: origins and earth history.

God Is Creator

The Bible begins with the statement, "In the beginning God created the heavens and the earth" (Genesis 1:1). There is perhaps no more succinct, pointed, nor beautiful statement in all of literature. We tend to pass over this statement too quickly and too lightly. First of all, this statement tells us who God is. According to the Bible, God is neither an idea nor a set of moral ideas and principles. God is the Creator of the entire material universe. He is the self-existent being, already existing at the moment the universe began.

A second point to be learned from this verse is that the universe is not self-existent. It is created. It is finite. According to the Bible, God is first; all else is second. This is God's world. It has been created; it does not have an independent, autonomous existence.

Man Is Created

The Bible also teaches that man is created. He is a being created in the image of the Creator. The statement "created in the image of God" does not mean man is shaped like God. It does not mean that God is made out of material substance. Material substance—atoms and molecules and the things which compose man's body—are created items. God created them. They had a beginning, but God did not. The statement "in God's image" therefore refers to God's personality image. Man is more than just the material chemicals composing his body. He is a being in the personality image of his Creator.

Man Is Fallen

One immediate consequence of having been made in God's image is that man has free will. Since the Creator possesses a will, man also has a will. The Bible teaches that subsequent to creation, man fell. Man used his will in an attempt to become autonomous. Fallen man seeks to be autonomous and desires to live and act independently of God, the Creator.

God, however, was not taken by surprise by the fall. He was not defeated by man's seeking to be autonomous and go his own way. In Genesis 3:15 we read, "And I will put enmity between you and the woman, and between your seed and her Seed; He shall bruise your head, and you shall bruise His heel" (NKJV). This verse should stand out like a neon sign. It refers to the Seed of the woman. In all the rest of the Bible, children are named through their father: Abraham's son, David's son, Solomon's son. In Genesis 3:15, however, we have the Seed of the woman. This is unique in all of the Bible. It is the first reference to the virgin birth of the promised Savior. Even though man had fallen, God was not taken by surprise. He promised to provide a Savior. Through accepting Christ as Savior, each individual in the human race, though fallen, has the opportunity to come back into fellowship with God. Each individual can have his sins forgiven and a new direction given to his life. He can begin moving closer to God instead of farther from him.

Two Great Classifications

The Bible thus divides the entire human race into two groups: those who know God and those who do not; those who love God and those who seek to oppose God; those who are seeking to move closer to God and those who are seeking to avoid Him. There is no middle ground. Jesus taught, "He who is not with Me is against Me, and he who does not gather with Me scatters abroad" (Matthew 12:30 NKJV). No one is neutral toward God. The Bible makes it very clear that people either open up to God or run away from Him. "This *is* the judgment—that light has entered the world and men have preferred darkness to light because their deeds were evil. Everybody who does wrong hates the light and keeps away from it, for fear his deeds may be exposed. But everybody who is living by the truth will come to the light to make it plain that all he has done has been done through God" (John 3:19-21, Phillips). Some, by an act of their will, choose to move away from God and His truth. They have an emotional reaction to God's light. They hate it. They actively oppose the truth with their mind, will, and emotions. Others, who accept God's forgiveness through Christ, move toward God's truth. They choose with an act of their will to move into God's light and to give Him credit for their new way of life. No one is neutral.

Man's Fallen Intellect

The fall, as we noted, however, was not limited just to moral direction. It affected man's intellect and reason as well. This is made amply clear in such passages as Romans 1. Unsaved man tries to cover his moral guilt by intellectualizing God out of the picture. He does this by inventing a naturalistic belief system such as evolution. He does this even though it means accepting a lie or flying in the face of evidence. Unsaved man tries to use his reason to destroy the Christian position.

> Now the holy anger of God is disclosed from Heaven against the godlessness and evil of those men who render truth dumb and impotent by their wickedness.

It is not that they do not know the truth about God; indeed he has made it quite plain to them (Romans 1:18-19, Phillips).

Unsaved man is not just neutral toward God's truth. He actively and strongly opposes it. He has a basic commitment to resisting the truth which points him toward God.

Unconverted man (natural man as the Bible refers to him) seeks to be independent or autonomous of God. He seeks to hide from God. He uses his God-given reason to move away from God. Natural man wants to run his own life. He wants to make his own decisions. He wants to decide at what job to work, what person to marry, where to live, how to spend his money, how to spend his recreational time. He does not want to submit to outside authority. He wants to be independent and autonomous. He therefore assumes the natural world is also autonomous.

Natural man consequently interprets the facts of the world around him using only his own mind. He resists using God's mind as a source of truth. Natural man tries to interpret all of his experience and all factual reality into a world view independent of God. He tries to assemble all the puzzle pieces as it were without regard to the picture on the box. It is important for Christians to understand how and why the natural man builds his world view if we are to reach him and evangelize him in our day.

Natural Man's World View

If we are going to present the gospel effectively to our generation we must understand the natural man's world view. We must understand how he thinks and interprets all of life. If we are to effectively challenge his world view, we must understand its basics. This is especially so in areas related to the Bible and science. We cannot hope to have any understanding of the creation-evolution controversy without some knowledge of the world view of natural man. In order, therefore, to better understand creation-evolution issues, let us examine briefly the nature of natural man's world view.

What Is Natural Man?

The term *natural man* comes from the Bible. "But the natural man does not receive the things of the Spirit of God, for they are foolishness to him; nor can he know them, because they are spiritually discerned" (1 Corinthians 2:14, NKJV). It is used to describe an individual who operates according to or is committed to a non-Christian world view. This is the case for all individuals up until the time of their conversion to Christ. It describes an individual whose philosophy is one of independence from God.

Anyone who has been a parent can appreciate the appropriateness of the term "natural man." Children have to be trained to be good; their natural tendency is to do wrong. They do not have to be trained to do wrong; that seems to be the way they naturally are.

Although we speak here of little children, adults have the same problem. Man naturally wants to be autonomous. He wants to be his own boss. He does not want to submit to authority; he does not want anyone else, including God, telling him what to do. This is natural man.

Autonomous Man, Autonomous Universe

Natural man builds his world view by beginning autonomously from himself with a set of assumptions or presuppositions. He then uses these assumptions to interpret all factual data. A Christian also builds a world view by beginning with a set of presuppositions, but he does not do so autonomously. He uses the Bible as a guide. A very basic assumption everyone must make concerns the nature of the material universe. Because natural man seeks to be autonomous, he also assumes the material universe is autonomous or independent of God. Instead of referring to the material universe as the creation, natural man calls it nature. Nature is assumed to have an existence independent from God. It is assumed to be self-contained, governed by a set of natural laws. Natural man tends to assume everything that happens occurs as a result of the operation of natural causes; all occurrences must be explainable in terms of the laws of chemistry and physics. Everything is reducible to chemistry and physics, including life, and even man's mind. Nature is considered to be autonomous. It behaves like a self-running machine, independent of any outside influence. A Christian scientist also assumes that the material world follows a set of laws, but the laws are dependent on God.

Infinite Regression of Cause and Effect

In natural man's view, everything that happens in the present, presumably everything that will happen in the future, and everything that has happened in the past is assumed to be the result of some previous natural cause. Each *effect* is preceded by a *natural cause*. That natural cause was itself an effect preceded by a previous natural cause and so on into the distant remote past. The present state of the universe is to be explained in natural man's system by following an infinite regression of cause and effect of natural laws into the remote past.

This infinite regression of cause and effect is reminiscent of a way I would amuse myself as a child. Standing a short distance in front of a large dressing table mirror, I would hold a smaller mirror directly in front of me. I positioned the smaller mirror such that images from the larger mirror were reflected into the smaller mirror. With this arrangement I could view my reflection in the larger mirror being reflected in the smaller mirror which was again reflected in the larger mirror, and so on *ad infinitum*. It was entertaining to see how many reflections I could count, one after the other. Each reflection caused another reflection. It was a type of infinite regression, each reflection being caused by a previous reflection.

Uniformitarianism

The process of using presently observable natural processes to extrapolate backwards into the far distant past is known as the principle of uniformitarianism. It is an infinite regression of effect and its previous cause. In particular, the doctrine of uniformitarianism specifically means two things. It means first of all the absence of divine "intervention." In this view, since nature is considered to be autonomous, any miracle must be an intervention into the laws of nature. In other words, to have a miracle, nature must be interfered with by some outside agency, and evolutionary uniformitarianism will not accept this.

A second principle of evolutionary uniformitarianism is that rates and processes occurring in the present have remained the same throughout history and can therefore be used to extrapolate into the far distant past. Events in the past are expected to be explainable in terms of present processes and rates. In discussing the nature of the Darwinian revolution, a well-known scientist and proponent of evolution remarks:

> Almost diametrically opposed to this (Divine intervention) were the conclusions of those who excluded all recourse to supernatural interventions. Uniformitarianism to them meant simply the consistent application of natural laws not only to inanimate nature (as was done by Lyell) but also to the living world (as proposed by Chambers). The important component in their argument was the rejection of supernatural intervention rather than a lip service to the word uniformity.[1]

As previously noted, extrapolation of present processes into the far distant past is very, very risky. The further into the past one attempts to extrapolate, the riskier the extrapolation. Even those who use this method sometimes recognize the danger:

> Geologists have used their observations of contemporary earth processes and products as a key to those of the past. Yet any reconstruction of the relation of time and the earth from a contemporary vista encounters formidable barriers. This is in large part because the amount of time available to man for observation, measurement, and experiment is infinitely

small relative to the rates of many major earth processes and to the length of geologic time. There is, of course, another imposing reason. Rock processes and the products we observe today reflect contemporary crustal environments. But these environments have changed with time, in space, in their proportions, and in kind. There was, after all, a time on earth when there was no "crust" at all—and very little earth.[2]

The doctrine of uniformitarianism is applied not only to geology, but to paleoscience in general. Paleontology, or as it is now often termed, paleobiology, also uses this principle.

Uniformitarianism is a direct corollary of the original assumption that nature is autonomous. Especially objectionable to those who hold to the doctrine of uniformitarianism is the idea of a biblical worldwide flood of Noah's day. Autonomous nature and the attendant assumption of uniformitarianism are in direct opposition to the idea of a flood. The suggestion of a worldwide flood is singled out for special scorn and ridicule:

> Geology was not a science until the legendary Noachian flood and six-day creation were replaced by explanations derived from careful study of rocks. The doctrine that past events should be explainable through no more than reasonable extensions of observable processes has played a vital role in substituting the plausible for the preposterous and the feasible for the fanciful in geology.[3]

Thus, one system for extrapolating into the past arises directly from the assumption that nature is autonomous.

A Dependent Creation

Now that we have outlined one of the two possibilities for approaching the past, we will consider the other assumption—that the natural world is not autonomous. Instead, it is dependent moment by moment on its Creator. In the dependent view, the world does not have an independent existence. The Creator did not create the world and then leave it. He created it to enjoy it. If the Creator is to enjoy His creation, He will not leave it but will interact with it. In the dependent view, which originates from the Bible, the whole created universe is upheld moment by moment by the word of the Creator's power (Hebrews 1:3). The Creator actually maintains the universe in coherence. He holds all things together (Colossians 1:17). The Creator interacts with His created universe, upholds it, and preserves it. "You alone are the LORD; You have made heaven, the heaven of heavens, with all their host, the earth and all things on it, the seas and all that is in them, and You preserve them all. The host of heaven worships You" (Nehemiah 9:6, NKJV). Thus in the dependent view, the whole universe, past, present, and future, is dependent moment by moment on the will of God. The Bible knows nothing of an independent nature.

> The New Testament proclaims again the message that there is no eternal cycle of nature or cycle of history. The history of the world moves toward its final destination and heaven and earth are destined to fall back into the nothingness from which they once emerged. Not only the creating, but also the upholding of the world belongs to God alone; that is to say, Jahveh is not a deistic supreme being who, after the creative act, leaves everything to the innate laws of nature, and He does not withdraw, like a platonic demiurge, into 'the way of being that belongs solely to Him'. He remains for ever the will and power behind all events—Christ 'upholds all things by the word of His power'. It is true that there is order in the living as well as in the non-living world; but this is order existing not in its own right, but as a testimony to God's fatherly care for man and animals. The Bible knows nothing of 'Nature' but knows only 'creatures', who are absolutely dependent for their origin and existence on the will of God.[4]

The dependent view as an assumption for interpreting all of earth history, past, present, and future, is not one which makes sense to the natural or pagan mind. The natural tendency for man is to reject it. Only one who has been led to repentance through the action of God's Holy Spirit is ready to consider rebuilding his whole world view from this assumption.

> But the unspiritual man simply cannot accept the matters which the Spirit deals with—they just don't make sense to him, for, after all, you must be spiritual to see spiritual things. The spiritual man, on the other hand, has an insight into the meaning of everything, though his insight may baffle the man of the world. This is because the former is sharing in God's wisdom, and
>
> > Who hath known the mind of the Lord,
> > That he should instruct him?
>
> Nevertheless, we who are spiritual have the very thoughts of Christ! (1 Corinthians 2:14-16, Phillips).

The unspiritual man has a natural tendency to reject the assumption that the material universe depends moment by moment on the Creator.

Opposition to the Supernatural

Natural man's world view, which begins by assuming nature to be autonomous with an infinite regression of cause and effect, is sometimes termed *naturalism* or a *naturalistic* world view. In our times it is popularly referred to as evolution. Naturalism assumes that everything in all of creation happens according to natural laws of cause and effect. These natural laws are considered to be self-existent and part of autonomous nature. Naturalism locks God out of the system by using the excuse that if God exists, He could not break His own natural laws. Someone using this system reasons that if God were to "intervene" in nature, it would be a violation of natural law, and God would not want to violate His own natural laws. Thus naturalism is opposed to any supernatural event and assumes such events do not occur. This means that God, if He exists, does not act on the system. Miracles do not occur. Thus some naturalistic explanation according to chemistry and physics must always be sought for anything claimed to be a miracle.

Another notable feature of naturalism is the way it redefines meanings of words. Naturalism redefines science to mean an autonomous approach to nature. Naturalism thus seeks to impose its own philosophical assumptions on the definition of science. It claims that its approach is scientific, and only its explanations are scientific. Any other explanation is nonscientific. Naturalism tends to label those who oppose naturalism as unscientific and anti-intellectual.

Science Redefined

The natural man defines his world view as science, and then using circular logic says that science cannot make the dependent universe assumption. The natural mind insists that the autonomous view fits reality. As mentioned earlier, the autonomous world view in our present culture is termed the evolutionary world view or the "scientific" world view. Those who hold to the autonomous view of the natural world frequently state that evolution is a fact. By this they mean that their own world view is the only acceptable description of reality, as opposed to creation, which they believe to be fantasy.

One of the reasons frequently offered by evolutionists for not accepting the dependent view of the natural world is that it would be unscientific. Their *definition* of science, however, is the naturalistic explanation of an autonomous world. Nothing can happen in this view that is not in line with the normal operation of natural laws. In short, their circular argument runs this way: (1) Nothing can happen that is not in accordance with natural laws; (2) science deals with things that happen according to natural laws; (3) therefore, any view other than things happening only by natural laws is unscientific. This type of circular argument is quite common. Sometimes it is even dressed up in sophisticated language and fairly lengthy statements.

When reduced to its simplist terms, however, it is simply the circular argument stated above.

The natural mind has a strong tendency to remain trapped in this circle. Even Christians can become trapped into adopting this same circular argument. According to the Bible, however, the autonomous view does not describe reality. In the biblical world view, the natural world is dependent moment by moment on the Creator. It is upheld by the word of His power. This is reality in the biblical view.

Science in the dependent view is *defined* differently from science in the autonomous view. A Christian can just as validly erect another circular argument. It would run as follows: (1) The natural world is dependent on God and is upheld moment by moment by the word of His power; (2) science is a study of the natural world; (3) therefore, any view other than the universe upheld by the word of His power is unscientific. Thus, the Christian scientist also reasons in a circle. The difference however is that it is not an autonomous circle. It follows the dependent assumption. Guided by the Bible, a Christian scientist also makes the assumption of the uniformity of natural causes (God's habitual way of working). But he also allows for God to will an event to occur in a noncustomary way.

The Bible clearly makes some statements about cases in which God acted other than in His habitual way. Thus the Bible is a necessary guide to the study of science. It is a guide to the study of reality. It is a guide for a scientific search for truth. The Christian, using the assumption of a dependent natural world, constructs a world view which is different from the world view of those who begin by assuming nature to be autonomous.

The autonomous approach to the natural world and the dependent approach to the natural world are thus totally different and antithetical philosophical views.

Blind Chance

In naturalistic thinking, life originated by a blind process without intelligence involved. Molecules interacting countless times by chance eventually produced life. This view that life is the product only of chemical and physical processes, without intelligence involved, is nearly universally presented in textbooks. For several generations, students in public schools have been presented with this as the only view accounting for the origin of life. Typically, these statements run somewhat as follows:

> Living creatures on earth are a direct product of the earth. There is now little doubt that living things owe their origin entirely to certain physical and chemical properties of the ancient earth. Nothing supernatural was involved—only time and natural physical and chemical laws operating with the peculiarly suitable earthly environment.[5]

Notice the dogmatism of this statement on the evolutionary view of the origin of life. Life just happened to develop on its own, without the interaction of intelligence. Life is autonomous.

A Universe without Design

No design or purpose is allowed in the evolutionary view. Design and purpose are repugnant to one who is trying to hide from a Creator. Interestingly, however, design and purpose seem to be so apparent when considering living things that many evolutionary biologists simply cannot resist using these terms. Design and purpose, however, have no place in evolutionary thinking. One biologist, aware of his colleagues' use of words such as strategies or design or purpose, attempted to correct what he considered a misuse of terms:

> The term "strategy" has become common currency among biologists of various persuasions from the molecular to the population level. We read of biochemical strategies exhibited by marine invertebrates and reproductive strategies in desert plants! . . . The term is therefore semantically quite incorrect but, far more important, it is philosophically grossly

misleading, as it implies that a process has occurred which is the very antithesis of the evolutionary concept of chance and necessity.

Let us therefore agree on the strategy to expunge this nasty little word from our biological vocabulary. . . .[6]

Even the suggestion of intelligent design or purpose is repugnant and has no place in evolution. *Evolution is the common term applied to the philosophical concept that nature is autonomous.*

Evolution is a total world view and was invented by fallen man as a means of avoiding responsibility to be in submission to the Creator. Man, the created being, chose to rebel against the Creator. Man willfully chose to make his own decisions about right and wrong rather than accepting the Creator's standards.

The fall had profound consequences, not only for man, but for all of creation (Romans 8:22). Human nature was permanently affected by the fall. That nature has passed right on down to us today. "Therefore, just as sin entered the world through one man, and death through sin, and in this way death came to all men, because all sinned—" (Romans 5:12).

It is a mistake to think that the fall is limited to moral and spiritual areas. The total man fell, and this affected man's intellect and reason as well. It also caused a series of separations. First was a separation between man and God. Man has a natural tendency not to do what is right.

The second area of separation was between man and his fellow man. Just as Adam tended to blame God and Eve for what he did, so we tend to blame others for our faults. Marriage partners, for example, tend to feel that theirs would be an ideal marriage if it weren't for their spouse. Or an employee may feel that his would be an ideal job if it weren't for the other employees or for the boss. We tend to blame others for our faults. The fall caused a separation between man and man.

A third area of separation is between man and nature. Instead of following the Creator's mandate to be good stewards over the creation, greed and selfishness lead man to exploit the natural resources. Thus we have pollution of the environment and the ecological crisis. The fall caused a separation between man and nature.

A fourth area of separation is that of man from himself. As a result, we all tend to be more or less schizophrenic. The good things we want to do, we end up not doing, and the bad things we don't want to do, we end up doing. There is a constant inner tension. The fall caused a separation of man from himself.

The fall helps explain many of the features of the creation-evolution controversy and has serious implications for present-day science. When Adam and Eve sinned, the Bible tells us they tried to hide from their Creator. I have often pondered whether evolution might not be modern man's way of hiding from the Creator. Anyone with even a little experience in discussing creation and evolution cannot help having noticed the seeming reluctance of many to accept creation as an explanation for origins. This is true for nonscientists as well as scientists. Man has an innate reluctance to accept creation, a fact that has been noted by a number of observers. "We are in the midst of another series of debates between creationism and evolution. But the real problem is not the age of man, the origin of life, or the creation of our universe. . . . The real problem behind evolution is the disposition of man *not* to believe."[7] Although Breckenridge is not a scientist, he strikes at the very heart of the matter.

E. H. Andrews is another writer who has done extensive study on the creation-evolution issue. He is an eminent scientist and has written an excellent little treatise, *Is Evolution Scientific?*

> Undoubtedly, however, the real answer to why the theory of evolution has gained such universal acceptance must lie within ourselves. Experience teaches us that we accept without question anything we find comfortable and resist ideas which cause us disquiet. . . . The idea of evolution is accepted without question by most of us because it relieves us of the

need to believe in God. Some, of course, accept both evolution and the existence of a God, but the *kind* of God who remains is no longer the Almighty Who called the worlds into being, and certainly not the God of creation and providence revealed in the Christian Scriptures.[8]

(Andrews's comments raise again the question of theistic evolution [i.e., God and evolution, too], but we will wait to say more about that in the next chapter.)

In a lecture to a college audience several years ago, I gave scientific evidence in favor of creation. Afterwards a middle-aged man, a non-Christian, remarked to me that the whole issue of creation raised some disturbing questions. If creation were true, and he thought it might be from evidence presented that night, then "the next question a person would logically be led to ask was, What is my relationship to the Creator?" He paused for a moment, as if thinking deeply, and then stated, "You know, that is a scary question. I don't think a lot of people want to ask that question." That man was unusually perceptive.

Henry Morris, a well-known scientist, speaker, and lecturer on the topic of creation and evolution, states, "Whether or not we choose to accept this framework [creation] is basically determined by whether or not we *want* to do so. Those who elect the evolutionary framework do so not because the facts of science require this, but because this is the philosophic thought-structure they desire. 'They did not *like* to retain God in their knowledge'" (Romans 1:28).[9]

Even though man normally tries to hide from God and is afraid of the Creator, this need not be the case. The Bible makes it abundantly clear that if anyone wants to make peace with God, it is entirely possible to do so. The Bible states, "For the wages of sin is death, but the gift of God is eternal life in Christ Jesus our Lord" (Romans 6:23). One who has made his peace with God through accepting Jesus Christ as Savior no longer has to hide from the Creator. He no longer has to accept evolution as the only possible explanation for origins. He is free to accept creation, just as the early scientists did. After being trapped in evolutionary theory, turning to creation can be a very exciting and rewarding experience. Many, in fact, have found this to be the case. Malcolm Muggeridge, the well-known writer, has commented on this point.

> Suddenly caught up in the wonder of God's love flooding the universe, made aware of the stupendous creativity which animates all life, and of our own participation in it—every color brighter, every meaning clearer, every shape more shapely, every word written and spoken more coherent. Above all, every human face, all human companionship, all human encounters recognizably a family affair; the animals, too, flying, prowling, burrowing, all their diverse cries and grunts and bellowing and the majestic hill-tops, the gaunt rocks giving their blessed shade, and the rivers making their way to the sea—all irradiated with the same new glory. This is freedom—the sense of belonging to God's creation, these are our human rights—to participate in the realization of his purposes for it.
>
> It is like coming to after an anaesthetic; reconnecting with reality after being enmeshed in fantasy, picking out familiar shapes and faces with delighted recognition.[10]

Creation not only serves as a good basis for science, but for all of life. It brings meaning to the totality of existence.

The doctrine of creation is also the basis of the gospel. If man was created and is now a fallen creature, he needs a savior. Creation and the fall are the basis for the whole message of the gospel. The worldly system has always been opposed to the message of the gospel, and that opposition continues. Because creation is so closely associated with the gospel, I believe this is one of the reasons it is under attack in our day. The attack is co-ordinated from the very headquarters of evil. It is a spiritual battle. Francis Schaeffer, commenting on the close association between creation, the fall, and the gospel, notes, "Take away the first three chapters of Genesis, and you cannot maintain a true Christian position nor give Christianity's answers."[11]

Chapter 5, Notes

1. Ernst Mayr, "The Nature of the Darwinian Revolution," *Science*, 2 June 1972, 985.

2. A. E. J. Engel, "Time and the Earth," *American Scientist* (Winter 1969): 459.

3. John S. Shelton, *Geology Illustrated* (San Francisco: W. H. Freeman and Co., 1966), 351.

4. R. Hooykaas, *Religion and the Rise of Modern Science* (Grand Rapids: Wm. B. Eerdmans Publishing Co., 1972), 8.

5. Paul B. Weisz, *The Science of Biology* (New York: McGraw-Hill, 1959), 21.

6. Gideon Louw, "Letters," *Science*, 9 March 1979, 955.

7. James Breckenridge, "A New Look at Evolution," *Christian Life*, June 1982, 40.

8. Andrews, *Is Evolution Scientific?* 3.

9. Henry M. Morris, *Studies in the Bible and Science* (Grand Rapids: Baker Book House, 1966), 110.

10. Malcolm Muggeridge, "The Fearful Symmetry of Freedom," *Christianity Today*, 21 April 1978, 15.

11. Francis A. Schaeffer, *The God Who Is There* (Downers Grove, Ill.: InterVarsity Press, 1968), 104.

Chapter 6

Truth and Consequences

*M*an at the fall began to develop a world view alien to the Bible. It is a world view based on the assumption that man and nature are autonomous; that is, that they can act independently of God.

Evolution is called on to explain the origin and development of all things within the assumptions of an autonomous nature. We constantly hear the term *evolution* being used. We are bombarded with it in a manner reminiscent of a propaganda attack. It is called on to account for the origin of the universe. Evolution is used to explain the processes taking place on planets in space. Evolution is invoked for the development of culture. Evolution is used to explain the progressions of new scientific developments, to account for changes in language, even to explain the origin and development of religious ideas, and much more.

What has been the reaction of the church and its leaders to this attack? How have leading theologians responded to evolution and the shift in philosophy accompanying it and to the popularization of science? Some theologians were aware of what was happening and courageously stood their ground against the rise of the new philosophy of materialism. They were not fooled by the antisupernatural bias of evolution posing as science.

Sadly, however, many theologians actually seemed to welcome the new philosophy behind evolution. They joined with the Darwinists to attack their more conservative theological brothers. It is interesting to speculate on reasons for this. Perhaps it was the high esteem in which science was held coupled with a desire for respectability. Perhaps they did not wish to appear ignorant or foolish. Often theologians were not well trained in science, and when scientists held to a particular view, they tended to go along with it uncritically. As Andrews notes, "To the ordinary man, science represents the objective truth about the real world in which he lives. Layman though he be, he therefore tends to accept whatever world-view appears to command scientific respectability."[1]

The temptation to conform to what is generally considered to be respectable is especially great for those in the academic world. In America, many of the prestigious institutions of higher learning were founded and presided over by dedicated Christians. What are now generally considered Ivy League universities were originally headed by theologians who were faithful to the Bible. Many of these institutions also had schools of theology. They were the training ground for those who were becoming church leaders. Reaction of leaders in the academic community to the widespread acceptance of Darwinian thought was generally one of compromise and of yielding to intellectual pressure.

> Although none of the presidents of the "best schools" in the United States would admit that evolution was being taught in their classrooms, the *Presbyterian Observer*, when challenged in 1880 by the *Popular Science Monthly*, could find only one American naturalist who would publicly repudiate evolutionary theory.[2]

It is interesting to note that at first, when evolution began to be taught in many universities and colleges, public relations officers for those schools did not mention it or even outrightly denied that evolution was being taught. Perhaps they feared losing grassroots financial support from church constituents.

Eventually, however, as evolution became ever more widely adopted, the same schools not only began to admit that evolution was being taught at their university, but actually proudly boasted of the fact. Evolution became the "in" thing. It was respectable. Academicians did not wish to be considered behind the times in accepting evolution. Theology departments actually led the way, in many cases. They wanted to be known as a modern religion department with a "scientific" world view. For them, all that was needed was retreat to a reinterpretation of Scripture. Genesis was no longer to be considered historical, but rather myth or saga. It was claimed that the Scriptures were not meant to tell us what had happened, but only Who was behind what happened. This was especially the case for the first eleven chapters of Genesis, which cover the time from creation up to that of Abraham.

Abraham was generally admitted to have been a historical character, but accounts earlier than Abraham were considered to be myth by many theologians. Coming in for special attack and scorn was the six-day direct creation account and the worldwide universal flood of Noah.

However, a normal straightforward reading of the creation account in Genesis indicates that simple historical statements are being made. Creation involved direct acts of the Creator. This means that creation came about by supernatural means rather than by natural means. Obviously a supernatural account of origins is in conflict with the naturalistic philosophy behind evolution.

Using the new naturalistic definition of science brought on by Darwinism, evolution thus became the "scientific" explanation for origins. Many people, not realizing that a change in philosophy had taken place as well as a change in the definition of science, continued to operate within the old definition of science. In the old definition, a scientific explanation was a true explanation or a description of what really happened. The constant assertion that evolution was scientific was then mistakenly interpreted by those still using the old definition as "evolution is a real description." Evolution was taken to be factual.

Those theologians who accepted evolution as fact and who were at the same time theists—that is, believers in God—tried to force biblical theology into conforming with Darwinism. This approach is known as theistic evolution, a concept that covers a broad range of ideas. Generally it takes the position that evolution happened, but that a Creator or intelligence was somehow involved in the process. Most theistic evolutionists will admit that direct acts of a Creator were involved at least to some extent, perhaps in an original creation of matter and energy and natural laws. Theistic evolutionists differ regarding the number and extent of the Creator's direct acts. But common to all the various theistic evolutionary views is the assertion that the creation account in Genesis is not to be taken in any literal or historic sense.

Atheistic and Theistic Evolution

Evolutionists fall into one of two camps regarding the existence of deity. One group is atheistic. They assume that creation did not take place because there is no creator. They deny the existence of a divine being who could create. Atheistic evolutionists assume an infinite regression of cause and effect. They assume that only autonomous natural laws operate in the universe, and that life arose by chance over a long period of time. No intelligence was involved, no creation took place, because there is no Creator.

The other group of evolutionists, as mentioned above, are theists and either assume or admit the possibility of a divine being. Because they are theists and also because they believe in evolution, they are theistic evolutionists. Theistic evolutionists, like atheistic evolutionists, make the same basic assumption that nature is autonomous. But theistic evolutionists also assume that God was somehow involved in the process, perhaps in an initial act of creation.

Many Christians have adopted some form of theistic evolution, but the Bible does not teach this approach. Theistic evolution arises from an attempt to remain a theist while accepting an autonomous nature.

Unavoidable Conflict

The Bible, however, teaches just the opposite of theistic evolution. What evolutionists refer to as *Nature* was created with purpose and design. It is not autonomous, but depends on God for sustenance.

Since the world view of the Bible is that nature is dependent and *not* autonomous, and since the world view of evolution is that nature *is* autonomous, then these two views *must* conflict. They are opposite philosophical views. As a consequence, facts discovered by scientists are interpreted entirely differently within each of these world views.

For a time theistic evolution was also the position I adopted. In high school, I made a commitment of my life to Jesus Christ. I accepted Him as my Savior and He began changing my life. I was converted spiritually and emotionally. Intellectually, however, many questions remained. From reading the Bible and attending a conservative church, I thought creation plainly seemed to be the Christian position.

My formal education, however, all through public grade school and high school, then into a private four-year college, and finally four years of graduate training ending with the Ph.D., was within the evolutionary framework. Evolution was presented as fact. But God is also a fact. It occurred to me that if God was fact and evolution was fact, then evolution must be God's method for creation. I adopted theistic evolution. All I had to do was to retreat from a firm stand on Scripture and reinterpret Genesis in a mythological manner. That way I could be a Christian and be scientifically educated, too—or so I thought. Further study, however, revealed extreme problems with the position, and I later rejected it in favor of direct creation.

After adopting theistic evolution, I had the uneasy feeling that I had compromised and downgraded Scripture. However, there were many theologians and many of my scientific colleagues who assured me that this was a respectable way to go. I became very sensitive and defensive when encountering those who were theologically more conservative and who held to a direct creation view. Any implication that the world was squeezing me into its intellectual mold (as Romans 12:2 warns against) was resisted fiercely. I wanted to be known as a Christian and a Bible-believer. But I also wanted to be intellectually respectable. There was, I suppose, a measure of pride in my new position. It made me tend to look down on those who were not as educated in science as I thought I was. The temptation was to look down on those who still believed in creation as not being well educated or as not being good scientists. Adopting theistic evolution, however, did not make problems go away. I had reinterpreted Scripture relating to creation, but where would the process stop? As one writer observed,

> Finally, the layman wants to know where this process of reinterpreting Scripture is going to stop. Will it affect our reading of the incarnation and resurrection of Christ?
>
> Until someone answers these questions, many a Bible believer will find himself more comfortable with literalist groups such as the Creation Research Society and the Bible-Science Association. But since that means flying in the face of science, the poor fellow may aptly be described as floundering haplessly in the Bible-science cauldron.
>
> We are indeed back to the boiling point.[3]

One of my questions centered around the assertion that creation "flew in the face of science," as mentioned above. What did this statement mean? At face value, it seemed to imply that creation contradicted factual information discovered in science. Is that really the case? If so, what are these facts which contradict direct creation? Is there no other valid interpretation of these facts? What is science, anyway? How does it work? An examination of that question seemed worthwhile.

Christian Students in Science

What happened to me is typical of Christian students in general. The evolutionary world view puts tremendous pressure on a student interested in science. Not knowing the naturalistic philosophical base of modern science, the student nevertheless observes the success of science. He soon realizes, however, that there is a conflict between the evolutionary world view posing as science and the creation world view. If he is a Christian, he knows that God is a fact. However, his science is presented as though evolution were a fact. Most students are bright enough to realize that creation and evolution are totally opposite viewpoints. If one is true, the other is false. How do they resolve this dilemma?

Can We Adjust the Bible?

What usually happens is that the student adopts some form of theistic evolution just as was my experience. He retreats into assuming that the Bible must be interpreted mythically, not historically, concerning the Creation account. The rationalization for doing this is usually that there are many interpretations possible for the Bible. Why interpret it narrowly? Why not take a very broad interpretation of the Bible so that whatever the view current in modern science, the Bible can be adjusted to fit it?

Thus the student seemingly ends his conflict between the Bible and what he has been told is science. There will be no conflict between them because the Bible has been harmonized with "science." Autonomous science then takes precedence over the Bible; autonomous naturalistic science is used to interpret the Bible. Theistic evolution uses the excuse that the Bible tells us who created, but not how he created. The how of creation is left to naturalistic science.

In my studies of science, evolution was the only world view presented. Creation was never presented as an alternative. If creation was mentioned at all, the impression was that creation had long since been discredited. Statements to that effect are common in the scientific literature, as illustrated by the following: "The American Association for the Advancement of Science, meeting in Washington, D.C., on January 4 [1982], passed a resolution declaring that 'creation science has no scientific validity' and poses 'a real and present threat to the integrity of education.' "[4] Derogatory remarks are consistently made toward those who believe in creation. These remarks are found not only in scientific literature, textbooks, popular media (television, radio, newspapers, magazines) but even in Christian publications. The pressure to conform to the world's way of thinking is extremely great and constantly applied. The problem for a Christian student of science has been aptly summarized by Joseph Dillow.

> At this point, the scientist who sincerely loves Christ and the Bible is confronted with a tension.
>
> Frequently, the apparently obvious interpretations of the Bible seem to contradict his scientific background. How is he to handle this?
>
> Because he is not trained in Biblical exegesis and theology, all too often he is content to fall back on the fact that there are many different interpretations.
>
> So he often feels a freedom to select from the maze of options the one that happens to be most consistent with his particular scientific background.
>
> This raises the question as to which of these different possible interpretations will be taken as the correct one. Or more precisely, what criterion does one use to select the correct one from these possible interpretations?
>
> The tendency of many Christians who are scientifically trained seems to be to select the interpretations that best fit with their personal scientific convictions. . . . It is highly improbable that the Bible is actually as ambiguous as these various interpretations would lead us to believe.[5]

Can We Reinterpret the Bible?

If the Bible is to be reinterpreted to fit the views of modern autonomous science, there is a real danger. Science continually changes its views. This means that the Bible must then also continually be reinterpreted as well. At one time, for example, evolutionary scientists supposed the universe to be a steady state universe. Then came the big bang theory for the origin of the universe. Present indications are that the big bang theory is in trouble and may soon be replaced.[6] Those who have reinterpreted the Bible to agree with continually changing views must also continually change their interpretation of the Bible. If the Bible is that flexible, it does not stand as ultimate truth. One cannot use it in a firm way for evangelism to convert a pagan world. One cannot use it to say, "Thus saith the Lord."

This lesson was driven home to me several years ago. Students at a public college in Washington state regularly had a discussion forum on Friday evening in the student union building. One Friday evening I was invited to speak on the topic of creation and evolution. After being introduced as a scientist who believed in creation, I stood up to speak.

Before I could say anything, however, a student from the audience quickly rose to his feet. He said, "Sir, before you speak, I want you to answer a question." He seemed to command a good deal of respect from the other students. Perhaps he was a leader in the discussion group; I didn't know for sure. He said, "Do you accept the Bible as literally true or not?" A hush came over the whole audience. I could tell by the reaction of other students to this question that it was an exceedingly important one to them. My answer could well determine whether I would further be allowed to say anything at all.

While I was thinking about an answer to that question, a number of thoughts raced through my mind. I knew that most students considered the Bible to be myth and scientifically inaccurate. The temptation was to tell them I took a compromising view and to be wishy-washy in my answer. I was tempted to think that perhaps by not giving a direct answer, the students might be more willing to hear me out on the discussion. However, I also realized this would be dishonest. It would be best to simply tell them the truth. I did take the early chapters of the Bible to be historical, or as my questioner phrased it, "literally true." The only honest thing to do was to tell them and leave the results to God. I said, "Yes, I do."

I shall never forget his response and the response of the audience. The tension in his face relaxed a bit, and he said to me, "That's good. You have something to say worth listening to. We may not agree with you, but your point's worth further consideration." From the reaction of the audience, it was apparent that they agreed with him.

That incident taught me a lesson and made a lasting impression on me. A direct straightforward reading of the Bible gives the impression that simple historical statements are being made. They are propositional truths about the real world. If I had hedged and called them myth, then that student felt I would already be on his side and would have nothing new to say. He already knew about evolution and the view that the first chapters of Genesis are myth. If evolution is true, and everything can be explained by natural means using chemical and physical laws, why add on the unnecessary hypothesis of a Creator? He had a point.

I did present that evening a scientific case for creation. The students listened politely and asked many questions. It was an interesting and enjoyable discussion. The opportunity could have been lost. However, since I was honest in stating that I did accept the Bible in a literal sense, it was not lost. Not all of the students agreed with the creation approach, but many of them expressed interest in further study. It made sense to them.

Theistic Evolution: An Unsatisfactory Approach?

After being pressured to accept theistic evolution as a compromise between science and religion (as already mentioned), I finally rejected that approach. There are a number of reasons it was unsatisfactory. First of all, deep down inside, it never seemed to ring true. Theologically, it just didn't make sense either. Genesis spoke of a finished creation. Theistic evolution, on the other hand, was a continuing naturalistic process over a long period of time, a process still going on now. It seemed very apparent that the Bible clearly spoke of *a finished creation in conflict with the idea of a continuing process*.

Second, it was logically inconsistent. It was put forward as a way of harmonizing science and religion, but it did neither. It sacrificed reason on the altar of compromise.

> "Theistic evolution" or "progressive creation" permits a belief in God, but assumes that He used evolution as the means of creation.
>
> Although I flirted with theistic evolution for quite some time myself, I finally had to give up on the idea. For one thing, "time and chance" are really the logical opposites of "plan and purpose." To give due credit, that's the real genius of evolution: a bold attempt to explain design without a Designer. If God used chance on purpose, would it really be chance? On the other hand, if it really were chance, how could it be purpose—except in George Orwell's *Animal Farm* where "love is hate" and "war is peace"?[7]

Theistic evolution not only was logically contradictory, but it was also theologically inconsistent as well. It seemed inconsistent to work so hard to exclude miracle from creation when it had to be admitted in the gospels. Why would a Christian want to fight to exclude miracle at one point in time but allow it at another?

Furthermore, evolution seemed to be against scientific evidence. It did not agree with the fossil record. The fossil record didn't show a slow gradual change of one species into another. It was also against the facts of biology.

> Scientifically, evolution could not be God's means of creation, simply because the evolutionary processes, mutation and selection, don't create. Those processes only vary and preserve traits that already exist, so they're effective only *after* creation has

already taken place. The evidence favors creation by special, completed acts, not by slow continuing processes.[8]

Evolution has severe problems with scientific evidence. It goes against the evidence. It goes against a direct reading of Scripture, has logical problems, and is theologically weak. Why would a Christian want to adopt such a position? Why would he insist that God used a method which is contrary to the evidence? Thus I rejected that approach.

Compromising Opposites

Theistic evolution did not come from science. Nothing in autonomous, pagan science insists that God was somehow involved with the process. Rather, evolution was invented and is held as an alternative explanation to creation. Supernaturalism is specifically excluded.

Theistic evolution also does not come from the Scriptures. One cannot show from Scripture that evolution was the process of creation. Theistic evolution did not come from science and it did not come from Scripture. It arose as an attempt to compromise two opposites. It came as an attempt to force the Bible to conform to culture rather than the reverse. Two totally different and antithetical world views were involved, and theistic evolution was an attempt to mix these two views. An undesirable consequence was compartmentalization of truth. Theistic evolution was forced to place religious and spiritual truth in a realm separate from scientific truth. Theistic evolutionists could thus be religious while at the same time accepting the views of a science independent of God.

Although I toyed for a while with theistic evolution, the logical inconsistency of putting religion into one realm and history and science into another realm was never satisfactory. It seemed to me that if truth existed, there should be a unity of truth. A Christian philosopher centuries ago made an observation that describes theistic evolution quite well. He stated: "the heart may be Christian, but the mind is pagan at the bottom."[9]

A Move toward Theistic Evolution

Theistic evolution, however, is accepted by many within the church in our time. This is true of nearly every denomination, though of some more than others. The liberal denominations have accepted evolution almost since Darwin made it popular. Many of the more conservative denominations and churches have unfortunately also gradually moved over to a position of theistic evolution.

Many, perhaps even a majority, of what have come to be known as Christian colleges have also moved to a position of theistic evolution. In the early 1970s a survey was conducted of science and mathematics faculty at institutions which were at that time members of the Christian College Consortium. Results of the survey showed that science faculty members in those schools took a theistic evolutionary position regarding creation and evolution.

With Christian colleges training many of the future leaders of churches, it is not surprising that there has been a move within churches toward theistic evolution. This has resulted in a negative effect on the church. The church's vitality has been deadened.

Consequences of Theistic Evolution

If theistic evolution is adopted, there are consequences. A straightforward natural reading of the Bible cannot be used. One must manipulate historical statements into myth. Hence one must always be on guard against using the normal, natural meanings of words in the biblical text on creation because they indicate real historical statements rather than myth. Such an approach tends to kill enthusiasm for Scripture. The creation account in Genesis, if studied in detail, is extremely exciting and fascinating. However, if one is told that it has no basis in historical fact and is just myth or poetic writing, the excitement vanishes. If one must superimpose myth on what seem like natural historical statements, why stop at the first few chapters of Genesis? What is to prevent later statements which seem like historical events from also being translated as myth? One could do this throughout the Old Testament and on through the gospels and the epistles as well. This not only greatly diminishes one's enthusiasm for reading the Bible, but it also leads to serious doctrinal consequences.

Another effect of theistic evolution is to diminish enthusiasm for evangelism. The burden of explaining to a non-Christian how to account for statements that seem historical but must be interpreted as myth is a massive burden. The first eleven chapters of Genesis are ones that talk about creation and the fall. If these are mythical, how then can we say that the fall is an actual event? If the fall is not an actual event, then why do we need a savior? If evolution is true and things have been continually improving, then perhaps man will work out all of his problems. Why must we be saved?

Pressure on School Children

In my experience, many of those who are now theistic evolutionists began by believing in creation. As young children in Sunday school, they were presented with creation using a natural, straightforward reading from Genesis. Children also think by using presuppositions even though they may not be mature enough to realize it. Reading the creation account in Genesis leads them to accept biblical presuppositions as natural. They have no trouble accepting miracle in creation. They also have no trouble accepting the miracles of Jesus. Later, however, especially after entering school, they begin to feel the pressure of a pagan world view. As one scientist, concerned about the issue, observes:

> A child is taught a set of values and a world-view in the home by parents who wish to instill certain concepts about God, the origin of man, and expected behavior. However, when the child enters public school, these values are no longer supported and reinforced as they once were. Frequently, the values are torn down and the child is compelled, under threat of academic failure, to affirm a contradictory

set of concepts. . . . The child is not presented with evolution as a theory. Subtle statements are made in science texts as early as the second grade (based on my reading of children's textbooks). Evolution is presented as reality, not as a concept that can be questioned. The authority of the educational system then compels belief and the attitudes are gradually molded without an honest statement of ultimate purpose.[10]

Tremendous pressure is thus placed on the child. He is pressured to accept a world view that conflicts with his own without really understanding what is happening. The child knows something is wrong and it causes severe trauma. I believe this is one reason for the rise in the number of students attending Christian schools and home schools. Parents do not want Christian values undermined and attacked by pagan values which are often presented militantly in public schools.

I have myself sat in class after class in the sciences and humanities in which any idea remotely religious was belittled, attacked, and shouted down in the most unscientific and emotionally cruel way. I have seen young students raised according to fundamentalist doctrine treated like loathsome alley cats, emotionally torn apart, and I never thought that this sort of treatment was any better than the treatment that religious prelates, who held authority, gave Galileo. Why scream about the inhumanity of nuclear war if you are also willing to force people of fundamentalist faiths to attend public schools in which their most cherished beliefs will be systematically held up to ridicule and the young children with it? These people are mostly too poor for private school to be an alternative. The state tries to prevent them from teaching their children at home rather than sending them to school. What choices do they have? Would you call it freedom? Do you call it fair?[11]

In the home and in Sunday school, the Christian child is normally taught to expect pressure from non-Christians in the area of Christian moral principles. All too often, however, he is not taught to expect intellectual pressure. While he does not expect to receive much help from non-Christians, he is also often denied intellectual help from the Christian community. Often he will be told, even by Christians, that his questions are not important or that creation is not an important issue. He will be told that it doesn't matter, since there are Christians who believe many things about the Bible. It's just a matter of interpretation.

Those who insist that it really doesn't matter are simply not being honest. If they actually believed that it didn't matter, they would be just as willing to accept creation as evolution. But I have not found them willing to do this. They always want the creationist to come over to the side of evolution.

One incident illustrating how students are sometimes denied the help they need happened in a church my wife and I attended a number of years ago. A particularly bright student attended the fifth grade Sunday school class at that church. The student asked a question in an area relating to science and the Bible. It was a good question, one often asked by older students. The response the student received to his question, however, was that it was a foolish question. The issue didn't really matter. Of what importance was it to the faith?

The disappointment of that student was overwhelming. Although he continued to attend that church for a number of years afterwards, I do not recall that he ever again asked another question in the intellectual area. Nor do I recall other members of the class asking questions. They seemed to get the message that Christianity did not have intellectual answers. Christianity was to be believed by blind faith. The intellectual side of life was to be left to the secular, pagan community.

Accusations from the Christian Community

Even more sad is the situation in which Christians side with pagans in attacking biblical presuppositions. Creation and those who believe in it come in for special attack by those within

Truth and Consequences   107

the church who have adopted theistic evolution. For example, from just three articles appearing in Christian publications receiving wide circulation within the Christian community, I find the following list of accusations hurled at those who believe in creation:

Creationists:
- Have a hidden agenda (are dishonest)
- Have poor strategy for Christian impact
- Are aberrational
- Are cultic
- Lack training in historical sciences (biology, geology)
- Have little contact with scientific community
- Appeal to uninformed audiences
- Do not make their case in established scientific channels
- Are not as honest as evolutionists
- Are unable to dent scientific orthodoxy
- Have a garbled message
- Have an incomplete message
- Have a message that is just plain wrong
- Have a message which often lacks accuracy
- Have a message which often lacks balance
- Magnify a particular view out of proportion
- Are hyper-literalists
- Sweep aside evidence
- Present a caricature of the true Christian view
- Are isolationist
- Are inflexible
- Are doing more harm than good
- Abandon science
- Are kibitzers of science
- Help perpetuate unbelief
- Commit logical fallacies
- Use verbal chicanery
- Misuse scientific theory

Misinterpret the Bible
Are guilty of the "growing edge syndrome" logic
Shadowbox with straw men
Strain factual data
Abuse reason
Use circular reasoning
Narrowly read Scripture
Flagrantly ignore scientific evidence[12]

Some of the accusations in the list are quite serious. These accusations come from those within the church, not those outside. Faculty members at Christian colleges are frequently the source of such accusations. In most cases the accusations come as a direct result of the accuser having adopted either consciously or unconsciously an autonomous view of nature.

A young person who is taught in Sunday school that God created, using miracle, and that the early chapters of Genesis are historically true faces a real problem. It is bad enough to be attacked by those outside the church, but when it comes from those who claim to be Christians, it can be very cruel.

A Ph.D. in science related to me his own experience. He was raised in a Bible-believing Christian home. In Sunday school, at an early age he learned the creation account as given in Genesis. Later he attended a well-known Christian college where he majored in one of the science areas. His faith in creation was attacked mercilessly. Being a thinking individual, he reasoned if the plain statements of Scripture could not be trusted when they talked about history and science, how could the plain statements of Scripture be trusted when they talked about salvation and forgiveness of sins?

The attack by theistic evolution hit him so hard that he suffered a nervous breakdown. He later recovered but still bears scars from that encounter. He now holds to a theistic evolutionary view. While discussing creation and theistic evolution, he told me that since his encounter at the Christian college, he resolved never again to take up a position that could be attacked by the autonomous view of nature. He was working out his religious convictions so there would be no point which could ever be proved wrong. He was not going to take a stand on any biblical issue which even in principle could potentially be disproved by factual evidence from science. In effect, he wanted to completely isolate his religious views from any contact with the real world.

I believe this man is a sincere Christian. Yet what a sad position to take! His position is the exact opposite of historic Christianity. Christianity is based on historical truth. In principle, these truths are open to verification or disproof. Christianity alone, of all the world's religions, is open to discussion in this way.

In an attempt to help him realize the logical consequences of his position, I asked him several questions. A foundational Christian doctrine is the bodily resurrection of Jesus Christ. The resurrection is a physical, not a figurative one. It is a basic tenet of Christian doctrine that Christ's bodily resurrection is historical fact. Using my friend's logic, however, even this doctrine would be called into question.

I asked him about it. I pointed out to him that here was a doctrine which, in principle, could be disproved by science. In principle, it might be possible to unearth a skeleton somewhere and show that it belonged to Jesus Christ. If this could be done, it would be proof that there was no resurrection. I asked him, "What about the resurrection and the possibility of its disproof by finding the remains of the body of Christ?"

The answer he gave amazed and saddened me. "What you say is true. In principle it might be possible for science to find the remains of the body of Christ. But it isn't important that Scripture be interpreted literally and historically. To me, it doesn't matter whether Christ literally rose from the grave or only figuratively rose. I can still be a Christian and accept Christ as my Savior."

At this point, I simply gave up and ended the discussion. He had been consistent in his logic all the way from Genesis clear through the New Testament. But what a sad position to hold. He had no firm basis for his faith and he was forced to deny a basic biblical doctrine. Scripture makes it clear that Christ physically and literally arose (1 Corinthians 15).

A Slippery Slope

Denial of the historical accuracy of the early chapters of Genesis is the beginning of a slippery slope indeed. It causes problems for institutions as well as individuals. Cases can be cited of institutions which have begun this course only to end up totally secular. Many of our well-known private colleges and universities began as Christian schools.[13]

Now, however, many of these schools have become totally secular and have no connection with the church that started them. Their move away from biblical Christianity began when nonbiblical presuppositions were adopted. It's like a cut flower bud. It may open and bloom for awhile, but it soon withers. Once cut off from the biblical roots, it was just a matter of time until the rest of Christianity was removed in those institutions as well. The end result of trying to mix two antithetical world views, as theistic evolution does, ends in ultimate disaster for the Christian position.

> There is no way to mix these two total world views. They are separate entities that cannot be synthesized. Yet we must say that liberal theology, the very essence of it from its beginning, is an attempt to mix the two. Liberal theology tried to bring forth a mixture soon after the Enlightenment and has tried to synthesize these two views right up to our own day. But in each case when the chips are down these liberal theologians have always come down, as a ship coming into home port, on the side of the nonreligious humanist.[14]

The consequences of accepting nonbiblical presuppositions are tragic, indeed. Man first tried this in the Garden of Eden and the whole course of history was changed. Consequences for individual civilizations have been recorded again and again throughout history. It happened repeatedly during

Jewish history as recorded in the Old Testament. Time and again God would bring them back to a biblical base, and time and again they would wander from it with sad consequences. These consequences are as sad for an individual as they are for institutions or a culture.

Another significant difference between the two world views concerns absolutes. The shift away from creation as a world view involved a shift away from absolutes regarding truth and morals.

> The present chasm between the generations has been brought about almost entirely by a change in the concept of truth. . . . Young people from Christian homes are brought up in the old framework of truth. Then they are subjected to the modern framework. In time they become confused because they do not understand the alternatives with which they are being presented. Confusion becomes bewilderment, and before long they are overwhelmed. This is unhappily true not only of young people, but of many pastors, Christian educators, evangelists and missionaries as well.
>
> *So this change in the concept of the way we come to knowledge and truth is the most crucial problem, as I understand it, facing Christianity today.* . . .
>
> The really foolish thing is that even now, years after the shift is over, many Christians still do not know what is happening. And this is because they are still not being taught the importance of thinking in terms of presuppositions, especially concerning truth.[15] [emphasis his]

One of the sad immediate consequences of moving away from absolutes, combined with the fact that the church has not recognized this problem, has been the departure of many young people from the church. Adults often wonder why young people leave the church when they reach teen years or young adulthood. Adults also are puzzled as to why young people seemingly have great difficulty in understanding the value system of Christian adults. Worse, young people have little knowledge of the Bible and do not recognize that it talks in absolutes. Citing some rather startling statistics, Dennis Miller discusses this topic and suggests some remedies.

> Fifty percent of Christian teenagers will sit in church next Sunday. Two years from now, 70 percent of those who graduate from high school will leave and never come back.
>
> Why this mass exodus? . . .
>
> But more teenage young people receive spiritual instruction today than ever in history. Why has it so little impact on their lives?[16]

Miller then explains the problem.

> Part of finding solutions to the mass exodus of teens from church is understanding how students today are conditioned to think. They determine their beliefs by comparing what they are being taught with what they consider valid.
>
> Most have been taught all through school that absolutes are only absolutes until the next discovery changes them. In short, they are taught there are no absolutes that are trustworthy. As a result, they determine their beliefs from their feelings. Most adults don't. . . .
>
> [A young person] determines what he believes by comparing information with his opinion and he acts upon what makes him feel good. This obviously places him at a great disadvantage when he considers Biblical absolutes and content-oriented Christian teaching.[17]

As a solution Miller suggests that in addition to teaching absolutes, the church must include life experiences as illustrations of absolutes.

Since students determine the value of truth by their experiences, the Church must begin to utilize life experiences more in teaching.[18]

From many discussions with young people, I have observed that they are quite capable of and willing to understand for themselves the situation concerning absolutes. It was not that they were not presented with absolutes early in their Christian training. They were. However, in case after case, after they entered school, confidence in biblical absolutes was eroded beginning with an attack on creation. The early chapters of Genesis which they had believed to be an account of real happenings were later presented as myth. A shadow was cast on the trustworthiness of Scripture.

This attack on the trustworthiness of Scripture was then subtly reinforced by cultural myths. As examples, young children are taught to believe that Santa Claus and the Easter Bunny are real. Later they find out that these were tricks played on them by adults. They were simply myths, and they then have difficulty separating these myths from true biblical events such as creation.

To remedy the problem and help students, we need to go back to where the problem began. Time after time I have observed that students who are allowed to see that creation is the basis of a valid thought system, a valid world view, are returned to the road toward spiritual maturity. The Bible becomes alive and exciting again. God seems much closer and a real Being. How does one help students in this area? What kind of specific information can one give them? First they need to understand the philosophic basis of the spiritual warfare we are engaged in. Then they need a general outline of biblical truths. Finally they need assistance with integrating biblical truths with their real world.

The move away from creation and toward the acceptance of evolution as a world view has not only had an effect on Christian young people, it has affected the entire culture as well. Many scholars have noted the relationship between acceptance of an evolutionary world view and the general decline in morality throughout our culture. Although strongly biased against creation, Stephen G. Brush, a historian, notes,

> Some people want creationism injected into the curriculum not because they favor it on scientific grounds but because they see evolutionism as part of a general trend toward atheism and immorality in society. They may be right about the historical *correlation* between acceptance of evolution and erosion of traditional moral values, but this does not prove that one caused the other, and it certainly does not follow that forcing biology teachers to present a scientifically discredited theory under the name of creationism will strengthen the influence of any kind of religious morality.[19] [emphasis his]

Brush is forced to admit that there may indeed be a correlation between acceptance of evolution and a decline in traditional moral values. Apparently, however, he is not willing to grant that one caused the other.

However, in implying that creation is a "scientifically discredited theory," Brush is either greatly misinformed on the topic or he is propagandizing for his particular viewpoint. Not only has creation not been scientifically discredited; it cannot be scientifically discredited. There is no way that past events can be put in the test tube and analyzed.

What Brush refers to as traditional morality is morality based on biblical absolutes. Moral standards derived from the Bible have given the highest standard of morality the world has even known. When these standards are set aside there is a decline in moral order throughout all of society. Brush as well as others have correctly noted that acceptance of Darwinism and attendant rejection of biblical authority are associated with a general moral decline.

Another observer, Josif Ton, spent many years in Marxist studies at school and university and had ten years of political education as a teacher in a communist country, Romania. He writes:

> Decline and abandonment of religion in Protestant countries began with the widespread acceptance of the theories of Charles Darwin. Many theologians capitulated to the new explanation of origins, and they tried to make their peace with science in other areas. Moral standards plummeted.[20]

Rejection of creation and acceptance of evolution started a general moral decline, and it has affected science as well. Science began to die. It was founded on the biblical ethic of truthfulness. The dying process was slow at first but has become increasingly rapid as evolution has become the dominant philosophy of science. Taking advantage of situations for selfish ends or for personal gain is not ruled out just because one is a scientist.

There is beginning to be widespread concern about moral values affecting science.

> There is little doubt that a dark side of science has emerged during the past decade. In ever-increasing detail, the scientific and general press have reported the pirating of papers and the falsification of data. Four major cases of cheating in biomedical research came to light in 1980 alone, with some observers in the lay press calling it a "crime wave." Federal investigators say two of these cases may end in criminal charges.
>
> In a profession that places an unusual premium on honesty, the emergence of fraud has created something of a stir.[21]

There is both general agreement that the problem is worsening and puzzlement as to the source of the problem. There is little doubt that it is having a drastic effect on science. When now an "expert" takes a position on a matter and supports that position with "factual" information, one can no longer be certain that even the factual information is correct. When factual data are falsified and cheating occurs in this area which is the very source of information for science, science is well along the road to dying. Science cannot continue to survive in any recognizable form when this activity becomes widespread.

The high standards expected of scientists and traditionally attributed to them were in fact established by the early modern scientists who were, as we have already noted, Christians. They held themselves accountable to the Judeo-Christian moral standard given by the Creator. As a consequence, they set the moral standards for science. It came to be expected of a scientist that he tell the truth.

It should come as no surprise then, when the Christian moral framework is rejected, that science begins to die. This is one of the reasons I believe evolution is antiscience. But science can again come alive by following the principles that made it great in the first place.

In speaking at various universities, I am finding that many young people are seeing the problem for what it is and are also seeing the solution. They are young scientists who are Christians and who are creationists. Given an opportunity, I believe we will see significant contributions being made by these dedicated young men and women. Time and time again I have observed the excitement and interest that is kindled in science when young people are given creation answers to some of the big questions facing science today.

The creation approach is tremendously motivating for the study of science, just as it was in the early days when modern science began. A young person using the creation approach can view each of the many, many individual data pieces of science as pieces that need to be fitted together to come up with an overall complete picture. These pieces, correctly fitted together, can provide answers and blessings to mankind just as science has done in the past. In his lifetime he will not be able to fit all the pieces together. New data will continually be appearing. But as more and more pieces of the picture are fitted into place, the picture becomes more and more complete and more and more reflective of the glory of our Creator and to the benefit of science.

Chapter 6, Notes

1. Andrews, *God, Science & Evolution*, 27.

2. David L. Hull, Peter D. Tessner, Arthur M. Diamond, "Planck's Principle," *Science*, 17 November 1978, 719.

3. Robert T. Coote, *Evangelical Newsletter*, 25 October 1974, 4.

4. "Creationists Lose First Round of a Long Fight," *U.S. News & World Report*, 18 January 1982, 34.

5. Joseph C. Dillow, "The Bible As a Scientific Text," *Moody Monthly*, January 1982, 132-33.

6. Professor Sir Fred Hoyle, "The Big Bang in Astronomy," *New Scientist*, 19 November 1981, 521-27.

7. Gary E. Parker, *Creation: The Facts of Life* (San Diego: CLP Publishers, 1980), 142.

8. Ibid., 143.

9. Malebranche, quoted by Hooykaas, *Rise of Modern Science*, 20.

10. Calbreath, "The Challange of Creationism," 10.

11. J. Willits Lane, "Letters: Creationism discussion continues," *Physics Today*, 8 October 1982, 103.

12. Edwin A. Olson, "Hidden Agenda behind the Evolutionist/Creationist Debate," *Christianity Today*, 23 April 1982, 26-30; David Singer, "What Christian Colleges Teach about Creation," *Christianity Today*, 17 June 1977, 8-11; William W. Watts, "Science and Logic with Key to the Scriptures," *Eternity*, October 1977, 54-57.

13. Robert Flood, *America, God Shed His Grace on Thee* (Chicago: Moody Press, 1976), 78.

14. Schaeffer, *A Christian Manifesto*, 21.

15. Schaeffer, *The God Who Is There*, 13, 15.

16. Dennis Miller, "Christian Teenagers—They're Leaving the Flock," *Moody Monthly*, September 1982, 11.

17. Ibid., 12.

18. Ibid., 13.

19. Brush, "Creationism/Evolution: The Case AGAINST 'Equal Time,'" 33.

20. Josif Ton, "The Socialist Quest for the New Man," *Christianity Today*, 26 March 1976, 8-9.

21. "On your honor," *Sigma Xi Newsletter*, December 1983, 2; William J. Broad, "Fraud and the Structure of Science," *Science*, 10 April 1981, 137.

Chapter 7

Theology and Science

*A*s we begin our discussion of a Christian theology of
science, we note that it is a positive approach to building a
world view and for interpreting the facts of science. Its emphasis is on truth. We begin with Scripture, with the God of the
Bible, and with presuppositions suggested by the Bible itself.
These presuppositions are used to interpret data both from the
external world and from man's own internal world, his inner
self. They encompass all of reality.

According to the Bible, man created in God's image is a
communicating being. Scripture is God's written communication to man. As the revealed Word of God, Scripture is the starting point man must use in learning truth. As Jesus said,
"Sanctify them by the truth: your [God's] word is truth" (John
17:17).

Scripture is the starting point for absolute truth in at least
two ways. First, it provides the correct assumptions or presuppositions from which man is to reason. Using these correct assumptions, man can properly interpret facts from the material
world and also interpret data from his own inner world.

Second, Scripture is a guide to truth because it gives some
of the final answers at which man must arrive when using his

reason correctly. It serves as a check for the correctness of our reasoning process. In our study of the natural world, we could draw the conclusion that it appeared to have been designed.[1] Checking that conclusion with the Bible, we find that it agrees. Man is finite and so is his reasoning. Only by having an absolute reference point can the results of reasoning be checked for absolute truth. Scripture provides this check.

Man is finite and his use of reason is limited because of this. God is not limited. His ways are higher than our ways. "As the heavens are higher than the earth, so are my ways higher than your ways and my thoughts than your thoughts" (Isaiah 55:9).

What is needed in a Christian theology of science is not only an exposure of the weaknesses of evolution, valid as that might be, but also the replacement of the evolutionary world view with one that is much more satisfying, both for interpreting the scientific evidence and the spiritual and social dimensions of man as well.[2] It is easy enough to criticize a particular view, but it takes work to put something better in its place.

A Christian theology of science based on the Bible as a foundation is not a new idea. Christian thinkers and philosophers have discussed some of the basic issues involved even from the earliest days of the church.[3] Also a substantial amount of development toward a Christian theology of science took place about the time of the Protestant Reformation and the beginning of the rise of modern science. Views of some of these early thinkers and philosophers on this point are available in the literature.[4]

In modern times, however, there has been a shift away from a world view founded on the Bible. That fact, coupled with much new observational evidence discovered by modern science, requires that a biblically based theology of science be continuously updated. The update needs to be expressed and presented in terms which are clear to a person raised in modern culture.

A detailed development of the many facets of a theology of science would require more space and time than is our purpose here. In this section, my intention is to show only that a valid theology of science can be developed and to point out some key features of that theology.

Development of a theology of science is really doing what Romans 12:2 asks a Christian to do. A Christian must be converted from paganism not only in his heart but also in his mind. "Do not conform any longer to the pattern of this world, but be transformed by the renewing of your mind. Then you will be able to test and approve what God's will is—his good, pleasing and perfect will" (Romans 12:2).

Challenging the Absolute Standard

Since the fall, however, man has sought to act independently of his Creator. As one writer observes, "Since the Fall the human mind has been wholly pagan."[5] The pagan mind resists submitting results of its reason against Scripture as a check. It even desires to stand as a judge of Scripture. There are just two ways to approach issues. Either we view everything through the Bible, or we view the Bible through man's autonomous ideas. Either Scripture stands as the ultimate standard to judge man or man seeks to act autonomously and use his own standards to judge the Bible.

Evolutionists are fond of referring to their own world view as scientific and to that of the Bible as religious. By this they intend to convey the idea that their view is more intellectually respectable than the opposing view. It is an example of *intellectual bullying*. Evolution begins on the same basis as any other view. It begins with faith in a set of beginning assumptions, just as any other view does.

Evolutionists have repeatedly pointed out that there is a conflict between what they term science and religion. As they define the word *science,* they are correct. The religious view as they refer to it is the biblical one that the natural world is not autonomous. There is a conflict; there must be a conflict. Nature cannot be autonomous and nonautonomous at the same time.

Science and religion, however, need not be defined as an evolutionist would define them. Science can be defined as a search for truth, just as it was by the early modern scientists who initiated modern science in the first place. It can be defined to agree with a biblical world view. If science is defined not as the evolutionist does but as a creationist would define the term, there is no conflict between the Bible and science (or religion and science).

The conflict is rather between two entirely different and antithetical philosophies of science: science in a biblical world view in which nature is not autonomous but dependent moment by moment on God, and science in an evolutionary world view in which nature is autonomous and independent of God. These two views will inevitably conflict. It is part of the age-old conflict prophesied in Genesis 3:15. "And I will put enmity between you and the woman, and between your seed and her Seed; He shall bruise your head, and you shall bruise His heel" (NKJV).

Creation and evolution are belief systems about origins and earth history, and these belief systems are built on assumptions that are diametrically opposed. There must, then, be a clash between these two views. There must be a conflict between creation and evolution. It is a part of the enmity mentioned in Genesis 3:15.

Did God Really Say . . . ?

In developing a theology of science, we will first examine the issue of the accuracy of the Bible. The pagan mind seeks to use its own standard and reasoning to judge the Bible. It is the old philosophy of the serpent from the Garden which asks, "Did God really say . . . ?" (Genesis 3:1b).

Pagan Mindset

The desire to be autonomous or independent of God is the root of the pagan mindset. The pagan mind challenges the accuracy of Scripture using a very subtle approach. It begins by assuming that there might be errors in God's Word. Then it sets itself up as an absolute standard to determine what those errors are.

The arrogance of this approach is almost unmatched. Finite wants to judge the Infinite. The only way to resolve a difference of opinion about whether or not something is true is to have an absolute source of truth for comparison. To judge God's Word using human reasoning is to elevate human reason above God's Word. It is to act as though man is the absolute reference point.

To use an analogy, suppose two people have wrist-watches, each of which states a different time. One says 3:30 while the other says 3:45. Which is correct? How could this difference be resolved? Each person could argue that his watch is correct. Another possibility is that both are in error. The only way to resolve this conflict would be to have an absolute by which error could be judged. If one considered telephone time the absolute, he could dial the telephone number and find out which of the two watches (if either) was correct in an "absolute" sense. The only way to determine which was correct would be by comparison with an absolute.

Likewise, to find out whether Scripture contains errors, one would have to have an absolute by which to judge error. The pagan mind wishes to set itself up as that absolute, independent of the Creator. The debate over scriptural *inerrancy* is not new. It began in the Garden of Eden and continues to the present.

A Challenge from Within

Sadly, the position that the Bible contains errors is found even within the church. One might not be surprised to find outsiders, non-Christians, maintaining that the Bible contains errors, but it comes as a shock to realize that the allegation of an errant Bible comes even from those within so-called evangelical circles.

> However, what has shaken the evangelical community in recent years is the growing numbers within its own ranks who have declared the Bible only partially trustworthy.

They defend the idea—the terms are virtually contradictory—of a *limited inerrancy*. Or, to put it more directly, they espouse Biblical errancy.

Though only dimly realized by the Christian in the pew, the widespread change of position today includes denominations, Christian colleges, theological seminaries, publishing houses, learned societies, and organizations.[6]

The author goes on to note that for almost two thousand years, the Christian church accepted a fully authoritative inerrant Scripture. It has only been since about the late 1800s that biblical authority began to be challenged from within the church. An errant view of the Bible has now spread to whole denominations. It is found in the majority of Christian colleges and seminaries. It is not that earlier minds had not considered the question of scriptural inerrancy. They had. But they also recognized the consequences of an errant view of Scripture and rejected that view.

This sad state of affairs today emphasizes the need for individuals to study the Bible directly. One needs to be careful of the opinions of "experts." It is well to remember that the Bible itself is the best commentary on the Bible. Its Author is the Expert on experts.

Input from Bible teachers is also helpful. Bible commentaries and dictionaries are also useful. Ultimately, however, each individual should study the Bible for himself and seek God's guidance in that project. The Holy Spirit is the guide for understanding Scripture. Jesus said, "But the Counselor, the Holy Spirit, whom the Father will send in my name, will teach you all things and will remind you of everything I have said to you" (John 14:26). "But when he, the Spirit of truth, comes, he will guide you into all truth. He will not speak on his own; he will speak only what he hears, and he will tell you what is yet to come" (John 16:13).

A helpful, though somewhat scholarly, treatment of the question of inerrancy appeared in a symposium entitled *God's Inerrant Word*. One contributor summarized the issue:

The center and theme of Christian revelation is that the perfect does come to earth: perfect God becomes perfect Man, with no loss of Godhead. But the pagan Platonist—and the naive Christian who has absorbed Platonic categories without realizing it—will not permit unqualified perfection to come to earth even when God Himself is responsible for it, as He is in the production of inerrant Scripture.[7]

Pressure from Without

Pagan culture puts tremendous pressure on a Christian to conform to its ways of thinking. It tries to get the Christian to conform to its world view. Scripture not only warns us to expect this pressure, but instructs us how to resist it (Romans 12:2). Pressure coming from outside can be resisted successfully by internal defenses; in effect, pressure pushing outward. This happens when God is made the source of ultimate truth. It happens when God "restructures" our minds. Even individuals who have become Christians early in life, have been raised in Christian homes, and have attended Christian institutions of learning will feel this pressure. It is even worse, however, for those who are converted out of pagan culture later in life, because they have more ideas to restructure.

God accepts us where we are. When a person accepts Christ as Savior, he may still have many vestiges of pagan thinking and culture within. At conversion, God does not squash our personality. Rather, He patiently allows us to grow in Christ. We begin to reorient our whole thinking pattern. Wrong ideas are displaced as God calls them to our attention. Nevertheless, there is a clear call not only to be spiritually and morally converted, but also to be intellectually converted. A non-Christian "must not be allowed to think that he can become a Christian and go on thinking that same old way. He must be told that Christ demands a *total* repentance—of heart, mind, will, emotions—the whole man. He must learn that Christ demands change in 'ultimate criterion.' And thus he must learn that even the evidentiary procedures he uses to establish biblical authority must be reformed by the Bible. He must learn that 'evidence' is at bottom an elaboration of God's self-witness; that 'proving' God is the same as hearing and obeying him."[8]

A True Communication

A Christian theology of science, then, begins with God and what He has truthfully revealed to us in Scripture. Scripture will be the source of our assumptions and presuppositions for interpreting the material universe. Scripture will also be the check on reasoning to make sure that our conclusions are not erroneous. "All scripture is inspired by God and is useful for teaching the faith and correcting error, for re-setting the direction of a man's life and training him in good living. The scriptures are the comprehensive equipment of the man of God, and fit him fully for all branches of his work" (2 Timothy 3:16-17, Phillips). "All branches of his work" *includes science.*

Is the Bible a Textbook of Science?

Frequently one hears an objection to this last statement. Those who object say, "The Bible is not a textbook of modern science." Now it seems perfectly obvious that the Bible is not a textbook at all. It is not a textbook on history . . . yet its historical statements have been tested and found to be true. It is not a textbook on geography . . . yet its geographical statements are correct. It is not a textbook on theology . . . but its theological statements are true.

One could say the same thing about an encyclopedia: "The encyclopedia is not a textbook of science." This would be a true statement. It would not mean, however, that when the encyclopedia listed information about a telescope, the information would be in error. It would not mean that when encyclopedia authors spoke of geological information, their statements would be incorrect. Just because an encyclopedia is not designed as a textbook does not mean its statements are untrue.

When someone says the Bible is not a textbook of modern science, he is usually implying that the Bible contains scientific errors. (Otherwise the statement seems meaningless. It is patently obvious that the Bible is not a textbook. Even if it were a textbook, textbooks contain errors and become outdated. The Bible does not.) It is faulty logic, however, to conclude that because the Bible is not a textbook of science, it therefore contains scientific errors.

The Bible does touch science in at least two ways. First, it provides the basic assumptions or presuppositions for building a framework within which the facts discovered by science can be interpreted. Second, the scientist can find within the Bible true information about earth history. Because the Bible is true, what it teaches about creation and events of earth history (such as the flood) is also true. Thus the Bible gives both starting assumptions and checks for scientific points of interest about origins and earth history.[9]

Genesis 1-11: History or Myth?

In addition to the statement that the Bible is not a textbook of science, the attack may take a more direct form by stating that the first eleven chapters of Genesis are not to be taken as historical; they are mythical or poetical or figurative. They are not meant to convey historical or scientific truth—only "religious" truth.

The first eleven chapters of Genesis cover the span of time from creation to the call of Abraham and include such events as the creation, the fall, the preflood world, the deluge, and the tower of Babel. Abraham is generally admitted to be a historical character, and events associated with him are usually considered historically valid.

However, an analysis of the form, style, and language of these eleven chapters indicates that they are in the same form as statements about Abraham and should be interpreted the same way. Further analysis of New Testament references to these same chapters and the events they describe show the writers took them as historical statements. Also, if these chapters were poetic, we could recognize that fact from their literary form. Poetic form is easily recognized, but Genesis 1 and 2 do not take this form; their form is historical. Furthermore, since these chapters have the same form as those about Abraham, who was obviously a historical character, these chapters must also be historical. If we insist that the first eleven chapters of Genesis are mythical, on what basis do we suddenly decide those discussing Abraham are historical? Might not Abraham and David and all the rest discussed in the same format and style of writing also be mythical? Additional evidence against a nonhistorical interpretation comes from the New Testament. It refers to these early chapters as if they were real events.

The Bible Makes True Statements

Francis Schaeffer has seen this issue clearly and has stated the options well.

> God has set the revelation of the Bible in history; He did not give it (as He could have done) in the form of a theological textbook. Having set the revelation in history, what sense then would it make for God to give us a revelation in which the *history* was wrong? God has also set man in the *universe* which the Scriptures themselves say speaks of this God. What sense then would it make for God to give His revelation in a book that was wrong concerning the universe? The answer to both questions must be, 'No sense at all.'[10]

In the Bible, God speaks *absolute truth* concerning God, man, history, and the universe. In the Bible, God speaks propositionally to man. This means that God makes statements which can be checked out for truth. If I say, for example, "There is a cat sitting on the porch," that statement is a proposition. It can be checked out for truth. One can look on the porch to see if a cat is sitting there.

In the same way, God has spoken propositional truth. He has made statements which contain information about the universe. The Bible says God created plants and animals to reproduce after their kind. This is a typical propositional statement. It is a statement related to an area of science we call biology.

As we noted before, the Bible is not a textbook of science. In biology, for example, it does not provide a detailed account of what one might see under a microscope when looking at plant or animal cells. Nevertheless, its statements in the area of biology are true. It does state that plants and animals will reproduce after their kind, and that is a true statement. Our own experience shows us that a dog does not produce cats. Dogs continue to produce dogs and cats continue to produce cats. Potatoes produce only potatoes. Animals and plants reproduce after their kind. This is a propositional statement, and it checks out with the real world.

Knowing Truly, if Not Exhaustively

At the same time we recognize that the Bible speaks truth about areas of scientific interest, we must not make the opposite mistake of assuming that the Bible provides an exhaustive list of truths and therefore all scientific study is worthless. The fact that we have true statements about biology does not mean that these statements are exhaustive and therefore all further biological study is worthless. The Bible makes true statements about science, but it does not exhaust the field.

The situation can be compared to mathematics instruction. We tell a first grade student that $2 + 2 = 4$. That is a true statement. But it does not exhaust the field of mathematics. It has not included algebra, or geometry, or calculus, or differential equations. A true statement need not be an exhaustive statement. Using the Bible as a guide, scientific study is still exciting and rewarding just as is assembling a jigsaw puzzle after seeing the picture on the cover of the box. Man can continue to study what God has created and learn some of the details, design patterns, and truths within the framework given by the Bible. Scientific study for a Christian can be a rewarding enterprise because he knows that it will ultimately make sense. The same Creator who made the world studied by science also designed our minds to understand that world. From our studies we are led to appreciate and worship our Creator.

Is Biblical Christianity against Science?

A scientist who is also a Christian can delight in his work and have absolute confidence in the framework of the Bible. With that confidence—and with that framework—he can understand the things he is studying. He knows they have final meaning and that they are there to bring glory to their Creator. The Bible says that God set man over the works of creation.

> [W]hat is man that you are mindful of him,
>   the son of man that you care for him?
> You made him a little lower than the heavenly beings
>   and crowned him with glory and honor.
> You made him ruler over the works of your hands;
>   you put everything under his feet:
> all flocks and herds,
>   and the beasts of the field,
> the birds of the air,
>   and the fish of the sea,
> all that swim the paths of the seas.
> O LORD, our Lord,
>   how majestic is your name in all the earth!
>
> (Psalm 8:4-9)

God intended that man should enjoy exploring creation and learning about it. In so doing, it brings joy to man and glory to God.

It is significant that Christianity has had a great and positive influence on the study of science. When Christians began to take the Bible seriously at the time of the Reformation, science began to blossom in its modern form. As we noted previously, many of the great early modern scientists were Christians. They not only studied science; they played a large part in developing both the ethic and the methodology which led to the rise and success of modern science. This methodology is still used by scientists in our own time, although there has been a move away from the biblical base. Even cultures that do not have a Christian base can have successful science by adopting the ethic and methodology put forward by these early scientists.

Some might argue that the rise of modern science was only coincidental with the Protestant Reformation. They would argue that modern science was not a result of the world view put forth by attention to the Bible, but was only accidentally associated with it. A historical analysis, however, refutes that thesis.[11]

Chapter 7, Notes

1. P. C. W. Davies, "The Tailor-Made Universe," *The Sciences,* May/June 1978, 6-10.

2. Andrews, *Is Evolution Scientific?* 3.

3. Bartz, *Luther and Evolution.*

4. Hooykaas, *Rise of Modern Science.*

5. Ibid., 21.

6. Harold Foos, "The Word of God: Why Inerrancy Is Paramount," *Moody Monthly,* January 1978, 35.

7. John Warwick Montgomery, ed., *God's Inerrant Word: An International Symposium on the Trustworthiness of Scripture* (Minneapolis: Bethany Fellowship, Inc., 1973), 34.

8. John M. Frame, "Scripture Speaks For Itself," in *God's Inerrant Word,* ed. John Warwick Montgomery, 179.

9. Andrews, *God, Science & Evolution.*, 72-73.

10. Schaeffer, *The God Who Is There,* 92.

11. Hooykaas, *Rise of Modern Science,* 162.

Chapter 8

Creation:
A Solid Foundation

*D*uring the time I was considering theistic evolution as a way to "harmonize" the Bible and science, the serious accusations hurled at the creation scientists both by atheistic evolutionists as well as those within the church who were theistic evolutionists did not escape my notice. At first it was a real deterrent to my giving serious consideration to creation. Even though a creationist may be a genuine Christian, he is not perfect and can be guilty of one or more of the accusations leveled against the creationists.

The real issue, however, is not whether creationists have made mistakes or are capable of committing wrong. This is only surface rhetoric. We must cut through the fog and get down to the real question: Is the creation position true or not?

Creation and Science

As I began my investigation into creation I found that many creationists were top quality scientists with excellent scientific credentials. Many had earned Ph.D.'s, some from prestigious universities. Scientific articles by scientists who believed in creation had been published in numerous professional scientific journals and other literature. Creationists were recipients of high scientific honors and awards. They were scientists in the best sense of the word.

Yet these men who thoroughly understood their science also believed in creation. Counted among their number were men and women who represented nearly every branch of science. I found that they were men and women who were not being dishonest with factual information. Also they were not ignorant. In many cases they were well-read and well-versed in both science and theology. True, these scientists seemed to be numerically in the minority, but that in itself did not make the creation position untrue. Jesus himself taught, "Enter through the narrow gate. For wide is the gate and broad is the road that leads to destruction, and many enter through it. But small is the gate and narrow the road that leads to life, and only a few find it" (Matthew 7:13-14). Truth is not decided by majority vote. It was truth I was after, not majority, "expert" opinion.

I began then to seriously consider what these scientists called creationists were saying. Repeatedly I found their answers to my questions satisfying and exciting. They were able to give acceptable answers to important questions. I found that the creation position, beginning with presuppositions suggested by the Bible itself, gave conclusions that were in agreement with reality. They were in agreement with both the external universe and the universe within, the universe of the human personality.

The Ring of Truth

The creation position seemed to me to have the ring of truth. At last, here was a position with which I as a Christian and as a scientist could relax. No longer need I always be on guard to explain away either theological truth or scientific truth. Truth could be a unified whole. Furthermore, I could read the Bible using the standard rules of communication. I could read it in a normal, straightforward manner; I did not always have to be on guard for some special or obscure interpretation.

The creation position began from an absolute reference point, the truth of God's Word. That was an exciting discovery for me. Truth could objectively and absolutely exist.

When I say Christianity is true I mean it is true to total reality—the total of what is, beginning with the central reality, the objective existence of the personal-infinite God. Christianity is not just a series of truths but *Truth*—Truth about all of reality.[1]

If science is a search for truth about the natural world, and if the Bible makes statements about the natural world, then the Bible can be a starting point for truth in the study of science. "The fear of the LORD is the beginning of knowledge, But fools despise wisdom and instruction" (Proverbs 1:7, NKJV). Using the Bible and the presuppositions it suggests about the natural world, we can then develop a sufficient theology of science.

Creation Ex Nihilo

A theology of science begins where the Bible does: "In the beginning God created the heavens and the earth" (Genesis 1:1). This and other supportive biblical passages form the basis of the doctrine of creation *ex nihilo*, the doctrine of creation out of nothing but pure spiritual power (cf. Nehemiah 9:6; Colossians 1:16-17; Hebrews 1:2-3; Revelation 4:11). According to the Bible, God did not start with energy, matter, and a set of natural laws and then order them into the present universe. God created out of nothing. He did not require pre-existing materials. He alone is infinite. Philosophically, one has a choice of either starting with matter as eternal or with Mind (God) as eternal. The material universe is finite; it was created. Only God is infinite and eternal. He existed before the beginning; he existed before time began. He is the self-existent one.

A frequent question encountered in discussions on the Bible and science is, Where did God come from? Biblically, this is a meaningless question. This does not mean that it is a silly or frivolous question, but a meaningless one. It begins with the wrong premise. It begins with the premise that time already exists above God, that he entered the scene at some point in time, that God is a captive of time. But biblically, God is above time. Time is one of the products of creation. God is infinite. All else, including time, is finite.

Out of nothing God created the whole space-time universe.

> By the word of the LORD were the
>   heavens made,
>   their starry host by the breath of his
>   mouth.
>
> . . . .
>
> For he spoke, and it came to be;
>   he commanded, and it stood firm.
>
> (Psalm 33:6, 9)

The Creator willed into existence the entire universe, a fact sometimes referred to as *fiat* creation. "At the beginning God expressed himself. That personal expression, that word, was with God and was God, and he existed with God from the beginning. All creation took place through him, and none took place without him" (John 1:1-3, Phillips). "And it is only by faith that our minds accept as fact that the whole universe was formed by God's command—that the world which we can see has come into being through what is invisible" (Hebrews 11:3, Phillips).

By an act of Divine will the universe came into being out of nothing. It was an act of instantaneous creation. No time was involved. One does not go from nothing to something by degrees.

The doctrine of *ex nihilo* creation is not a new concept, although it is an often neglected one. Some of the perceptive early thinkers associated with the rise of modern science were aware of the implications of this doctrine. Malebranche (1638-1715) was one of these.

> Malebranche recognized that mechanistic philosophy could fall easily into the error of believing that, once God had created the world, the world then existed in its own right. In his opinion, however, this would amount to independence, and he preferred to think that, as soon as God stops willing the world to exist, it will cease to exist. . . . The universe . . .

has been brought forth from nothing, and it so completely depends on God that it would be reduced to nothing if God ceased to maintain it by His will.[2]

The doctrine of *ex nihilo* creation is thoroughly biblical and (to phrase it colloquially) allows one to give big answers to big questions. It is also a uniquely biblical doctrine; it did not come from pagan religions. Nonbiblical religions either worship nature itself, as in pantheism, or assume that nature is independent and autonomous. "It is interesting to note that the concept of an *ex nihilo* creation is peculiarly Judaeo-Christian and although there are many creation myths from different ancient cultures, the idea of a creation from nothing is exclusively biblical in origin."[3]

"I Am Not Ashamed . . ."
I believe one of the major reasons Christians are often on the defensive in presenting the gospel in today's culture is that they are not adequately instructed about the power of the doctrine of creation ex nihilo.

Beginning with that doctrine, creation science can put the Christian back on the offensive again in defending and presenting his faith.

This was certainly true in my own case. The apostle Paul stated that he was not ashamed to present the gospel of Christ. "For I am not ashamed of the gospel of Christ, for it is the power of God to salvation for everyone who believes, for the Jew first and also for the Greek" (Romans 1:16, NKJV). As a young person I memorized that verse in Sunday school. However, when on the college campus, I found myself being ashamed—literally afraid—to present the gospel of Jesus Christ.

One reason for this fear was my inability to provide adequate answers to questions I received from unbelievers. These were deeply penetrating questions about big issues and deserved big answers. My response to them was less than adequate and it resulted in my getting shot down in flames, as it were, more than once. Those were painful and unpleasant experiences, and I did not wish to repeat them. Yet one of my biggest lacks was in not recognizing the philosophical base from which the questions came.

In reading Romans 1:16-20, I at first thought Paul just had more courage than I. No doubt Paul was a courageous man, but that was not the whole explanation. A closer reading revealed an interesting new truth. After stating that he was not ashamed, Paul then listed his reasons for his boldness. Not the least of these is an adequate response regarding creation. Thus Paul was able to give big answers to big questions. He proceeded from an adequate base.

A More Complete Picture

How can the doctrine of creation *ex nihilo* put the Christian on the offensive in presenting his faith? It does so by giving a more complete picture of reality. It steps back behind the material universe to the spiritual reality upholding it. The material universe is not all there is; the material universe *and* the spiritual power behind it describe reality.

These are deep and basic truths that may be difficult to grasp easily. Borrowing somewhat from an idea suggested elsewhere,[4] the situation might be compared to a boat floating on a lake. A limited view would consider only the boat and the water. Such a view could describe motions of the boat on the lake, actions of waves and wind, and so forth. It could not, however, explain why there was a lake. A broader view, however, would consider not only the boat and the lake, but would admit that beneath the lake, even though it could not be seen, was a continuation of the shore. Earth material (clay and rock, etc.) constitutes a solid earth shore which continues up to the lake edge and then continues on beneath the water, out of sight, across the whole bottom of the lake, coming up again on the opposite shore. Without the bottom to the lake, there would be no lake. The lake and the boat can be compared to the material universe. The bottom of the lake is like the spiritual power behind the material universe. Without it there could be no material universe.

Not only were matter, energy, space, and time brought

into existence by an act of the will of the Creator, but the habitual ways matter and energy interact were also willed by him. These normal ways of interaction are the basis of our laws of science. Creation *ex nihilo* forms the foundation of our expectation that the universe is one of law and order.

Laws of Science

What do we mean when we use the term *scientific law?* Let's take a moment here to review and discuss this term. Science is a study of the present universe. Scientists observe the material universe in its present state and describe what they see. From a large number of observations of some object or phenomenon, scientists observe that the universe behaves in a certain orderly way. Scientific laws or laws of "nature" are simply scientists' descriptions of this orderly behavior.

An example is the law of gravity. From a large number of observations, scientists formulate a law which states, "If an object is released above the surface of the earth, it will tend to move toward the earth." We say an object falls because of the law of gravity.

It is well to note that science did not invent the way nature behaves; it simply describes it. Scientific laws are man's formulations of his observations about the way the material universe behaves. Laws did not come into existence because science exists; science exists rather because nature behaves in a predictable way. Science, then, is a description of the way nature behaves. We express these descriptions in generalizations known as scientific laws and these laws are understandable and can be communicated by rational minds.

We believe the descriptions or laws truly describe the way the universe operates, and we assume these laws to be valid throughout the entire universe. The same rules that govern falling objects here on earth will also govern falling objects on the moon or on the planets or even as far out into space as our telescopes can observe. That is why the laws are spoken of as universal laws.

A basic question arises: Why are the laws of science as

they are? Why, for example, does the speed of light have its particular value? Why isn't it three times this value or half or some other multiple? Out of the limitless possible values for the speed of light, why is it what it is?

The same question could likewise be raised for the law $E = MC^2$. It might have been MC^3 or MC^5 or $MC^{1/2}$. Why are the laws as they are when so many other choices are theoretically possible?

Creation *ex nihilo* answers this question. The laws of science are as they are because God willed them to be that way. This is not a simplistic answer, but a most profound one. An act of the will, a choice, implies intelligence. It implies intelligence or mind behind the universe. As one writer succinctly puts it,

> Without intelligence there is no true choosing but only a response to the rules of chance. But before even *those* rules existed, a choice or distinction was made as to what they should be! The unavoidable conclusion is, therefore, that intelligence pre-existed the natural universe and the laws by which it functions. The only escape from this argument lies in a total agnosticism concerning the fundamental nature of scientific law.[5]

That God willed the laws to be as they are is a big answer to an important question.

Another major question requiring a big answer is, From where does the human mind originate? Two answers can be given to that question. Either mind is only a product of chemical and physical processes going on in the brain, or it has an existence independent of matter. If mind is just the result of chemicals and electrical impulses going on in a particular organ of the body, then thought and all reasonings are a mirage. Even the question, What is mind? is just the result of certain electrical impulses moving through a particular momentary arrangement of chemicals making up an organ called the brain. These chemicals and electrical impulses move about by chance. If they are the basis of reason, then reason is just an illusion, as are mind, will, and emotion. They are only the result of chance.

A naturalist starts out thinking but ends by undermining all thought. He must use his mind to prove his philosophy, but then his philosophy affirms that all reasoning is mere cerebration by a physical brain. If reasoning is just an electrochemical operation in the material brain, then why should a naturalist ask anyone to accept his thought as "true"?[6]

Thinkers and philosophers through the ages have struggled with this same question, What is the nature of mind? There is no doubt that mind uses the brain or is associated with or rides upon the brain, perhaps like the message in a sentence rides upon the symbols used to construct that sentence. The symbols themselves, however, are not the message. If mind is only the brain—just matter and energy and their interactions— then reasoning about the nature of mind is an illusion.

The only other possibility is that mind is separate from the material universe. Mind has an existence independent of atoms and molecules and matter and energy, even though our minds are bound by the restraints of the brain and body. Even non-Christian thinkers and philosophers most radically committed to an evolutionary philosophy are forced to admit that mind has an existence independent of matter.

A close scrutiny of the way 'mind' manifested itself in the course of evolution supplies arguments that, in my opinion, make *dualism* look like the most plausible approach. I shall therefore argue that the category of 'mind' (we shall try later on to formulate this concept more precisely) exists autonomously and independent of matter.[7]

In addition to arriving at this conclusion by analyzing the situation philosophically, experimental research also seems to support this contention.[8]

A Solid Philosophical Base
Why can man expect to use science to understand the universe? Creation gives an answer to this question. In the creation

view, man's mind and the material universe both flow from the same source, the mind of God. *The universe is not a chaos; it is a cosmos, designed and bearing evidence of a Designer.* Reason, a product of mind independent of matter, can therefore be used to rationally understand the universe using methods of science. Furthermore, this understanding, in the form of natural laws, can be intelligently communicated. Natural laws can be formulated and expressed in concise ways (for example, mathematically), and these ways can be intelligently communicated. Another scientist, using his rational mind, is able to understand that communication and understand its significance.

For the Gospel

Furthermore, man's inward universe—that of being, desires, emotions, and will—is a natural consequence of mind. Mind is more than just brain, which is part of the material universe. The biblical doctrine of creation *ex nihilo* shows that the spiritual and material world co-exist. The material universe is dependent upon the spiritual—behind material reality is spiritual reality. Both mind and matter ultimately come from the same source, God. This means that man is morally responsible to his Creator, a fact man knows even if he denies it. He lives in God's world even though he would like to pretend he does not. This point is made quite clear in Scripture:

> [S]ince what may be known about God is plain to them, because God has made it plain to them. For since the creation of the world God's invisible qualities—his eternal power and divine nature—have been clearly seen, being understood from what has been made, so that men are without excuse.
>
> For although they knew God, they neither glorified him as God nor gave thanks to him, but their thinking became futile and their foolish hearts were darkened (Romans 1:19-22).

Creation *ex nihilo* is thus the basis for the gospel: man was created but chose to act independently of the Creator; he exercised his will and sought to be autonomous. The fall is a historical fact, and man as a created and then fallen being needs a Savior.

For Doctrine

Creation is also the foundation for other important Christian doctrines. It is the basis for hope beyond the grave. Man is more than just body and brain. His spirit-mind (soul) lives on.

Creation *ex nihilo* is also the basis for the hope of a new creation, promised in Scripture by God Himself. The same one who brought the present material universe into existence by an act of the will also said, "Behold, I make all things new" (Revelation 21:5, NKJV).

Again, the doctrine of creation *ex nihilo* is the foundation for our expectation of providence in the present universe and also the basis for our expecting answers to prayer. "You alone are the LORD; You have made heaven, the heaven of heavens, with all their host, the earth and all things on it, the seas and all that is in them, and You preserve them all. The host of heaven worships You" (Nehemiah 9:6, NJKV). God did not just create the world and then leave it; He upholds it by the word of His power. He preserves it moment by moment. The entire universe is subject moment by moment to the will of God. Thus, when a believer prays, he can be logically consistent and expect an answer to that prayer. The answer can come through providence in an ordering and timing of circumstances. It can also be a direct act of God's will in a localized change of the laws of nature. A direct miracle can occur in answer to a believer's prayer. " 'If you abide in Me, and My words abide in you, you will ask what you desire, and it shall be done for you' " (John 15:7, NKJV).

Creation: a Philosophical Base for Science

Creation thus forms a solid philosophical base, not only for science but for all the important doctrines of the Bible as well. It is in agreement with the external universe, and it is in agreement with the internal universe, that which is inside man, what man honestly knows he is.

Unlike creation science, evolutionary science cannot explain ultimate origins, a fact begrudgingly admitted by evolutionists. Even if one adopts the evolutionary world view of infinite regression of cause and effect, he finally reaches the point at which it is not possible to regress any further.

This can be illustrated with the presently popular cosmological theory of origins known as the big bang. If one were to calculate backwards and move all the material of the universe backwards in time until the motions met at the point of the big bang, that would still be an origin for the universe, even though some may not wish to admit it.[9]

Thus, even using naturalistic or evolutionary assumptions, one is brought to an origin for the universe.

Of course, one can try to escape this conclusion by going off into an area where we have absolutely no physical evidence whatsoever. One can postulate that the universe endlessly expands and contracts, big bang after big bang. However, it is a philosophical leap of blind faith because there is no evidence to support such a contention. A well-known scientist who is not a creationist, commenting on this whole situation, said, "Theologians generally are delighted with the proof that the Universe had a beginning, but astronomers are curiously upset."[10]

For the Operation of the Universe

The doctrine of *ex nihilo* creation also explains the present operation of the universe. The natural world acts in a consistent way because God wills it to act in a consistent way. He upholds the universe moment by moment. Scripture tells us that the Creator interacts with the universe and enjoys it.

> May the glory of the LORD endure forever;
> may the LORD rejoice in his works (Psalm 104:31).

The universe is not left to run as a self-acting machine. It is not as the deists thought, a clock which has been wound up with no further interaction from the Creator. God interacts moment by moment with the universe. To use a theological phrase, He is immanent in the universe, He is present.

Limiting Reality

Each scientist is biased by a philosophical background into which he fits the observations he is making. Evolutionary science uses the bias that nature is autonomous; it assumes the laws of nature are independent. Nature is a machine, as it were, that acts independently of any outside influence such as that of a sustaining Creator. Evolutionary science is thus hampered by a limited view of reality. It is only a partial description because it rules God out from being actively involved with his creation.

It is important to point out here a mistake that is commonly encountered. Evolutionary science (science studied within an evolutionary philosophy) is often equated with science itself. This is a gross error. When science is equated with evolutionary science, it is not only wrong but causes a great deal of confusion. It can be especially confusing to Christian young people who begin by believing in creation and then draw the incorrect conclusion that they must either accept science and give up their faith, or keep their faith and ignore science. It causes them to be caught in a false dilemma. It is a grave mistake to equate science with evolutionary science because science can also be creation science.

Creation Science

Creation science is science carried on within a different philosophical framework. It begins with the assumption that the material universe (nature) is dependent on God. Creation science takes a broader view and is capable of giving big answers to big questions.

However, science carried on within an evolutionary framework can only give limited answers since it only admits to a limited reality. Evolutionary science thus has a severe built-in limitation.

We have seen that the conflict between creation and evolution is one between differing belief systems. It is a philosophical conflict. Science is concerned with making observations of the present universe, and these observations are formulated into what are known as natural laws. Yet science is studied within a philosophical framework or belief system. That philosophical framework can be evolutionary, which begins by assuming that the material universe is autonomous and follows an infinite regression of cause and effect. However, this philosophical system gives only a partial view of reality. It does not answer the question of why there should be laws of science or why the laws of science are as they are. It does not answer questions about the inward universe, the nature of man, nor does it give an answer to the question of mind.

Chapter 8, Notes

1. Schaeffer, *A Christian Manifesto*, 19.

2. Hooykaas, *Rise of Modern Science*, 21.

3. Andrews, *God, Science & Evolution*, 51.

4. Ibid., 37.

5. Ibid., 36.

6. Arlie J. Hoover, "Naturalism: Philosophical Smuggler," *Christianity Today*, 2 July 1971, 12.

7. Hoimar von Ditfurth, *The Origins of Life: Evolution as Creation* (New York: Harper & Row, 1982), 227.

8. Arthur C. Custance, *The Mysterious Matter of Mind* (Grand Rapids: Zondervan Publishing House, 1980).

9. Timothy Ferris, "The Spectral Messenger," *Science 81* (October): 66-72; P. C. W. Davies, "The Tailor-Made Universe," *The Sciences* (May/June, 1978): 6-10.

10. Robert Jastrow, *God and the Astronomers* (New York: W. W. Norton, Inc., 1978), 16.

Chapter 9

God, Creation, and Man

*I*n reading the creation account in Genesis, it is important to note another basic principle, what I call the *telescope principle*. One who has had the experience of looking through a powerful telescope or pair of binoculars will understand what I mean. Suppose, for example, that on a clear day we were to view a mountain some distance off. With the naked eye we could discern the general outline of the mountain and perhaps whether it had timber or other cover on it. However, if we were to look at the same mountain through a telescope of low power, we could discern trees and maybe a few buildings on the mountain. By inserting a higher-power lens and using greater magnification, we could observe more detail. We would see not only a building but perhaps even windows and doors on the building. As the power of the telescope increased, we could see objects on the mountain in greater and greater detail.

Although higher power would provide us with greater detail, it would at the same time limit our field of view to a smaller area. We would see less of the mountain, whereas with the naked eye we observed the entire mountain.

I believe the same telescope principle applies to the reading of Scripture, a point easily missed in our fast-paced, modern day. People are impatient and anxious to get to the point at hand. Perhaps you have spoken with someone who has jumped into a discussion of a subject and you have no idea what he is talking about. You respond by saying, "Wait a minute! Back up a little bit. What are you talking about?" And then the speaker has to back up and give a broad overview so you know the context in which he is making his remarks. Then he can provide greater details, and you will be better able to follow the discussion. The Bible is not in such a hurry as many modern speakers. It frequently gives us an overview of the topic and then begins to look more closely at the details.

We observe this principle utilized in the creation account in Genesis. "In the beginning God created the heavens and the earth" (Genesis 1:1). This verse is like a grand overview of the entire space-time universe. It is a simple statement of absolute creation and includes all things. The universe is not self-existent but is the product of an act of God's will. "When we consider the universe, and the questions arise in our minds, 'Who made these things? What was their origin?' the first verse of Genesis gives an answer. And it answers with the simple declaration that God created the heaven and the earth."[1]

Then, in the next few verses, the power of magnification is increased and our field of view is cut down from the whole universe to just planet Earth. This allows us to have a few more details about the earth itself, its surroundings, and about the earth's plant and animal life forms. Then in chapters 2 and 3 we focus down even further, to a small part of the earth—the Garden of Eden.

Thus the Bible begins by giving us a complete overview of God's creation of the entire universe. It then provides a few more amplifying details about the earth and its life forms. Finally it focuses down to giving details about the Garden of Eden and individual man and woman. This provides a solid foundation for understanding all that follows in Scripture. The rest of the Bible is a discussion of the interaction of God with man. In order to appreciate this biblical discussion, however, we need the overview and we need to understand the context in which the interaction of God and man would take place. This context is provided by the first three chapters of Genesis.

A Recurring Pattern

This same telescoping pattern can be found elsewhere in Scripture. It is a recurring pattern and not unique to Genesis. For example, in talking about the birth of Jesus Christ, the Gospel of Matthew begins, "A record of the genealogy of Jesus Christ the son of David, the son of Abraham." This gives the overview. Then it begins at Abraham and runs through a genealogical table, coming finally to the engagement of Joseph and Mary and the conversation between the angel and Mary. Then in chapter 2 we have further amplifying details: "After Jesus was born in Bethlehem in Judea, during the time of King Herod." This provides the time and place setting. Next, details about the wise men are listed. Finally, the account ends with the wise men finding Jesus. We have here first an overview and then more and more details. The rest of the Gospel of Matthew gives us the fine details about Christ and his earthly ministry.

The telescope principle allows us to know exactly what is being talked about. We do not have to wonder about the subject matter. Recognizing this principle avoids some of the problems encountered in creation-evolution discussions when this principle is ignored. For example, some will ask if chapter 2 of Genesis isn't a separate creation account. The answer is, No, it is an increasing magnification of details of events given in chapter 1. It is a simple continuation, just as chapter 2 of Matthew is a simple continuation of Matthew 1 about the birth of Christ. The telescope principle thus aids in understanding not only the account of Christ's birth, but also the creation account given to us in Genesis.

As noted earlier, the form of the early chapters of Genesis is not poetical. They make statements about events that actually took place, as do statements later in the book of Genesis which are beyond any doubt historical. And the New Testament refers to these events as real events.

Genesis one is not poetry or saga or myth, but straightforward, trustworthy history, and, inasmuch as it is a divine revelation, accurately records those matters of which it speaks. That Genesis one is historical may be seen from these considerations. 1) It sustains an intimate relationship with the remainder of the book. The remainder of the book (i.e., The Generations) presupposes the Creation Account, and the Creation Account prepares for what follows. The two portions of Genesis are integral parts of the book and complement one another. 2) The characteristics of Hebrew poetry are lacking. There are poetic accounts of the creation and these form a striking contrast to Genesis one. 3) The New Testament regards certain events mentioned in Genesis one as actually having taken place. We may safely allow the New Testament to be our interpreter of this mighty first chapter of the Bible.[2]

The Problem of First-Day Light

As we move beyond introductory overview of Genesis 1:1, we encounter a series of divine fiats. God says, "Let there be." The repeated use of "Let there be" statements indicates direct acts of a Creator, or divine fiats. At each of these points, the Creator acted. In plain language, a miracle occurred. God said, "Let there be light," and there was light. This event was a divine fiat. God willed light to come into existence and light came into existence.

It is interesting to note here that this was before the creation of light bearers or luminaries. "If we read Genesis 'without prepossession or suspicion' we receive the impression that the author meant to teach a creation in six ordinary days and, more than that, to teach that the earth was created before the sun, moon and stars."[3]

According to Genesis, light was not associated with light bearers until the fourth day of creation.

It has seemed curious to me that skeptics would argue that this is proof the Bible is scientifically inaccurate. Modern science, skeptics say, shows that light comes from the sun, moon, and stars. (Light coming from the moon, of course, is reflected sunlight.) Therefore, they conclude the Bible must be in error because we know that light now comes from astronomical objects. How is it possible to have light without a body to emit it?

This line of reasoning is odd in view of the fact that modern science also insists it is possible to have light coming from empty space itself. Modern theorizing about the universe includes such items as black holes. Theory says that if black holes exist, they are associated with certain physical effects. One of these effects is that empty space itself must emit light. "The radiation being described here is not coming out of any kind of matter—the usual source of light energy. The region around the black hole is quite empty of matter. Instead, this radiation is coming directly out of the empty space itself!"[4]

If modern scientific theory insists on the possibility of light coming out of empty space (in other words, without light-bearing objects), it is inconsistent to criticize the biblical idea that light existed on the first day of creation without sun, moon, or stars. To persist in that criticism is to illustrate the bias a pagan mind has against truth coming from Scripture.

The fact that Genesis talks about light existing before the appearance of sun, moon, and stars seems rather to be evidence of divine authorship for the Bible. It was inconceivable to pagan thinking that life could exist without the sun and its light. Hence, pagan religions worshiped the sun as the source of light and heat. The Hebrew people were surrounded by this pagan thinking, yet in Hebrew Scripture there is a remarkable absence of these ideas. The Bible is unique in stating that the sun is of secondary importance. God is first cause. The biblical emphasis is upon God as the Creator who is therefore worthy of worship. It is in Him that we live and move and have our being (Acts 17:28).

"God called the light 'day' and the darkness he called

'night.' And there was evening, and there was morning—the first day" (Genesis 1:5). When did the first day begin? The first day began with creation (Exodus 20:11).

Evening and Morning

The phrase, "there was evening, and there was morning—the first day . . . second day . . . third day," occurs throughout the creation account. At first, I wondered why evening was listed before morning. In our culture, of course, we think of a day as proceeding from morning until evening. This is an illustration of the strong influence our surrounding culture has on us as we read the Bible. It should remind us of the danger of judging the Bible by our culture, rather than judging our culture by the Bible. In Hebrew culture, on the other hand, a day begins at 6 P.M. and runs through the night, ending at 6 P.M. the following day. In each Hebrew day, light follows darkness. This is illustrated by the Hebrew Sabbath which begins at sunset on Friday and continues until sunset on Saturday. It emphasizes the pattern of light following darkness recorded in the creation account. The Hebrews have more justification for their pattern than our modern culture.

God called the Hebrews to be the recorders and caretakers of Holy Scripture. In honor of the creation of the world in which God called the light out of darkness, the Hebrews instituted their pattern for the beginning and ending of days. Each day reminded the Hebrews of their relationship to the Creator. Each new day in which light followed darkness reminded them that they were created and not the product of a mindless universe.

Miracle and Process

The divine fiats of chapter 1 indicate that miracle was involved in creation. However, we need to be careful at this point not to make the opposite mistake of assuming that since miracle was involved, no natural process at all was involved during creation week. It does not follow that because miracle was involved, all normal process is ruled out. Already, at the moment of the creation of the entire universe, God had created the laws of nature. It would make no sense at all to have matter and energy created without also first having the laws which govern them. Creation of the matter and energy of the material universe thus implies also creation of the laws by which the material universe would function. "And yet his work has been finished since the creation of the world" (Hebrews 4:3). The whole plan was complete before any part of the material universe came into existence.

Plant life was created on the third day. Plants immediately began to operate according to laws of plant biology. Root systems were taking in nutrients; light, which had been created on the first day, caused photosynthesis in leaves. Geological processes were also occurring. Land, after it had been separated from water, must have been acted upon by the water. We can logically deduce, for example, that not all land was at the same elevation. Genesis 2:10 mentions a river that went out of the Garden of Eden. Rivers are channels in which water moves from a higher elevation toward a lower elevation. After the creation of land, water would begin operating according to its normal processes. As the animals were created, they began breathing air. Normal processes of respiration were occurring. During creation week, both miracles and process were occurring. It is a logical mistake to assume that because miracle was involved with creation, normal processes were not also functioning.

Limiting Miracles

We need to be on guard against allowing extrabiblical assumptions to crowd out biblical assumptions. Pressure to accept extrabiblical assumptions comes from the pagan world view which assumes that *only* natural processes occur; miracles are ruled out.

All Christians, insofar as I am aware, would insist that miracle was at least involved in the formation of matter, energy, and natural laws. However, Christians often submit to the pressure of pagan thinking and assume that no further miracle occurred during creation. As we discussed earlier, this view, theistic evolution, sees only natural processes and no miracles involved after the original formation of matter and energy; it comes from the idea that nature is autonomous and is an evolutionary view. In the biblical view, however, miracle was clearly involved subsequent to the original creation of matter and energy.

A Risky Extrapolation

Science in the biblical view is a search for truth. Truth about the physical universe is also obtained by what the Creator Himself has told us about the universe.

Those who insist that the only scientific approach is to limitlessly extrapolate presently observed natural processes into the far distant past are making an unjustified, risky assumption. It is risky even in the naturalistic framework because there is no guarantee that the rate of processes may not have changed even within the framework of natural laws.[5] It is also wrong to assume that natural processes have not been interlaced with miracle because the Bible clearly indicates they have. We must not allow ourselves to be trapped into assuming that nature is autonomous.

Christians who fall into this trap are forced to downgrade the authority of Scripture. If one begins by making the assumption that nature is autonomous, he must come to the same conclusion the pagan mind reaches when using these assumptions. Otherwise the only way out is to assume that any miracles which have occurred must be divine intervention; God must *interfere* with the machinery, as it were. A miracle is thus *super*natural. One who holds to autonomous nature assumes that anything like miracle must be a meddling in nature or a breaking of natural law. This is inconsistent, and the unbelieving mind rightly objects when Christians use this inconsistent logic.

Upholding the Basic Principle

As we have already discussed in the chapter on a theology of science, natural law is nothing more than the habitual working of God's will. When God wills to act in a different way (miracle), the creation (natural world) follows that will. Thus a miracle is not breaking natural law; rather, it is upholding the basic principle behind all of nature. Nature follows, moment by moment, the will of God. The Bible teaches that creation (nature) is not independent; it is not autonomous.

> The Bible, however, attributes *all* events, however insignificant, immediately to God. Natural things are nothing but His instruments, and the order of nature is founded not on an immanent logic, but on God's care for his creatures. God does not intervene in an order of nature which is semi-independent; He acts either according to a regular pattern, or else in a more exceptional way, or even in a unique way.[6]

Biblically, a miracle is not an intervention into or interference with the laws of nature. A miracle is not supernatural. A miracle is simply a noncustomary act of the will of God or even a unique choice that God decides should happen at that moment. Occasionally we must use the term *supernatural* simply because our culture does not understand or have a term for the biblical teaching of the moment-by-moment upholding of creation. The term supernatural conveys a meaning to our culture that God is doing something. But God is always doing something. He isn't just involved in the "supernatural." He is also involved in the natural or "normal" course of events.

To insist that science must assume that God only works in His customary way (the normal laws of science) is to put God into a straitjacket. He works the way He wills to work. It is especially misleading to insist that God must work only in the way He usually wills to work and then label that way science. Science so labeled is a nonbiblical science. It ceases to be a search for truth because it is not open to allowing God as an intelligent being to will to work in any other way. In those cases in which He did will to work in a way other than His habitual way of working, one would be forced to continue to look for a false naturalistic explanation, whereas the actual situation would be otherwise. Adopting the premise of autonomous nature and calling it science closes off science from being a search for truth.

The Question of Time

A notable illustration of this last point is the topic of *time*, one of the key areas of contention between creation and evolution. Topics which occur again and again in creation and evolution discussions include the age of the earth, dating methods, and the length of the days of creation ("Were the days of creation long periods of time? Were they figurative or literal days?"). The assumptions behind these questions are seldom stated explicitly. Usually the tacit assumption is that nature is autonomous. Also, with so much discussion about the question of time, it is strange there is so little discussion of the philosophical basis for time. Although evolutionist and creationist literature frequently discusses length of time for earth history, there has been little discussion about the nature of time or its philosophical foundations.

What is time? We are all aware of its passage, but what is it? To delve into that question very deeply at all would take more space than is appropriate here. Because of the importance of this issue, however, a few comments seem in order.

Time Is Created

First, time is part of the creation. It is one of the items created by God. Time is somehow the background against which events in the material universe occur, sequentially separating one event from another. It is also somehow associated with the rate at which sequence occurs. We all have an intuitive feel for time. We speak of a long time or a short time. We have certain expectations about the rate at which certain events occur and by which we perceive longness and shortness of time.

Consider, for example, events which can be expected to take place between one sunrise and another (that is, suppose one day is our standard for measuring passage of time). Events which occur or are expected to occur with great frequency during a day, such as the tick of a clock, we say have a short time duration. On the other hand, events which occur only infrequently with respect to a sunrise and sunset we associate with a long time. Many sunrises and sunsets occur between one Christmas and the next. We tend, therefore, to think of this as a relatively long time. Thus our concept of length of time is associated with the frequency with which an event occurs or can be expected to occur compared to some other regularly occurring event, such as sunrise.

Returning to creation and evolution, has it been a short time or a long time since creation? In answering this question, we need to examine some of our assumptions about time.

Assumptions about Time

Concerning the nature of time, we need to be very careful about the assumptions we make. Wrong assumptions can lead to wrong conclusions, conclusions that conflict with the biblical view and therefore with reality. Hence it is important to have an adequate philosophy or theology of time when discussing events related to the passage of time.

To illustrate, suppose we have a smoothly flowing river several hundred kilometers long. A number of highway bridges cross this river at intervals of thirty to fifty kilometers. While standing on a bridge near the mouth of the river, we spot an empty soft drink can floating in the water under the bridge. We pose the question, "How long has the can been floating down the river?"

At this point, we must make some assumptions. We could assume that someone threw an empty can into the river near its source. If we make the assumption that man (intelligence) was involved only at a point near the river's source, then because of the slow flow-rate of the river and its long length, we would conclude that the can had been floating for a very long time. We arrive at this conclusion because of our original assumption that the river has been closed off from man everywhere except at its source.

Suppose, however, while standing on the bridge, we also find a notebook lying nearby. Picking up the notebook and reading the first few pages, we find a brief description of the river and its bridges. Additional statements in the notebook inform us that its author threw a soft drink can into the river two bridges up from the one on which we are standing. The can landed in the water and began floating down toward the mouth of the river. We then calculate the length of time the can has been floating in the river based on the assumption that the notebook statements are true. This calculation leads us to the conclusion that the can has not been floating in the river for such a long time after all.

Different Assumptions, Different Conclusions

From our observations of the floating can alone, there is no way to tell whether it began at the source of the river or whether it was dropped from a bridge downstream. A can dropped from a bridge follows the same natural laws of the flow of the river as a can starting from the source of the river. Now, man is perfectly capable of tossing a can into the river near the source. Man is also capable of tossing an empty can from a bridge near the mouth of the river. Both events would be caused by an act of the human will. How would we know which had occurred? If we chose to trust the notebook record, we would draw one conclusion and it would be in agreement with science. On the other hand, if we made an assumption that men are only willing to toss cans into rivers at their sources rather than from bridges, we would not believe the notebook record and would reinterpret it some way. We would make a different assumption about how long the can had been in the river. (This illustration should remind us of the age of the earth questions encountered in creation-evolution discussions.)

Events in the universe follow the will of God moment by moment. When God chooses an event to occur in a noncustomary way, we term it a miracle and that event enters the normal stream of time. From that event onward, objects associated with the miracle obey all the normal laws of science. If we try to extrapolate backwards, using normal processes, we would make an error in how much time had elapsed since the miraculous event occurred. It would be similar to making the error about the floating can. Extrapolation regarding past events is at best a risky undertaking.

In the Bible God has given us statements about the "river." If we believe those statements, we will draw conclusions different from those who do not believe those statements. We were not there to witness the events of the past. We can only interpret them on the basis of believing or disbelieving the account of the One who was there. Dropping a can from a bridge is like an event we would term a miracle. After the event has occurred, there is no way of proving which bridge, if any, the can was thrown from, or whether it floated for a long time all the way from the head of the river. Likewise, after a miracle we have no way of differentiating the miracle from normal events in the flow of time. The only way to tell is to trust the notebook record.

Miracles and Time

It is important to realize that science cannot say that miracles do not happen. God, who willed the universe into existence and also the normal ways it interacts, could certainly choose to act in a different way in a local area at any point in time. Furthermore, the Bible tells us that He has done so. The unusualness, unexpectedness, or uniqueness of the event would call it to the attention of those who witnessed it. The purpose is to get people to think about God and cause them to wonder if God was involved. It is an indicator of God's love for His fallen creatures.

Consider Jesus' first miracle, that of turning water into wine, recorded for us in chapter 2 of John's gospel. At one moment the containers held water. An instant later, they contained wine. The wine that had just been formed immediately began to follow the usual natural laws of the universe. Recalling the bridge and stream illustration, wine which had come from water entered into the stream of time. Those who tasted the wine and did not know its source recognized it immediately as good wine because it obeyed the normal natural laws. It tasted like wine, it smelled like wine, it had the color of wine. It obeyed all the laws of wine.

If the governor of the feast had thought about the age of the wine, he would have assumed that it had been formed quite some time previously. In truth, however, it had an age measured only in minutes. It had been in the stream of time only a short distance. How can this be? Evolutionary science, of course, has no answer. Creation science, on the other hand, can accept such an event. In creation science, all events are the moment-by-moment outworking of the will of God. God can drop something into the stream of time, as it were. God willed that water should become wine and the material universe obeyed that will.

A Moving Sequence

When we perceive a sequence of events one after another, we associate the series with the passage of time. A motion picture film is really just a series of snapshots. When these individual pictures are shown rapidly, one after the other, they give the appearance of motion. Each individual frame in a movie film is an individual snapshot of the scene. If the film is moved through the projector rapidly, the motion will appear to speed up; time will appear short between events. If the film is moved slowly through the projector, we will see the scene in slow motion; time will appear long between events.

Might not time be the rate at which a series of snapshots of the universe move past one another? The real world, then, might be compared to a super movie camera. What we call time, as perceived by motion of an object or sequence of events, might simply be a series of instantaneous snapshots of the whole universe on this camera. The camera would photograph the entire universe and all objects in it. If the film were moved through the projector, we would perceive each new picture as the next event. In principle, there might be a long distance (time) between one picture and the next. However, from our perception here on earth, since the next picture is the next event, we would think of it as coming immediately after the previous one—in short time.

When God performs a miracle, such as turning water into wine, perhaps from His point of view there is a picture of the whole universe and He simply slips in a new frame. The new frame is on the reel in subsequent pictures, and we perceive it thereafter to follow the normal laws of science.

To my finite mind, this is the analogy I think of for creation week. When God said, "Let there be . . . ," He in effect slipped into the motion picture a new frame which then continued to be part of the overall movie from that point on. The six days of creation week contained a series of "Let there be's." Each time God slipped in a new frame, and it then became part of the over-all picture. It was as quick and as rapid as turning water to wine.

Creation Is More Scientific

There are two antithetical possibilities for the origin of the universe: direct creation or evolution by natural processes. Both of these assumptions cannot be simultaneously true. If we as Christians choose evolutionary presuppositions, and if direct creation is the actual case, then we will draw wrong conclusions about the material universe and about the nature of time. We will be trapped, as the pagans are, into saying that creation is un-scientific. If in actuality, however, creation is the true case, then it is a more accurate description of the origin and operation of the universe, and therefore a more scientific explanation. The creation explanation, allowing for the moment by moment out-working of the will of God, is a more scientific explanation because it describes reality as it is.

Evolution, on the other hand, ignores part of reality because it wrongly assumes nature is autonomous and that it is therefore not possible for God to slip another frame into the movie. Evolutionists object to direct creation. One of the reasons they offer for doing so is that it is not possible to observe the original acts of creation and therefore that removes them from science. This is an invalid objection for two reasons. First, it is based on a limited assumption about and definition of science. An ancient Indian arrowhead, for example, can be studied by science even though scientists were not there to observe its formation. The assumption that it had a maker does not remove it from the realm of science. Second, creation by divine miracle must be scientific if it actually happened, regardless of whether or not it was observed. It is also inconsistent for evolutionists to contend that creation is unscientific because it was not observed. The origin of life by evolutionary processes was also not observed, but evolutionists term such an origin as scientific.

True, we cannot use process logic to mentally reconstruct what happened during creation week. Process logic assumes only natural processes occurred and does not allow for direct miracle in creation. A miracle during creation week or any time thereafter is an illustration of the fundamental principle that the entire universe follows moment by moment the will of an intelligent Creator. If this is a basic principle of the natural world, and if science is based on fundamental principles, then the fact that creation involved direct miracle does not make it unscientific. Science must consider all the data.

The Bible as Data

Part of the data creation science considers are the words God has given to us. They are true data about the universe in the same sense that a sample we would observe in a test tube is also true data about the universe. Evolutionary science ignores or refuses to consider as evidence what God has said. Creation science is not closed to that evidence. Part of the evidence available to scientists are the statements in the Bible about creation. To the extent they are ignored, science will be that much in error about the real situation.

As an illustration of how science will be in error by omitting part of the data, let us use an analogy of an automobile with 65,000 miles registering on its odometer. Using the assumption that only process logic applies, we rule out the possibility that an intelligent driver guided the automobile over a series of streets, roads, and highways. If we thus limit ourselves to examining only the automobile, we cannot tell all the individual roads and places it has traveled during its lifetime to cover 65,000 miles. Regardless of how diligently we theorize about the travel history of the car, using only process logic we will have little hope of ever knowing it. However, if we also allow the assumption of an intelligent owner-driver, one could check the owner's travel log to determine what roads had been traveled. Using the owner's log together with process assumptions would allow real progress in a scientific study of the automobile. For example, the type of mud under the fenders would make sense if we read in the log that some of the roads traveled were dirt roads.

The creation account in Genesis not only tells us information about all creation—the material universe—but it also tells us something about the nature of the Creator. Consider the statement that God saw everything He had made, "and it was very good" (Genesis 1:31). This statement can tell us something about the Creator as we consider the following. Genesis 1:26-27 tells us that we (mankind) were created in the image of the Creator. The image is that of personhood and does not refer to material substance. This is the basis for our expectation that human beings have a mind as well as some of the other qualitative features of the Creator's personality. Humans have a mind and a will because we are the product of a Creator with a mind and a will.

We observe that one of the basic urges or drives in all human beings is the drive for creativity. For some it may be art, for others it may be inventing something, for still others it is handwork or craftwork of one type or another. Also, we find enjoyment in our creative urge. We like to observe and enjoy the results of our creativity.

When the Creator looked at what He had created and saw that it was good, it implies He thoroughly enjoyed creating. It was fun for Him. It was a good creation and a source of enjoyment.

Ex Nihilo
According to the Bible, God is first; all else is second (Colossians 1:17). Matter, energy, space, time, and the principles or laws by which interactions between them were to occur, did not always exist. They came into existence as an act of God's will at the moment of creation.

A Finished Creation
Further, the Bible tells us the creation was finished at the

end of creation week and that it was a good creation. The Creator made everything necessary for the whole universe to be in harmony. Everything necessary for life on earth was provided in just the right amounts. The nutrients for plant life were present. The climate necessary for plants to grow was made just right. Animals had nourishment. Man not only had nourishment, but it was pleasant nourishment.

> Now the LORD God had planted a garden in the east, in Eden; and there he put the man he had formed. And the LORD God made all kinds of trees grow out of the ground—trees that were pleasing to the eye and good for food. In the middle of the garden were the tree of life and the tree of the knowledge of good and evil (Genesis 2:8-9).

We learn from this account and from other passages in Scripture that the Creator not only made a good creation, but he was good to man whom he had created.

Fallen man frequently has a warped, distorted idea of God and does not believe that the Creator is good and that He loves man. I recall a discussion with a young woman from a private college on the West Coast. She claimed to be an atheist. I asked her to describe the God she did not believe in. She thought for a moment and said, "God is a nasty, mean-tempered, gray-haired old man in the heavens who wants to stop people from having any fun." After giving this negative picture of God, she sat silently for a moment. Then, before I could respond, she said in half-surprise, "You know, maybe it's not God that I don't believe in. Maybe it's my idea of God." That was a perceptive observation. Many people have a distorted, limited view of the Creator. They do not know Him and are afraid of Him. They don't realize He loves them and sent His Son to die for the sins they have committed. They don't know that the God Who created them also loves and cares for His creatures.

Biblically, then, the creation model begins with creation *ex nihilo*. God is good and He created a good, completed creation.

God saw all that he had made, and it was very good. And there was evening, and there was morning—the sixth day.

Thus the heavens and the earth were completed in all their vast array.

By the seventh day God had finished the work he had been doing; so on the seventh day he rested from all his work (Genesis 1:31-2:2).

Days of Creation

The biblical account tells us that creation was finished in six days. A straightforward reading of the biblical text also leads one to conclude that they were normal days. Evolutionary science will not accept this conclusion because it refuses to accept God's Word as data and assumes instead an infinite regression of natural causes and effects.

Science cannot directly examine the past. Therefore it cannot determine that creation was not in six literal days. Science can only extrapolate into the past by making certain assumptions. How far back is the extrapolation valid? An evolutionist would extrapolate limitlessly into the past. This is like trying to extrapolate backwards over all the roads that an automobile with 65,000 miles on the odometer had traveled. Just as one cannot do this with any degree of confidence, so one cannot safely extrapolate back to creation week. But just as one could ask the owner of the automobile which roads had been traveled, so one can search the Scriptures to see what the Owner of the universe says about earth history.

There is no indication in the biblical text that the days of creation week were not normal days, and there are strong indications from the text that they were. One biblical scholar who has studied this topic thoroughly enumerates several of these indications.

In view of the widespread resistance to this concept [ordinary day] in some Christian circles today, it is surprising how many strong Biblical arguments are available in its support if the time-honored, historical-grammatical system of Biblical hermeneutics be accepted. *First,* the use of a numerical adjective with the word *day* in Genesis 1 limits it to the normal day. It is true that the word *day* is used in two or even in three different senses in the creation narrative (of a twelve-hour period of daylight in 1:5, 14, 16, 18; of a twenty-four-hour day in the rest of the chapter; and of the entire creation week in 2:4, though this verse may refer only to the first day of creation), but in each case the context shows what sense is to be understood. In historical narratives the numerical adjective *always* limits the word to the twenty-four-hour period.[7]

Whenever there is a number associated with the word *day,* it always means a normal day. If the text reads "first day," "second day," or "thirtieth day," it refers to a normal day. Where the word *day* is not associated with a number, it may mean a normal day or it may refer to a period of time. Meaning in such cases is determined from context. However, of the many times the Hebrew word *yôm* (day) is used throughout Scripture in historical contexts, whenever it is associated with a number it always means a normal day.

Moreover, the qualifying phrase, "and there was evening and there was morning," attached to each of the days indicates that they were normal days. In addition, there is an association with ordinary days clearly indicated in Exodus 20:11. Here man is instructed to work six days and rest the seventh, in the same pattern God used during creation week. There is no reason to think these were not ordinary days as one would understand from a direct reading of the text.

Not only are the days literal; they are also consecutive. As E. J. Young[8] has shown, textual evidence clearly indicates consecutive days. The consecutive numbering of the days given in the creation account indicates that the days themselves were also consecutive.

The suggestion that the days of creation were not literal days did not come from a careful study of Scripture. The attack on literal days came rather from extrabiblical assumptions asociated with an autonomous view of nature. The attack came from evolutionary presuppositions and not from scientific data. No observations of either the present or the past universe have shown that the days of Genesis 1 were anything but normal days.

The Nature of Man

Genesis 1 does not give us all the details we might be curious about. It does, however, provide an absolute reference point and initial assumptions as well as an outline from earth history. It gives a basis for understanding man.

> Then God said, "Let us make man in our image, in our likeness, and let them rule over the fish of the sea and the birds of the air, over the livestock, over all the earth, and over all the creatures that move along the ground."
> So God created man in his own image, in the image of God he created him; male and female he created them" (Genesis 1:26-27).

Mankind is in the image of the Creator, but because man is only finite while God is infinite, man's personality is only a finite and perhaps dim reflection of the rich, full, and infinite personality of the Creator.

Consider some of man's personality traits: love, creativity, sense of humor, appreciation for beauty, sociability, abstract thinking or reasoning, will, and intelligence, among others. God possesses each of these personality traits in infinitely greater amounts than man. Man is only finite and a dim representation of the Creator. Each individual has within himself a different capacity for a particular personality factor compared with other individuals. Each individual is different: no two individuals are exactly alike. They have been created to have different intensity factors for their personality traits.

Men and women are also different. Certain of the personality traits tend to be intensified in women. Others tend to be intensified in men. Thus, when the Bible says that God created man male and female, we see a difference in intensity of personality characteristics but not in "mankindishness." It takes both the unique personality characteristics of men and the unique personality characteristics of women even to begin to reflect the infinite personality of our Creator.

Downgrading Women

By not taking into account the creation narrative and related Scriptures and their teaching on who man is, both society and individuals within it suffer much needless pain. History has shown us that women especially have suffered in societies rejecting scriptural teaching. Scripture teaches that both men and women are beings in the image of their Creator. Their personalities, biochemistry, and created roles are different, but they are both fully equal in personhood. Perhaps because men are physically stronger than women, in some societies women have been considered little more than personal property. When the gospel has been received by those societies, the status of women has improved.

In modern westernized cultures we are again witnessing an attack on the status of women as these cultures depart from their once Christian base. Rejecting the creation account given to us in Scripture, the feminist movement tries to blur the distinctions between male and female. God created men and women each with unique abilities to fulfill the roles He intended for them. Feminists reject that truth and attempt to force men and women out of the high roles God created for each. Consequences for marriage and the family have been particularly severe. The next generation is society's most precious resource and yet feminists denigrate child raising and homemaking. Little girls are instead being taught to admire professions traditionally occupied by men. The unnaturalness of this approach is illustrated by data from one social experiment.

In the early 1950s in the state of Israel, communal living

groups were organized in which sexual role equality was to be the ideal. Each communal living group was known as a *kibbutz*. Men and women were to have equal jobs, equal responsibility. What has happened since? Although young children were socialized so as to minimize all sex differences (except perhaps in dress or personal names), they still demonstrated significant sex differences. Boys' behavior was different from that of the girls. As adults, these same children tended to gravitate toward a division of labor. Men did the physically harder labor of farm work while women cared for the children and the homes. One observer noting this phenomenon writes,

> Marriage and the family have increased in importance, although both institutions had been regarded by the "pioneers" as obstacles to the collectivist spirit and to the emancipation of women. There has been a "return from radical feminism to femininity." A beauty parlor now operates within the Kibbutz. . . . Not only has the definition of equality been changed from one of "identity" to one of "equivalence," the women themselves are content to view their present condition as more "natural."[9]

Even though young children were socialized and raised by their kibbutz to believe that the distinction between males and females could be eliminated, their behavior, subsequent socializing, and mental outlook spontaneously returned to a pattern closer to that of the Bible. Men and women were created to be different and that difference was intended by the Creator as a delight and something to be enjoyed by both sexes. The Bible describes man as he really is. It is in agreement with reality.

Coming Back into Dependence

Creation is the basis not only for understanding the nature of God and the nature of man, but for the rest of creation as well. The universe was created and fitted for understanding. Man was given a mind to understand it, though that understanding is limited by man's finiteness. Through science man observes and studies God's handiwork. The Bible as God's Word is intended to serve as a guide to the study of the universe. The Bible shows the universe was intended to be interpreted by the Word of God even before the fall.

> To properly interpret the trees in the Garden of Eden, for example, man had to be supernaturally informed not just with respect to their ultimate cause but also with respect to their specific qualities (Gen. 2:15-17). In the Biblical position there has never been a "prehistoric" era devoid of special revelation from God (Isa. 40:21) and this constantly available special revelation has necessarily been inseparably linked to historical, observable events in the physical world (Deut. 4:32-35).[10]

In the Garden of Eden, God gave man instructions for interpreting his physical surroundings. All thought has a starting point; Adam was to use God's Word as the starting point for interpreting the world around him; for example, which fruits he could eat. Adam knew that his thinking and reasoning were dependent on God.

We also learn from Genesis 3 that man was tempted to start his reasoning independently from the Creator.

> Now the serpent was more crafty than any of the wild animals the LORD God had made. He said to the woman, "Did God really say, 'You must not eat from any tree in the garden'?"
>
> The woman said to the serpent, "We may eat fruit from the trees in the garden, but God did say, 'You must not eat fruit from the tree that is in the middle of the garden, and you must not touch it, or you will die.'"
>
> "You will not surely die," the serpent said to the woman. "For God knows that when you eat of it your eyes will be opened, and you will be like God, knowing good and evil" (Genesis 3:1-5).

The serpent did not question the actual words God spoke. Instead, he tempted Eve to question the interpretation of those words. The temptation was to use new assumptions for interpreting data about the material world. By reinterpreting what God had said, man could act independently of God. Paraphrased, the temptation was, "Why go to God to begin your thinking? If you eat this fruit, then you can decide for yourself what is right and wrong. You can begin your thinking independently of God."

This is the same temptation faced by people today. The temptation is to reinterpret what God clearly has said. Man has a natural tendency since the fall to want to be independent. He wants to run his own life. He wants to make his own presuppositions and to assume that he is autonomous. As a result of the fall, man attempts to use his own reason to judge the very words of God. He elevates his own reason above the revelation from God. Fallen man considers the idea of beginning his thinking with assumptions given by God as foolishness.

However, when an individual confesses to God that he has been attempting to live his life independently of God, God will forgive him. "If we confess our sins, he is faithful and just and will forgive us our sins and purify us from all unrighteousness" (1 John 1:9). Then as the forgiven individual allows God to reorient his thinking, he can use the biblical world view to integrate all of reality. Life will begin to make ultimate sense.

Moral Responsibility

As a result of the fall, man tried to hide from the Creator: "Then the man and his wife heard the sound of the LORD God as he was walking in the garden in the cool of the day, and they hid from the LORD God among the trees of the garden" (Genesis 3:8). From that point on, the natural tendency of man has been to erect world views independently of the Creator. Man erects independent systems of thought. He also wants to be morally independent. Because of his immoral living, he then thinks up a system to justify it.

Man has a choice: either he can *live* his way into a pattern of thinking, or he can *think* his way into a pattern of living. Fallen man has moral guilt and he does his best to think up a world view to remove the guilt. He lives his way into a pattern of thinking. The Christian who has made his peace with his Creator through accepting Christ as Savior can approach life on a firmer basis. He can think his way into a pattern of living.

Some of the strongest proponents of the evolutionary world view have been honest enough to admit this situation. Aldous Huxley is one example:

> I had motives for not wanting the world to have a meaning; consequently assumed that it had none, and was able without any difficulty to find satisfying reasons for this assumption. . . . The philosopher who finds no meaning in the world is not concerned exclusively with a problem in pure metaphysics, he is also concerned to prove that there is no valid reason why he personally should not do as he wants to do, or why his friends should not seize political power and govern in the way that they find advantageous to themselves. . . .
>
> For myself as, no doubt, for most of my contemporaries, the philosophy of meaninglessness was essentially an instrument of liberation. The liberation we desired was simultaneously liberation from a certain system of morality. We objected to the morality because it interfered with our sexual freedom; we objected to the political and economic system because it was unjust. The supporters of these systems claimed that in some way they embodied the meaning (a Christian meaning, they insisted) of the world. There was one admirably simple method of confuting these people and at the same time justifying ourselves in our political and erotic revolt: we could deny that the world had any meaning whatsoever.[11]

The Bible indicates repeatedly from Genesis to Revelation

that man with a moral problem tries to hide from his Creator. He knows he is guilty and erects systems of thought to justify his activities. Romans 1 outlines some of man's efforts to this end.

The Moral Problem

Biblical creation implies moral responsibility to the Creator. God is a moral being. Therefore we are morally responsible to him because we live in his universe. We are his creatures and therefore responsible to him. The biblical model of creation not only explains man's origin, but why man acts as he does. Man has a moral flaw and tries to avoid facing up to his guilt. This last point is documented with research done by some secular sociologists.

Secular sociologists and psychologists using the evolutionary model of man have erected elaborate rationalizations for criminal behavior. Such behavior is often attributed only to social conditions, environmental background, or genetic flaws. This view downgrades man. It downgrades him by making him less than a person responsible for his own actions. An individual in the evolutionary view is not morally responsible for his actions because his actions stem from the natural chemical and physical laws in nature. Man in this view behaves as he does because of chemicals going through his brain or because of the chemistry and physics of his particular environment.

Much of the present-day treatment of criminals and their behavior is based on the evolutionary world view. Because this view is not consistent with who man really is, it does not lead to success in criminal treatment. It cannot be successful because it has a wrong view of man and draws wrong conclusions about him.

Choosing Wrong

Several years ago a study of a large number of habitual criminals was carried out by a psychologist and a psychiatrist. These scientists were trying to get the criminals to change from a lifestyle of habitual crime to one of social responsibility. In the course of the study, the criminals were confronted with a view of themselves that was contrary to that being espoused by the liberal academic community, which assumed the criminals were not responsible for their behavior but were merely the products of their heredity and environment. The scientists conducting this study, however, assumed the men used their free will and chose to act in a criminal way. The two doctors confronted the criminals with who they really were:

> They were told of their wayward childhoods, their lying, and their general life-styles as well as regaled with their assumptions about themselves and others. According to the authors [the psychiatrist and the psychologist], the subjects were often reduced to speechlessness or bewilderment by the accuracy of the accusations.[12]

The criminals themselves readily recognized that they chose their lifestyle as an act of their free will. They were amazed at the scientists' accurate analyses of their behavior. They knew they were doing wrong. They had willfully chosen the criminal lifestyle.

In the biblical picture, man was created with a will. He could choose to submit to the authority of God or he could choose to disobey. Thus, when criminals were treated from the point of view that they had a free will—that they chose their lifestyle and were therefore responsible for it—substantial progress could be made toward their cure. A significant percentage of these "hopeless" individuals was totally cured by what amounts to the biblical approach. The biblical approach is thus far more loving than the usual approach, and even though fallen man may not wish to admit it, is in agreement with what is.

God's World

Fallen man lives in God's world, even though he may think he is autonomous. The nature of man is as Genesis says it is. He did not originate from the animals. He did not originate by chance. Man is in the image of his Creator. This means that man has a will and can make real choices.

Paul used this argument in his discussions. We see, for example, in Romans 1:16-20 that Paul used both the nature of man and evidence of the natural world in support of biblical claims: "The wrath of God is being revealed from heaven against all the godlessness and wickedness of men who suppress the truth by their wickedness" (Romans 1:18). Man lives in a created world. He is subject to that world even though he may pretend there are no moral absolutes and that he is only the product of evolution.

This verse brings to mind an incident from a number of years ago. I was invited to lead a discussion group with university students, most of them science majors. We discussed a number of topics including creation and evolution. In the course of these discussions, I made the statement that most of the clergy of the city did not believe the Bible was reliable, but that it contained errors of history and scientific fact. They considered it to be a generally unreliable document.

Most of the students in the discussion group were not Christians. They expressed surprise at my statement concerning the clergy and challenged it vigorously. They responded, "But they have to believe the Bible. That's what they're paid for!"

I challenged them. "Well, let's be scientific about it. Let's go interview them and ask them what they believe about the Bible." The students then selected several large churches from the Saturday church page of the newspaper and picked out the names of ministers from these churches. I then made appointments with them. These clergymen knew nothing about us, other than the fact that most of the group were science majors. (It is interesting that upon learning the group consisted mostly of science majors, a majority of the ministers automatically assumed the students were agnostic or non-Christian. It was an interesting comment on their perception of the relationship of science to Christianity.)

In preparation for the interviews, the students composed a number of questions. They tried to word the questions in such a way that the ministers would answer with what they really believed, not what they thought the students expected them to believe. One of the questions was, How reliable is the Bible? I can still remember the response from a minister serving one of the largest and most respected churches in the city. He was an older man, perhaps in his sixties. As nearly I can recall, his reply was, "Completely unreliable." The students were surprised by that answer, and one asked him, "Then why are you in the ministry?" The minister became sober, looked the questioner straight in the face, and responded, "I have been in the ministry for over forty years. I have observed the lives of many people. My observation is that those who live with a faith in God consistently get more out of this life than those who do not. With me, being in the ministry is a practical matter. I want to help people get more out of life."

That was a significant answer. Even though this minister did not believe the Bible, he had made the observation that those who lived as if it were true, those who lived as if there were a moral Being to whom we are responsible, consistently get more out of this life than those who did not. Those who lived as though this were God's world were richer, fuller persons. Even though one might not believe the Bible, it still describes reality. It describes the way things are. I have never forgotten that incident and the lesson it taught me.

Man is free to choose his own way, but he is not free to escape the consequences of that choice. God chooses the consequences. As the Bible puts it, " 'Just as they have chosen their own ways, and their soul delights in their abominations, so will I choose their delusions, and bring their fears on them; because, when I called, no one answered, when I spoke they did not hear; but they did evil before My eyes, and chose that in which I do not delight' " (Isaiah 66:3b-4, NKJV).

In the creation account, the world was created and was very good. At the time of the fall, evil entered the world and all creation was affected. Man was changed and the whole creation began a decay and dying process—the consequences of choosing autonomy.

It is important to note that for man the fall included not only moral areas, but those of reasoning and intellect as well.

Reorientation Is Hard Work

Even after receiving God's forgiveness in Christ, it still takes a lot of effort to rebuild one's thinking patterns. One must reinterpret almost everything he has been taught. He must re-examine and reinterpret things in light of new assumptions. He must extract himself from the pagan world view and bring his thinking into agreement with a biblical world view.

Dr. Gary Parker, who holds a Ph.D. in biology, began as an evolutionist. Later he became a Christian and adopted a biblical world view. Dr. Parker mentions the tremendous amount of effort involved in restructuring one's thinking. "When I ask you to think about the relative merits of creation and evolution, I realize I am asking no small thing. It's like asking, 'why don't you take a little time off, read through this little book, and re-think your entire world-and-life view, your concept of yourself and place in the world! That's not easy!'"[13]

Believe Moses

At the time of the fall, man's whole being was changed. He sought to act independently in morals; he sought to act independently in his presuppositions about the natural world; he sought to act independently in reasoning. In short, man as he had been created to be no longer existed. God had told him, "The day you eat, you will die." And man died. True enough, his body was still alive, but even that began to die. It began to age and decay until finally the last thing we read about Adam was that he lived 930 years and died.

The Bible also tells us that at the time of the fall, God instituted changes throughout all of creation. Not only were there changes in man's intellect and his body, but there were changes in the material world as well. Thistles and thorns and weeds were brought forth. The New Testament, commenting on the fall, makes it clear that changes were effected throughout all of creation. "We know that the whole creation has been groaning as in the pains of childbirth right up to the present time" (Romans 8:22).

Because of the fall, man needs a Savior. The gospel begins in the first three chapters of Genesis. I believe this is why this portion of Scripture in particular comes under so much attack in our day. The forces of darkness do not want men to realize the light of the gospel. These first three chapters, read in a straight-forward historical manner, provide the foundation for the whole Christian position. If these chapters are denied or explained away or reinterpreted as myth, the whole foundation for the gospel is removed.

Jesus himself said, "For if you really believed Moses [the first five books of the Old Testament, including Genesis], you would be bound to believe me; for it was about me that he wrote. But if you do not believe what he wrote, how can you believe what I say?" (John 5:46-47, Phillips).

Without accepting a literal creation and fall, there is no sound basis for accepting Jesus as Savior either.

Chapter 9, Notes

1. E. J. Young, *Studies in Genesis One* (Phillipsburg, N.J.: Presbyterian and Reformed Publishing Co., 1973), 7-9.

2. Ibid., 105.

3. Ibid., 66

4. P. C. W. Davies, "Uncensoring the Universe," *The Sciences* (March/April 1977): 7.

5. Henry M. Morris "The Late Great Principle of Uniformitarianism," *Good News Broadcaster*, April 1983, 45.

6. Hooykaas, *Rise of Modern Science*, 13.

7. John C. Whitcomb, Jr., *The Early Earth* (Grand Rapids: Baker Book House, 1972), 27.

8. Young, *Studies in Genesis One*.

9. Judith K. Brown, review of *Gender and Culture: Kibbutz Women Revisited* by Melford E. Spiro, in *Science*, 26 October 1979, 441.

10. Clough and Fredricks, "Creationist Science," 47.

11. Aldous Huxley, *Ends and Means* (New York: Harper & Brothers, 1937), 312, 315, 316.

12. Constance Holden, "The Criminal Mind: A New Look at an Ancient Puzzle," *Science*, 3 February 1978, 513.

13. Parker, *Creation*, 140.

Chapter 10

The Early Earth

*I*n our culture the nonbiblical world view is often presented vigorously and aggressively. The Christian must challenge that world view. He must present a Christian alternative with equal vigor and enthusiasm. This will require work and intense, continued effort.

The Christian can expect a fierce and continuing battle as well. It is a spiritual struggle and very intense. "For our fight is not against any physical enemy: it is against organisations and powers that are spiritual. We are up against the unseen power that controls this dark world, and spiritual agents from the very headquarters of evil" (Ephesians 6:12, Phillips). The battle is not just a battle of the intellect. It is not simply a battle between two sets of ideas. The struggle is a spiritual one against the very rulers of evil themselves. It is against the father of lies, the master deceiver. Fortunately the Christian is not alone in this battle. He has been promised God's armor and the help of the Holy Spirit.

Biblical Creation: an Outline

In challenging the evolutionary world view, it is not enough to point out fallacies and errors in evolution (and there are many of them). It is not enough to point out where evolution is contrary to factual evidence (and it is). While these things need to be done, Christians must also expound a Christian alternative to take the place of evolution. We must present an even better explanation within a theology of science which is not only consistent with the factual evidence from science but also more satisfying for explaining man and his being. If we care about and are to reach the non-Christian in today's culture, we need not only to challenge evolution but to replace it with something more satisfying both for science and for the whole man.

We need to do this not only for the non-Christian, but for the Christian as well. One who is converted out of the pagan world system needs to grow and mature in his new faith. A sound theology of science will help him do so. We can count on the help of God in this process. It was, after all, the Holy Spirit who worked in the individual to bring about his conversion in the first place. The Holy Spirit will also help the new convert grow in his faith.

In the pages that follow, we will outline a creation approach to origins and earth history in answer to the question, "If evolution is not true, what do we put in its place?" The Bible itself serves as a primary reference source for the assumptions and historical data used for constructing a biblical creation interpretation of origins and earth history.

As we mentioned previously, our task will be somewhat like assembling the pieces of a jigsaw puzzle. The Bible serves as the picture on the puzzle box. It gives us the overview. We shall have to work, however, at fitting individual pieces into place.

In these pages we will not do more than outline a few key features of the creation approach. For more in-depth details one may consult some of the excellent books and films on the topic appearing in recent years.

A Broad Outline

Because the Bible gives only a broad outline and limited details of origins and earth history, creationist scientists and individuals who have studied scientific data will sometimes differ on details. There is a surprising amount of agreement, however. Even those who come from different scientific, social, cultural, and religious backgrounds and who have studied independently of one another come to strikingly similar general conclusions.

The quality of scholarship from creationists is also excellent in many cases. The Christian need not be ashamed of the creationist position from a scholarship point of view. There are excellent scientists and scholars who hold this position and expound it with clarity and accuracy.

Earth History

We have talked briefly about origins in the previous chapter. This brings us to the next point of contention between creation and evolution, that of earth history. We want to try to reconstruct some of the details about events of the past. In doing this, we shall use the Bible as a guide, realizing that it only outlines major events of earth history. Details must be filled in either by reasonable extrapolation or by study of historical records and artifacts. This process of trying to reconstruct a picture of earth history is what I call "unveiling the past."

As we begin this process it must be emphasized that we are attempting to fill in details of a historical process. A creation scientist is free to make assumptions in line with the broad biblical outline. Those who take the evolutionary approach to earth history also make assumptions within the broad outline of their original premise that nature is autonomous.

Modern scientists, of course, were not there to observe the past as it was happening. In going about our task of unveiling the past, we must therefore rely both on eyewitness accounts and physical data. Eyewitness accounts include the Bible and documents from ancient history. Physical data include artifacts left by man and other archaeological data as well as data from geology and earth sciences.

It should be remembered that any secondary assumptions we make may be wrong. As new data arrives, secondary assumptions may need to be modified. This of course is the very basis of the scientific approach. With limited data, one makes a hypothesis; if further data confirm the hypothesis, then one can advance it to a theory. However, if further data do not confirm the hypothesis, then a new assumption and new hypothesis must be made. A creation scientist uses this approach as freely as does the evolution scientist. This means that in attempts to reconstruct history, one creation scientist may not agree in all details with another creation scientist. What is agreed on, however, is the world view of the creation approach as well as those points specifically stated by the biblical record.

In this section, my goal is simply to provide an outline of earth history and to show that such an approach can be in agreement with observational data. I do this in order to counter the argument of the evolutionists that a creation approach cannot be used because it is in disagreement with facts. The exact opposite is true. The creation approach *is* in agreement with the facts and I shall illustrate this as our discussion continues.

Veils to Understanding the Past

In unveiling the past, the ideal situation would be to have a complete description of what the original earth was like. If we had this description, and knew in detail the various components, then in principle it would be possible to add in the changes which have occurred since that time and we would arrive at what we observe today. That would be the ideal case. In actual fact, however, we are far from the ideal. We do not have many of the details of what the original earth was like.

Furthermore, the Bible gives only a brief description of some of the major events that have brought changes to the original earth. That means we must make secondary assumptions and continually search for new data to test these secondary assumptions. Thus, in reconstructing earth history, there are a number of "veils" to our understanding of the past. These veils make it difficult to get a clear picture of what the original earth was like and hinder our attempts to interpret the changes which have occurred since the creation.

The Six Veils

There are six major veils that make it difficult to reconstruct earth history from a creation viewpoint. These veils are
like thin curtains over a window. Looking out through a cur-
tained window, one can make out broad outlines, but the curtain
prevents us from seeing much detail. We can see if objects are in
motion and perhaps see rough outlines and sizes, but all we can
see is the broad outline. In a similar way, these six curtains to
our understanding of earth history prevent our perceiving clear
details about events which occurred in the past.

The Fall

The first of these veils is the fall. The Bible tells us that the
original creation was changed at the time of the fall. The
changes were general and involved all of creation as Romans 8
explains, but the extent and the details of those changes are not
listed for us. Thus the first veil to understanding the past is the
fall and changes associated with it.

The Flood

A second veil to unraveling the past is the worldwide flood
of Noah's day. The flood caused extensive changes on the surface of the earth. This affected not only artifacts of interest to archaeology but to geology and paleontology as well. The flood
caused perhaps the most extensive changes that have occurred
since creation.

The Bible clearly indicates these major changes. This is
true not only from the account given in Genesis but also from
comments given elsewhere in Scripture.

Peter writes, "By water also the world of that time was del-
uged and destroyed" (2 Peter 3:6). The world of that time
perished, so the conditions that existed up until the time of the
flood no longer existed after it. Major changes occurred at the
time of the flood. Since we do not have a detailed list of all of
these changes, the flood constitutes a second veil to our unraveling of earth history.

Time

A third veil to our understanding of what the original earth was like, and therefore how changes which have occurred since have affected it is the factor of time. By ordinary human standards, creation took place a long time ago. Even if we take the position that creation took place a few thousand years ago, this is still a long time by human standards. A lot of changes can take place in even a thousand years. Time itself has erased many of the details and much of the evidence. Some of the human artifacts may have rotted completely while others have deteriorated; geological features, erosion, and other physical changes have destroyed some of the original evidence. Time is one of the major veils to our understanding of the original earth and to our attempts to reconstruct its conditions.

Cultural Conditioning

A fourth curtain making it difficult to reconstruct earth history from a creationist point of view is cultural conditioning. We live in a culture which is antagonistic to the creationist view point, and this conditions our thinking. Our culture places relentless pressure all the way from childhood through old age to accept the prevailing cultural view. Historical data relating to earth history are constantly being interpreted for us by those with a world view antithetical to that of the Bible. Data are repeatedly displayed and interpreted within a world view which assumes that nature is autonomous.

This is done in newspapers, magazines, and museums, to name a few. I have yet to see in major communication media a creation interpretation given to the discovery of a new fossil skull or bone. Newspapers and other media consistently provide an evolutionary interpretation of such data. Earth history at museums is pictured as evolutionary. I have yet to visit a public museum where a creation interpretation was ever given to any of the data.

Furthermore, creationist views are held in near total contempt at most academic institutions. In high schools and universities, the creation position, if it is even mentioned, is usually discussed in derogatory terms. Creationists are referred to as ignorant, anti-intellectual, and unscientific.

Cultural conditioning thus plays a major role in veiling the past. A good many ideas suggested by the autonomous world view and its attendant evolutionary claims have to be overruled and one's thinking restructured to consider the creationist point of view; one must almost rethink everything he has learned in modern culture.

Primitive Man

Veil five is a specific example of cultural conditioning and concerns modern culture's ideas of early man. Our culture, steeped as it is in evolutionary thinking, has conditioned us to think of early man as primitive. Because evolution views man as having ascended from the animal stage, the further back in time one goes the more animal-like and primitive should be man's features and culture. This present day idea that man in the past was primitive even affects Christians in reading the Bible.

One frequently encounters, even in Christian writings, the idea that the people discussed in the early chapters of Genesis were not scientific. They mean by this statement that these early people were unsophisticated in their knowledge about the natural world. There is no hint in the Bible, however, that early people were unsophisticated. Just the opposite is true. Adam named all the animals, indicating a high level of mental ability.

Evidence from archaeology also indicates that early man had a high level of intelligence and a fairly sophisticated technology. He had what we would call a high level of science. Those who have held to the evolutionary view of man are continually being "surprised" by the discoveries of ancient artifacts which indicate early man's high level of sophistication. Of course, what the evolutionist usually does when confronted with this evidence is to simply push backwards in time man's development from the animal. Nevertheless, the idea that early man was inferior to modern man is quite widely held. In the last part of this chapter, we will look specifically at the nature of early man.

The Educational System

Veil six is a second example of how our fallen culture has made it difficult to unravel a true picture of the past. This veil is our educational system. Textbooks used in schools are strongly influenced by the prevailing thought-forms of the surrounding culture. Fortunately some individuals and educators are beginning to recognize this. One who has is Dr. Thomas S. Kuhn, and he is considered controversial as a result. Nevertheless, he has carefully argued his case. Kuhn observes that scientists are guided by a set of biases, theories, standards, methods, or a world view which he refers to as a paradigm.

> A new paradigm cannot build on the one it succeeds; it can only supplant it. Science is not the cumulative process portrayed in the textbooks; it is a succession of revolutions, in each of which one conceptual world view is replaced by another. . . .
>
> The notion of science as an enterprise that draws constantly closer to some goal set by nature is one that is deeply held. That may be in part, says Kuhn, because of the way that scientific textbooks persistently rewrite the past in terms of the prevailing paradigm. The aim is pedagogic efficiency, so that the student does not have to master all the "wrong" ideas of the past. But the effect is to create a quite spurious tradition of uninterrupted progress, of the cumulative acquisition of knowledge. This revisionist practice explains the invisibility of scientific revolutions; the victors of each revolution, who write the textbooks, present the past as if scientists had always striven for the objective embodied in today's paradigms.[1]

Students tend to believe if something is in print, it must be true. If it is written in a textbook, it must be fact and it must be what has always been believed.

In fact, some evolutionists were unsatisfied with the rate at which evolution was being absorbed by the younger generation.

They became impatient with the fact that creation was still believed. In order to speed up the process of incorporating their world view into textbooks, evolutionists solicited money from the federal government, a fact they openly admit.

> The American creationist movement is not new. It has a long history in politics and education. For decades after the Scopes monkey trial, even though the conviction was later overturned on a technicality, the subject of evolution was for the most part absent from high school textbooks. Then, in the 1960s, the National Science Foundation put $7 million into the Biological Sciences Curriculum Study, which developed and published new textbooks as part of the post-Sputnik effort to improve American science education. These books included evolution, and commercial publishers began to follow suit.[2]

It was not only in science textbooks that this was done. Social science textbooks were also rewritten to push the evolutionist's world view. Even more money was spent on this project. The creationist position leads to moral absolutes; people are responsible to their Creator for their moral behavior. Evolutionists, on the other hand, did not like young people to be raised to believe in moral absolutes. They wanted to rewrite the textbooks to put in moral relativism. To accomplish this, they sought the power, prestige, and money of the federal government; tax dollars were used to incorporate their particular religious views.

> The condition for creationists was exacerbated by expansion of NSF support into the social sciences. "Man; A Course of Study" (MACOS) is a curriculum module stressing, among other concepts, human cultural adaptation to environmental conditions. The fact that groups such as Eskimos have from time to time sanctioned infanticide in order to limit the population to a size the environment could support is seen by social scientists as a demonstration of man's

majestic ability to cope with his surroundings. As seen by some religious fundamentalists, this example is an unjustified relativist attack on value absolutes such as the sanctity of life and the prohibition against killing. Not only did the new biology curriculum promote evolution and the new social studies course endorse cultural relativism, these purposes were accomplished with the overt support of the federal government. Over a hundred million dollars in tax revenues had been spent by NSF for development of these heresies.[3]

When Christians objected to having textbooks rewritten with a world view contrary to that of the Bible, evolutionists were infuriated. It appears they thought no one had a right to challenge what they were doing. They labeled those who disagreed as right-wing fundamentalists and anti-intellectuals. They accused them of being unscientific and against education.

The type of cultural conditioning received by students has put tremendous pressure on them to accept an evolutionary world view. It has created a thick curtain to unraveling the past. Thus the task for one who is a creationist is almost overwhelming. The veils to understanding the past hinder him greatly. In order to truly get a fresh look at historical data, one almost has to begin his education all over again. He will get little help from the educational system. Nevertheless, these are the kinds of odds God likes. God is not overwhelmed by man's railing against revealed truth.

It is written:

I will destroy the wisdom of the wise,
And the prudence of the prudent will I reject.

For consider, what have the philosopher, the writer and the critic of this world to show for all their wisdom? Has not God made the wisdom of this world look foolish? For it was after the world in its wisdom had failed to know God, that he in his wisdom chose to save all who would believe by the 'simple-mindedness' of the gospel message (1 Corinthians 1:19-21, Phillips).

One of the encouraging signs of our day is to see the large number of young people who are beginning to realize they are being manipulated by the educational system. In my lectures on university campuses and elsewhere, I am encouraged by the increasing awareness of young people to this problem. More and more young scientists are interested in searching out the creationist explanation for origins and earth history. Some excellent creationist research is also being accomplished by these young people even at the graduate level. They are not receiving much encouragement from the educational establishment, but they are going ahead anyway.

The Scriptures are the guide for truth to these young people, and they take to heart the verse which says, "Let God be true, and every man a liar" (Romans 3:4). Man's ideas, beginning with the assumption that nature is autonomous, simply cannot give big answers to big questions, and many young people now realize it.

In deciphering earth history within a creationist framework, we know the overall view, but we must still fit together individual pieces according to the picture on the box. Some statements in the Bible are clear and definite, and we can use those as solid data bases for deciphering the past. However, there are many details that are not provided by Scripture. We must arrive at them by logical deductions from scriptural statements combined with physical data. Other details will be educated guesses based on the broad scriptural outline and reasonable extrapolations from presently observed data.

In making educated guesses about how the individual scientific facts or pieces of the puzzle fit together, sometimes one has to tentatively position a piece into a location. Later, as the puzzle becomes more complete, it will be found that the placement was incorrect. Scientists must also tentatively place some details until further data either confirm them or show that they must be reinterpreted.

This tentativeness is not unique to the creationist viewpoint. All earth historians face a similar situation. However, the creationist viewpoint actually gives the scientist a head start because he already knows the true broad outline of earth history. The events mentioned in the Bible serve as checks for his reconstruction. The evolutionist does not have this advantage because he tries to work from a limited view of reality. He excludes certain data coming from the Bible (such as eyewitness accounts of the worldwide flood).

Many scientists, both ancient and modern, have worked at reconstructing earth history from a creationist point of view. Some excellent work has already been done and more is currently being done. The creationist framework provides a viable tool for interpreting data from science and also for making predictions of new research areas.[4] A creation approach will solve some of the major problem areas associated with paleoscience.

The Conditions on the Early Earth

A few remarks about the condition of the original earth as it existed following creation are necessary in order to have a foundation on which to build. From geological evidence and from statements made in Scripture, we can assume the early earth had a warm, subtropical climate.[5] It did not have the extremes in warm and cold that we have today. Genesis describes the Garden of Eden:

> Now the LORD God had planted a garden in the east,
> in Eden; and there he put the man he had formed.
> And the LORD God made all kinds of trees grow out
> of the ground—trees that were pleasing to the eye
> and good for food. In the middle of the garden were
> the tree of life and the tree of the knowledge of good
> and evil" (Genesis 2:8-9).

Combining this statement with Genesis 2:5—"The LORD God had not sent rain on the earth" indicates that meteorological conditions were different from today and supports the idea that the early earth had a climate very different from what it has now.

Every tree that was pleasant to the sight and good for food was present in the garden. The fossil record tells us that we have only a dim representation of life forms today compared to what existed in the past. If a large number of trees existed together in the garden of Eden, that means there must have been a warm, subtropical climate. It is not possible for wide varieties of trees to exist in colder or temperate climates. In subtropical areas, it is not uncommon for several hundred different types of trees to grow within an area of one square mile.

Further evidence that the earth once had a uniform warm climate from pole to pole is furnished from geological observations. Areas that are now desert, such as the Sahara or the great American desert, were once lush with green vegetation and had a moist climate. The ginkgo tree, which requires a warmer climate, once grew in the semi-arid high desert region of central and eastern Oregon and Washington. Even in the Canadian province of Alberta, near Drumheller and nearby dinosaur beds, there is evidence of a warm climate. The same is true of areas in what are today Siberia and Alaska. In the Bering Sea off the coast of Alaska are fossil coral reefs. Coral grows in warm water, not cold. In Antarctica, scientists have found fossils of plant remains such as palm leaves and coal, indicating a warm, subtropical climate.

Scholar A. M. Rehwinkel's book *The Flood,* though written a generation ago, still stands as an excellent reference on the flood's relationship to earth history.

> God had created a perfect abode for man, the crown of His creation. It was perfect and complete in every detail. There were no thorns and thistles in that world. The earth brought forth abundantly of everything that was needful to provide for the wants, comforts, and pleasures of man. There was no need of a struggle for an existence either between man and man or between the beasts and their companions. There were no Saharas, no barren wastes, no bleak and sterile hills, no rigors of the arctic and no

disease-breeding heat of the tropics. The most enchanting islands in the subtropical area of the South Seas today are but an imperfect replica of what that world was which received the verdict "very good" from its Creator.[6]

The world of Adam and Eve at creation was much different from our world today. We have just faint shadows of what it was like.

With respect to climate, the fossils show that there was a uniformly mild climate in high and in low latitudes of both the northern and the southern hemisphere. That is, there was a perfectly uniform, non-zonal, mild, and springlike climate in every part of the globe. This does not mean that the climate was of necessity the same in all parts of the earth. There were differences, but not the present extremes.[7]

A Different Atmosphere

Apparently there was associated with the warmer climate of the original earth an atmosphere with a composition somewhat different from today's atmosphere. If the climate was warmer, the atmosphere may have held considerably more water vapor than it does today. Even more important, however, the atmosphere may have contained a higher percentage of carbon dioxide. There is considerable evidence from geological studies to support this idea. Fossil fuels, such as coal and oil, would suggest a higher composition of CO_2 in the atmosphere at some time in the past. We know that coal was formed from plant material. Plants get their carbon by photosynthesis using carbon dioxide from the atmosphere. The carbon now found in the millions and millions of tons of coal located around the globe was at one time in the atmosphere. A slightly higher concentration of carbon dioxide in the atmosphere would produce a warmer climate. Geologists refer to this phenomenon as the "greenhouse effect."

Carbon dioxide also is a sort of atmospheric "fertilizer." It has been demonstrated that plants grow more readily in greenhouses which have a supplemental supply of carbon dioxide. The combination of warmer climate and sufficient source of carbon dioxide would have resulted in a land surface covered with a rich, thick vegetation layer. Areas of the globe now devoid of plant life (either because of desertification or because they are now too cold) at one time had a thick covering of plant material.

One Land Mass

The Bible also may hint that all the land masses were essentially in one piece at one time on the early earth. We cannot be dogmatic on this point, but it would not be out of line with the statement in Genesis 1:9, "Then God said, 'Let the waters under the heavens be gathered together into one place, and let the dry land appear'; and it was so" (NKJV). If the waters, or the seas, were in one place, then it seems logical to conclude that the land was also in one piece elsewhere. If that were not the case, waters would have been in several places, as today, with multiple continents. If the waters were in one place, then it is a hint that perhaps there was one giant continent and the multiple continents we observe today came some time after creation.

A More Uniform Earth

Globally the climate of the early earth was much more uniform than today, but that does not mean there were not also some variations. The variations, however, were not so extreme as those observed today, nor were there the extremes of elevation on the earth's surface. There may have been high hills, but not the high and rugged mountains observed now. Nor did the ocean basins then have the extremes in depth. The earth's surface was much smoother and less wrinkled than it is now. The geological record seems to indicate this. Evidence indicates that most mountain building is of comparatively recent origin and that ocean basins sank as mountains rose. Such a process is also in agreement with Psalm 104:8.

Of course, differences in elevation on the surface of the land prior to the flood would also be associated with differences in temperature. At higher elevations, air temperature would have been cooler while at lower elevation it would have been warmer. From our perspective in the present world, it is difficult if not impossible to say exactly how extreme were the elevations on the early earth.

Normal Process vs. Creative Activity

It is also difficult to work out geological features of the early earth, but we can make some reasonable deductions. The land surface must not have been just barren, smooth rock when creation was finished. There had to be soil for plants to take root and grow. There may have been different types of soil, such as clay, or sandy loam, or humus-type soils. Since the time of creation, rocks have been continuously weathered into soils by natural processes.

However, from this we must not make the mistake of assuming that since soils now are produced from weathering, weathering is the only way God could have made soils for the early earth. The Bible clearly tells us that direct acts of creation were involved. Creation implies a completed project. Soils were likely created as part of the creative fiats. Some features of the geology of the early earth, if viewed from the process assumptions, would lead to wrong conclusions, especially regarding the time involved. It is wrong to insist on using process assumptions where creation assumptions apply.

Time Factors

A careful study of the Bible seems to show that one of the principal differences between events associated with normal processes and those associated with creative activity has to do with time factors. Normal processes, whether geological or other, occur during the passage of time, whereas creation events do not. Thus, if we use process assumptions for creation conditions or events, we will draw wrong conclusions about time.

From a human point of view, perhaps God willed the present universe to be responsive to both normal process and creative activity. Subsequent to the original creation week, creative conditions or events (miracles) would call man's attention to the existence of God. Intelligence is behind all events in the universe, whether they are normal events associated with God's usual way of working or whether they are creative or miraculous events, His unusual way of working. A miracle, however, may be the way a loving Creator draws the attention of fallen man.

Fallen man, however, wants to be autonomous and so he assumes that nature is also autonomous. To him, normal events are just the outworkings of natural physical and chemical laws. This allows him to believe that no intelligence is involved either for origins or the continued upholding of the universe. However, when he encounters creative situations or events, their unusualness draws his attention to the fact that the natural world is dependent. It shows him there is more to the universe than just material. The material universe has been created and constructed in such a way that it is responsive to acts of an intelligent will. This intelligent will can be God's or, on a much smaller scale, man's will.

To illustrate, suppose we were to enter a room and find a book lying flat on a table, and then later enter the same room a second time and find the book standing on end. What would we conclude? There are two possibilities. One is that a natural process such as an earthquake bounced the house and the table in such a manner that the book accidentally was vibrated from its flat position to a standing one. This would be an explanation using only natural chemical and physical processes.

A second possibility, however, and one more likely, is that while we were absent from the room, a person entered the room, picked up the book, stood it on its end, and left the room again. On entering the room the second time and seeing the book standing on end, we would conclude that intelligence was involved—someone stood the book on end.

One can think of many situations that occur every single day in which we conclude that intelligence has acted. By intelligence we mean the activity of will or mind. The opposite conclusion, as in the case of the book, is so improbable as to teach us by experience to differentiate those situations in which·

intelligence is involved and those in which only "natural process" has been involved.

The events of creation week are similar to our room and book experience. If we were to visit the early earth at one point in time and then come back a day later, we would have seen changes which would make us realize intelligence was involved. Creative activity had occurred. It's foolish to insist that God cannot act in such ways, especially when He has told us in His Word that He has.

Consider the creation of Adam. If one had entered the early earth at one point in time, there would have been no man. If one returned a day later, one would then have found an adult human being. Adam did not go through the process of growing from a baby to young adulthood and finally to manhood. He was created as an adult. Furthermore, Adam was created with a vocabulary. God could communicate to him in meaningful ways. He knew the meaning of words and rules for communication.

Eve also was created as an adult. Adam had the experience, in fact, of entering the "room" before and after creative activity had taken place. When Adam went to sleep, there was no woman present; when he awoke, he found a full-grown adult woman. Eve was created with a vocabulary. She could communicate with God and with Adam. She also carried on an intelligible verbal communication with the serpent. Creative activity and situations thus bypass normal process, which involves time. Creative activities do not involve time.

All subsequent children born on earth went through a process involving time. These children experienced conception, birth, and growth to maturity. On the early earth, process was involved subsequent to the initial creation events. Adam and Eve were created in surroundings that already had food and other supplies necessary for living. Perhaps it was not surprising to Adam to have another adult appear suddenly; he was not yet experienced with normal process. It was only subsequent to creation that he learned how much time was involved in growing from infanthood to adulthood. Only after creation was he able to learn process functions.

Miracles as Creative Events

It is difficult for modern man to step out of his normal, process-operating world and imagine or understand what it was like for creative events to be happening. We have a natural tendency to hang on to things we already understand. We have a natural tendency to want to explain things by process assumptions, since they are familiar. Because creative situations and events are not normally part of our experience—at least not events of the magnitude of creation week—we have a natural reluctance to accept those events as real or historical. This is understandable, but it does not make those events any less likely or real. All events depend on God and His will, and He can will creation events or situations to occur as easily as He can will normal processes.

Creation situations and events are not associated with passage of time. We do have some hints of what it must have been like to observe creative activity, however. As we look at the life of Jesus and his acts, we get a picture, although on a much smaller scale, of what creative activity was like. Let's take a look at two such events associated with creative activity. In each case we note that the activity was associated with intelligence and that time was not a part of the activity.

The Feeding of the Five Thousand

First we have the miracle of the feeding of the five thousand (Matthew 14:15-21). Five thousand hungry men in addition to women and children were fed and filled from just five loaves and two fish. In fact, by fishermen's standards, the fish were small fish (John 6:9). After the people had eaten all they wanted and were filled, there was still enough left over to fill twelve baskets.

This was a creative act. Time was not involved with this miracle. If normal process had been involved, a good deal of time would be associated with providing this much food. Grain would have to be planted and then grow to maturity, be harvested, ground, and cooked into bread. Fish would have to be caught, brought to shore, and prepared for eating. However, in this creative situation with Jesus time was not involved.

Water to Wine

A second case is the first recorded miracle of Jesus, that of turning water to wine (John 2:1-11). As soon as the waterpots were full of water, servants began to take out the liquid and it was wine. Normally, if process had been involved, grapes would have needed to grow and mature, juice would need to have been squeezed out and processed. Creative activity does not include time processes.

We see from examples such as these that there is a difference between creative events and process events. One involves time and the other does not. Clearly one cannot use process logic to describe creative events without arriving at errors in timing.

A second point to be noted is that one cannot predict when a creative event will occur by using process reasoning. The guests at the wedding could not have predicted that water would become wine. The disciples, when asked to feed the five thousand men plus their women and children, did not expect that five loaves and two fish would have been adequate. They protested when Jesus asked them to use such limited supplies to feed the people. They were not expecting the creative activity because they were accustomed to think in terms of process, as we all are. There is no way to predict from routine process activity when a creative event will occur. God wills in His own wisdom to cause such events. The natural world is dependent on the will of God moment by moment. We also are dependent on God and his revelation through the Scriptures for our understanding of the natural world.

It is incorrect to use process reasoning to object to the account of creation given to us in Genesis. It is a logical fallacy to assume that only process can occur there. Clearly, if creation is possible at all, then process assumptions cannot be the only ones used for describing things in the past. They can only be used when we have a clear indication that creative activity did not occur.

Capability of Early Man

Physically, early man's body was far superior to our bodies today. In the years since creation, many degenerative effects have been accumulating. This has greatly reduced the health of man today compared to what it was in Adam and Eve's day. Man was fresh from the hand of his Creator, and his body had not deteriorated. Congenital diseases (diseases inherited through genetics) such as sickle cell anemia or diabetes have become much more prevalent since creation.

Mentally, early man was extremely alert and intelligent. Mental powers have also decreased since the days of Adam and Eve. Adam, for example, named all the land-dwelling animals and birds. "Out of the ground the LORD God formed every beast of the field and every bird of the air, and brought them to Adam to see what he would call them. And whatever Adam called each living creature, that was its name. So Adam gave names to all cattle, to the birds of the air, and to every beast of the field. But for Adam there was not found a helper comparable to him" (Genesis 2:19-20, NKJV). The implication here is that Adam sized up the characteristics of each animal and, on the basis of its characteristics, gave it a name. The name was so fitting that people continued to call it by that name.

This naming of the animals on the basis of their characteristics implies high mental capability. It is difficult even for one who has studied animals to be able to name from memory all the animals in the United States, let alone the entire world. Adam, however, thought the names up on the spot. This suggests high mental capabilities and keen observational powers.

A Faint Reflection

In the modern world, we have just dim shadows or hints of what man closer to creation was like. Some of the good genetic qualities that early man possessed have been preserved in certain individuals today. But it is difficult, if not impossible, to find in one person today all the superior characteristics associated with early man. Some individuals may exhibit unusual athletic ability. Others have unusual mental ability. And still others have unusually great musical talents. We classify them as geniuses. They are much above average in retaining some of the original perfection associated with early created man. We have read of individuals who have "photographic" memories. Such individuals could walk into a grocery store, make a quick glance at a shelf, turn away again, and tell you the exact number of items on the shelf. Others have unusually astute memories. A case is reported of an individual who goes by the code name "S."

> He was able to recall perfectly lists of as many as 70 arbitrary words or numbers presented once. Moreover, 15 or more years later he could faithfully reproduce these lists without ever confusing any of them.[8]

It is often objected that the sixth day of creation must have been longer than an ordinary day because it would be impossible for one individual to name all animals in such a short period of time. The error in this logic, however, is in extrapolating from today's inferior average mentality back to Adam. In truth, we have deteriorated a long way from Adam. It was no problem at all for Adam to name all the animals in a short time. We have just a dim reflection of what his capabilities were as we observe certain isolated pockets of humanity today.

Early Civilization

Keen powers of observation, undegenerated high intellect, physical health and soundness, and ideal environment combined to allow early man to begin to develop a high level of civilization. Even though conditions began to deteriorate at the fall, living conditions on early earth were less harsh. A warm springlike climate made the struggle for food and shelter less intense. Time and energy could be used for cultural development. By our standards early man developed a surprisingly high level of science and technology.

Being closer to creation, they had not experienced the accumulated degenerative effects that we have. Their bodies aged at a much slower rate and their life span had not degenerated to such a short one as ours. Up until the time of the flood, the average life span of individuals was 930 years. With such ideal conditions, they could rapidly develop a high level of civilization.

My specialty is chemistry, and I have studied it for over a quarter of a century. I like to believe that I know a little about chemistry. However, it is nothing compared to what I could learn if I were to study chemistry for three, four, or five hundred years—or more. We can imagine a similar case for early man. These early individuals with their long life spans and keen intellects could study the environment and have time to develop their observations into a high technological state. Furthermore, those who had these skills could directly pass them on for hundreds of years to succeeding generations. This would make learning much more efficient than in our day.

However, it is not our purpose here to go into detail regarding these matters. We want only to provide an outline of early earth and attendant conditions. And Scripture provides many hints about that early situation. In Genesis 4, we learn that farming was well-developed. Cain was a tiller of the ground. He did not just gather fruit; he actually tilled the soil. Abel was a keeper of sheep. Early man was not just a hunter; he practiced animal husbandry. Jabal lived in tents and raised livestock.

Early man also took time for luxuries such as the arts. These early individuals not only invented music, but they invented the musical instruments on which to play it (4:21). Stringed instruments and wind instruments are both mentioned here. Archaeology provides clues that these instruments were of high quality.

They also forged and worked in metals (4:22). Iron is mentioned, and bronze, which is an alloy of tin and cooper. The chemistry for producing these substances is quite sophisticated, indicating that early man had developed a fairly sophisticated technology.

There was also an adequate labor force. A veritable population explosion was taking place.

> And Adam lived one hundred and thirty years, and begot a son in his own likeness, after his image, and named him Seth. After he begot Seth, the days of Adam were eight hundred years; and *he begot sons and daughters*. So all the days that Adam lived were nine hundred and thirty years; and he died. Seth lived one hundred and five years, and begot Enosh. After he begot Enosh, Seth lived eight hundred and seven years, and *begot sons and daughters*. So all the days of Seth were nine hundred and twelve years; and he died. Enosh lived ninety years, and begot Cainan. After he begot Cainan, Enosh lived eight hundred and fifteen years, and *begot sons and daughters*. So all the days of Enosh were nine hundred and five years; and he died (Genesis 5:3-11, NKJV).

Each of these individuals had numerous children. Even by extremely conservative estimates, they must have had large families. Let's assume they were not in any hurry to have children and only had one child every twenty years. That's certainly not breaking any records. If they continued to have children for, say, eight hundred years, that would be forty children per family. These children were growing up and in turn having children, and their children were having children. Reproductive years were spread out over hundreds of years, enabling a large population to develop quite rapidly.

It is also interesting that present-day people from various parts of the globe have folklore and legends of a former golden age in the distant past. This folklore includes longevity and high technical achievements. Perhaps these accounts refer to the preflood conditions and civilization.

The Flood

Even in those ideal conditions, however, man sought to be autonomous and stood in rebellion against his Creator. Consequently man began to turn the near paradise of early earth into a virtual hell. Social conditions continued to worsen until by the time of Noah, conditions were so bad that the Bible describes them in near universal terms:

> Then the LORD saw that the wickedness of man was great in the earth, and that every intent of the thoughts of his heart was only evil continually. . . . The earth also was corrupt before God, and the earth was filled with violence. . . . And God said to Noah, "The end of all flesh has come before Me, for the earth is filled with violence through them; and behold, I will destroy them with the earth" (Genesis 6:5, 11, 13, NKJV).

The horror and terror of living in that kind of society is difficult even to imagine. The terrorism and violence of our own day perhaps gives us a reflection of what it may have been like then. God did not want man to be wicked and violent against his fellow man. As a consequence of man's continued rebellion, God prepared a judgment.

One of the things we learn from Scripture, however, is that even though man deserves God's judgment, God is exceedingly merciful. Before a judgment, God always sends a warning. We see this same situation in the case of the flood. God warned Noah of the approaching flood and told him to begin building an ark. "And the LORD said, 'My Spirit shall not strive with man forever, for he is indeed flesh; yet his days shall be one hundred and twenty years'" (Genesis 6:3, NKJV). We learn that mankind had over one hundred years warning that such an event was coming. It did not come unannounced out of the clear blue. While Noah was building the ark, he was also preaching. For God "did not spare the ancient world when he brought the flood on its ungodly people, but protected Noah, a preacher of righteousness, and seven others" (2 Peter 2:5). Everyone on earth at that time had a warning that a catastrophe was coming. Furthermore, they had a graphic object lesson in the construction of the ark.

Noah's warning went unheeded, however. The people did not believe him. They could not believe that a catastrophe was imminent; they assumed nature was autonomous. They used process thinking. Everything in their experience indicated that processes were uniform, and they extrapolated from that into the future and assumed that nothing other than what had been happening could occur. Only some of Noah's immediate family believed him.

Chapter 10, Notes

1. Wade, "Thomas S. Kuhn," 144.

2. James Gorman, "Scientist of the Year: Stephen Jay Gould," *Discover*, January 1982, 60.

3. James Guthrie, "Curricula and Political Conflict," *Science*, 13 May 1977, 753.

4. Robert Flood, "University Professors Probe Flood Geology," *Moody Monthly*, January 1981, 96-98.

5. Richard A. Kerr, "How to Make a Warm Cretaceous Climate," *Science*, 17 February 1984, 677-78.

6. A. M. Rehwinkel, *The Flood* (St. Louis: Concordia Publishers, 1951), 1.

7. Ibid., 7.

8. Jack McCarthy, "How's Your Memory?" *Northwest Magazine*, 24 August 1980, 3.

Chapter 11

The Flood and Earth History

O ne of the things that has impressed me in reading Scripture is that when God says something is going to happen, it happens. God said the flood was coming and it came. God caused the flood to occur. Exactly where in the normal course of history He acted in a non-usual way to cause the flood we do not know. One possibility is that He did not act until the flood actually began. He actually willed at that moment for the fountains of the great deep to begin breaking up and the windows of heaven to open. It is also possible that He acted further back in time and then simply allowed the consequences of that action to follow the normal process of events until the flood occurred. We cannot be dogmatic on this point.

I have often wondered, however, if God's action which caused the flood might have been taken at the time of the fall along with the other changes that occurred in nature at that time. At the time of the fall, God instituted a number of changes in the natural world. We are reminded of thistles and thorns appearing in the plant world. Perhaps one of the changes also instituted at the time of the fall would eventually lead through normal natural processes to the flood when these processes had fully matured.

Suppose, for example, the instituted change was to allow the earth to begin to radiate into space more heat than it was taking in. As a consequence, the earth would begin a cooling process. If the initially warm earth began to cool, there would be a number of expected normal consequences associated with that cooling. For one thing, the atmosphere would begin to become supersaturated with water vapor.

Even more important, we know that a cooling object shrinks in size. The earth has a rock crust on the outside which is solid. Inside the earth, however, is liquid material. As the earth began to cool and therefore shrink, tremendous pressure would be put on the rocks and on the liquid interior. It would be similar, I suppose, to taking an orange, placing it in both hands, and squeezing it tightly from all directions. An orange being squeezed from all directions, if then pricked with a nail, would squirt juice out in a fountain. As the earth continued cooling, rocks built up greater and greater amounts of stress.

Catastrophe

When these rocks reached the limit of their strength, sudden fracturing occurred and liquid rock began to squirt out all over the earth. As the Bible says, "all the fountains of the great deep burst forth." Worldwide volcanic activity would suddenly take place. Underground reservoirs of water would also be opened up. Volcanic dust and debris would be shot high into the atmosphere, initiating rain. The water vapor placed above the atmosphere on the second day of creation would rain down in torrents since it now had dust nuclei for condensation. The entire preflood equilibrium would be upset. Ocean basins would be uplifted. Continents would split apart and be moved. Tectonic or mountain-building activity would be going on. Tremendous amounts of geological activity would take place. Erosion and deposition, and re-erosion and redeposition would occur. There would be an entire collapse of the preflood atmosphere. The magnitude of this catastrophe is almost beyond comprehension.

Even such an event as the massive eruption of Krakatoa in August 1883 would only dimly mirror this catastrophe. When Krakatoa erupted, the explosion was so great that it destroyed an entire island. Sunsets all over the world were red for three years from the dust of that explosion. A tidal wave—a wall of water moving out across the ocean at a height of one hundred feet or more—occurred. We know this because there are trees washed up to that height above the present-day ocean level. Krakatoa was a gigantic explosion, yet it was miniscule compared to the geological catastrophe taking place at the time when all the fountains of the great deep burst forth.

There had never been an event like that before and there has never been one since. The entire globe was involved. Waters continued to rise for a total of 150 days, or about five months, as Genesis 7:24 tells us. It is no wonder that all in whose nostrils was the breath of life, all that was on the dry land, perished except those who were in the ark. In addition to rising water, great cataclysmic geological activity also continued undiminished for 150 days.

Then the floodwaters began to recede and the geological activity began a slow, gradual return to normal.

> Then God remembered Noah, and every living thing, and all the animals that were with him in the ark. And God made a wind to pass over the earth, and the waters subsided. The fountains of the deep and the windows of heaven were also stopped, and the rain from heaven was restrained. And the waters receded continually from the earth. At the end of the hundred and fifty days the water decreased. Then the ark rested in the seventh month, the seventeenth day of the month, on the mountains of Ararat. And the waters decreased continually until the tenth month. In the tenth month, on the first day of the month, the tops of the mountains were seen" (Genesis 8:1-5, NKJV).

The Waters Recede

According to Scripture, things began a slow return to normal at the end of five months. Whether the readjustments involved only God's normal way of acting (what we term normal process) or whether one or more direct acts of an unusual nature were involved (miracle), it is difficult to determine. Either way, the waters began to recede over a period of many months and even years.

Genesis 8:3 says "the waters receded continually from the earth." The waters went down gradually and continuously. Verses 4 and 5 tell us, "the ark rested in the seventh month," but the tops of the mountains were not seen until the tenth month. It took two months for the waters to go down enough for the ark to come to a halt on the mountains of Ararat. After the ark landed, three additional months were required for the water to recede sufficiently for the tops of the mountains to be seen.

The earth's surface was wrinkling and buckling as a new thermal equilibrium was being established. This wrinkling resulted in some land areas being elevated while other places were sinking. There were areas where mountains were being shoved up. As mountains rose, ocean basins sank. The wrinkling process would be much like taking a book lying horizontally and tipping it upward at an angle. As one part of the book tips upward, the other part tips downward. As the continents were lifted up in this manner, water was washing off from them in all directions. Hints as to what was happening are also given in Scripture:

> He set the earth on its foundations;
>   it can never be moved.
> You covered it with the deep as with a garment;
>   the waters stood above the mountains.
> But at your rebuke the waters fled,
>   at the sound of your thunder they took to flight;
> they flowed over the mountains,
>   they went down into the valleys,
>   to the place you assigned for them.

You set a boundary they cannot cross;
　never again will they cover the earth.
(Psalm 104:5-9)

An analogy might be to consider a pie pan filled with sand. If the pan were held below the surface of a tub of water, and then elevated above the surface, water would wash off from the pan in all directions. As the water moved rapidly over the sand on the pie pan, it would tend to move sand along with it. This would cause erosional channels. High and low spots would trap water in pools to form inland "lakes." This is similar to what was happening on the surface of the earth.

Toward Equilibrium

The readjustment on earth's surface took many months. In fact, the final equilibrium took hundreds or even thousands of years. In some cases we are still feeling the effects of that readjustment. The amount of geological activity during the time of the flood was extremely high, yet all geological activity associated with the flood did not stop with the flood. It took many centuries for the new thermal equilibrium to be reached.

Scripture also outlines several other interesting details.

"As long as the earth endures,
seedtime and harvest,
cold and heat,
summer and winter,
day and night
will never cease" (Genesis 8:22).

This is the first mention in the Bible of seasons associated with warm and cool temperatures. Prior to the flood a water vapor canopy above the earth and an atmosphere of different composition provided the earth with a greenhouse effect. However, sudden removal of the greenhouse effect would also remove the nearly uniform climatic conditions stretching from pole to equator. A likely effect would be the appearance of warm and cool seasons for the first time. We cannot be dogmatic on the meaning of this verse, but it correlates well with what we know of meteorology and the scriptural mention of a rainbow following the flood. Agriculture was practiced before the flood (Genesis 4:2) but possibly on a continuous, not periodic basis. After the flood, however, there was a definite time for planting and harvesting associated with seasonal temperature variations. This interpretation is also consistent with Genesis 1:14 where astronomy was used for marking seasons or telling time, since no characteristic seasonal temperature changes would have been available for marking it.[1]

We know also that differences of climate and temperature are associated with different latitudes. We now have arctic, temperate, and tropic zones. In the preflood world, however, these zones were not present, as indicated by geological evidence of a worldwide warm climate. The geological data show that the change in climate was sudden and not gradual, and this is consistent with the flood and its effects.

A further point is also mentioned:

> "Thus I establish My covenant with you: Never again shall all flesh be cut off by the waters of the flood; never again shall there be a flood to destroy the earth." And God said: "This is the sign of the covenant which I make between Me and you, and every living creature that is with you, for perpetual generations: I set My rainbow in the cloud, and it shall be for the sign of the covenant between Me and the earth" (Genesis 9:11-13, NKJV).

That God promised never again to destroy all life by a flood is one of the evidences the flood was worldwide and not simply a local event. Those who have argued that it was only a local flood have difficulty with this passage. Obviously there have been great local floods in various localities since Noah's day, yet God said there would never again be another flood of this magnitude. Either God was not telling the truth or the flood was worldwide. The new climatological and geological equilibrium was also worldwide. They could not have been just local changes because the equilibrium adjustments necessarily involved the entire earth, lithosphere, atmosphere, as well as biosphere.

God also said he would use the rainbow as a reminder that he was keeping his promise of no further worldwide floods. Meteorological conditions prior to the deluge were not such that a rainbow would be seen "in the clouds." Now, however, meteorological conditions were changed so that rain refracting sunlight could produce a rainbow. This is not just a nice legend that we tell Sunday school children to entertain them; rainbows associated with clouds had never been seen on earth before. From a scientific viewpoint, the conditions simply were not present for them to be seen. Those who rebel at the authority of Scripture want to attribute rainbows to a simple legend. Instead, rainbows are a reminder that God keeps his promise. When God said a great judgment happened in the past and would never happen again as long as the earth remains, he will keep his promise. It is a fact based on the solid promises of God and is verified by solid scientific evidence. Additional details and scientific documentation are available elsewhere.[2]

Following the flood, a new equilibrium began to be established. Earth's crust was continually placed under new stresses as cooling and readjustments continued to be made. The whole surface of the globe was greatly altered as a result of this worldwide catastrophe. Evidence abounds for this great event.[3]

One of the amazing features of our current society, however, is the vehemence with which the flood of Noah is systematically denied. Worldwide evidences clearly pointing to this event have been systematically denied or reinterpreted in an attempt to hide from this event. This denial is largely a modern phenomenon. Two hundred years ago, scientists in general accepted the worldwide flood and the attendant evidence.

The Results of the Flood

Let us look now at some of the changes brought about by this worldwide, singular catastrophe. An immediate effect, of course, was the burial of a large amount of plant and animal materials. The results of this burial are observed today as the great fossil beds located in various locations around the globe. Also, much of the lush, thick vegetation covering the preflood land mass would have washed from the land and formed great rafts of floating matter. Large quantities of this material would subsequently be buried under soil eroded from the surface of the land. Voluminous amounts of plant material buried in this way later were changed into fossil fuels of coal and oil.

Coal and Oil

Evolutionists are fond of insisting that oil and coal took millions of years to form. Careful study of these materials, how-ever, combined with actual laboratory experiments, indicates that long periods of time were not involved.[4] This is one of many examples of evolutionary thinking hindering the process of sci-ence. Evolution, with its need for and insistence upon a long time scale for earth history, completely misled the direction of research which sought to understand the formation processes of coal and oil. Considering our critical dependence upon energy, it is a tragedy that this research was not carried out earlier. Clearly, the biblical information suggests a far superior ap-proach to research in this area. Actual laboratory experiments have now demonstrated that coal and oil formation occurs in a relatively short time.[5] This information could perhaps have been obtained much earlier if it had not been for the hindering effect of evolutionary thinking.

Sedimentary Rocks

Following the flood, tremendous layers of water-laid sedi-ment covered the earth's surface. Most of the rocks on the sur-face of the earth are sedimentary rocks, which are formed by materials settling out of water. Immediately following the flood, these sedimentary layers were still in the form of soft mud. Chemical processes soon began to operate, turning these materials into stone, a process known as lithification. In some cases this happened relatively rapidly and in other cases it happened more slowly, depending upon local conditions and on the chemical components involved.

Another feature of the great deluge is interrelated with the chemical composition of the atmosphere before the flood. Carbon dioxide, which probably was in higher concentration before the flood, is soluble in water. As the rain of the flood began to fall, it dissolved carbon dioxide as it passed downward through the atmosphere. Carbon dioxide dissolved in rain water formed carbonate ions. The carbonate ions subsequently combined with calcium ions normally contained in seawater to form a precipitate known as limestone (chemical name, *calcium carbonate*). Thus, one would expect great limestone deposits to have been formed as a result of the flood. Again, this is observed at many points on the earth. Many of the limestone deposits also contain fossils. This again would be expected from the mechanism of the flood. Dead plant and animal matter would be covered with freshly formed calcium carbonate as it precipitated out and settled to the bottom. Many forms of life would be covered by these precipitates. One would expect limestone deposits to contain fossils.

The flood mechanism suggested here can also explain other geological features. Volcanic dust and gases shot high into the atmosphere would have subsequently shielded out some of the sun's rays. At the earth's poles, this would cause deep cooling and perhaps snow and ice formation on a broad front. Once the snow and ice were present on the earth, the whiteness of snow would tend to reflect back into space more heat and light. The effect would be self-amplifying and there would be quite a large area of snow and ice in the northern and southern extreme latitudes.

Climatic Changes

Warm air from the equatorial regions would also have strongly interacted with the cold air masses from the polar regions and intense storm systems would have resulted. Immediately following the flood and for many years thereafter, storm systems were probably much more violent than at present. As the atmosphere began to cool, partly as a result of removal of carbon dioxide and removal of the greenhouse effect, the cooler air would also contain less moisture. The net result of these changes would have been a gradual drying of the earth's climate and increased formation of deserts. This again is observed. Plant and animal remains found in the great desert regions of the world, such as the Sahara, indicate that these were not always deserts. At one time the Sahara was covered by lush greenery. It was a well-watered and verdant area whereas today it is dry and sandy. Remains of ancient river beds in the Sahara Desert have been discovered using satellites and have also been confirmed by observations on the ground.[6] Evidence of dramatic climatic changes are present throughout the globe.

Erosion

During later stages of the flood, as we have seen, the land surfaces were being lifted up. Water was washing off the surface of the land in great torrents, back into the ocean basins: "[the waters] went down into the valleys, to the place you assigned for them" (Psalm 104:8). Because the sedimented mud layers had not yet had time to harden into rock, tremendous amounts of erosion took place as the waters were returning in torrents to the ocean basins. If one flies over the earth, one can observe the tremendous erosion which resulted as the waters moved off the continents. In many cases it is even possible to tell the direction of the flow from evidence left behind. Sometimes the water went immediately back into the ocean; in other cases it was trapped by natural land formations for many centuries afterward.

In one such case, water washed back into the ocean basins in what has been called the great Spokane flood. Water trapped in the area of Idaho and eastern Washington and Oregon was eventually released in the Columbia Gorge and washed down toward the Pacific Ocean. The fact that tremendous amounts of water washed over the area is very evident. In the Grand Coulee region of Washington state there exists today what is known as

Dry Falls. No water washes over the falls now, but from a study of the geology of the area it has been estimated that hundreds of cubic miles of water rapidly washed over Dry Falls at one time in the past. The rushing waters carried the soil away as it moved over the land surface above and below the falls. On inside bends in the present day Columbia River, in the Palouse Region, there are giant ripple marks left by the receding water. These ripple marks are composed of giant gravel bars, fifty feet high and three hundred feet apart. A tremendous movement of water is required to form such features.

Fossil lakes were also left behind. Much of the western United States bears evidence of these lakes. In the Bonneville basin, as the land surface was rising after the flood, water was trapped and later evaporated; because of natural barriers it could not run off into the ocean. As it evaporated, its salt content was left behind, forming the Bonneville Salt Flats and the present-day Great Salt Lake. On the hills surrounding the Great Salt Lake, hundreds of feet above the present lake level, one can see evidence of ancient shore lines where wave action etched the banks of the hills. Similar features can be found in other parts of the world as well. Thus there is much geological evidence which clearly points to the catastrophe of Noah's flood. It is not because of a lack of evidence that the flood is denied.

Evidence for Catastrophe

It is interesting that, for the most part, geologists early in the last century were catastrophists. The evidence clearly pointed in this direction. Even science historians who are evolutionists admit this fact.

> The reason why catastrophism was adopted by virtually all of the truly productive leading geologists in the first half of the 19th century is that the facts seemed to support it. Breaks in fossil strata, the occurrence of vast lava flows, a replacement of terrestrial deposits by marine ones and the reverse, and many other phenomena of a similar, reasonably

violent nature (including the turning upside down of whole fossil sequences) all rather decisively refuted a rigid uniformitarian interpretation. This is why Cuvier, Sidgwick, Buckland, Murchison, Conybeare, Agassiz, and de Beaumont, to mention a few prominent geologists, adopted more or less catastrophist interpretations.[7]

Geological Evidences

The evidence that pointed to catastrophism has not disappeared. It is still the same today. In fact, even more evidence of catastrophism is being continually discovered. The evidence has not changed; only the assumptions used to interpret that evidence have changed. Most geologists of the past used biblical assumptions, and catastrophism fit. It is no longer the case that most geologists use biblical assumptions, but there may be a return to catastrophism if it can be divorced from biblical views.[8]

Sometimes new discoveries suggesting catastrophism are so striking that they make the news sections of scientific publications. It is interesting to read letters to the editor following such announcements. An example of this occurred in the weekly magazine of the American Chemical Society, *Chemical & Engineering News*. The news section of the magazine reported the finding of an interesting fossil in a diatomaceous earth quarry in Lompoc, California. Diatomaceous earth was formed by microscopic organisms with hard exterior skeletons or shells. When these skeletons collected together in large numbers, they formed a deposit which now is mined for use as an abrasive or filtering agent. *Chemical & Engineering News* reported the following news item.

> Workers at the Dicalite division of Grefco Inc. have found the fossil skeleton of a baleen whale some 10 to 12 million years old in the company's diatomaceous earth quarries in Lompoc, Calif. . . . The whale . . . is one of the largest fossils ever collected anywhere. . . . The whale is standing on end in the

quarry and is being exposed gradually as the diatomite is mined. Only the head and a small part of the body are visible as yet. The modern baleen whale is 80 to 90 feet long and has a head of similar size, indicating that the fossil may be close to 80 feet long.[9]

Subsequent to the publication of this news item was a letter to the editor regarding the find.

SIR: K. M. Reese made no comment concerning the implications of the unique discovery of a baleen whale skeleton in a vertical orientation in a diatomaceous earth quarry in Lompoc, Calif. However, the fact that the whale is standing on end as well as the fact that it is buried in diatomaceous earth would strongly suggest that it was buried under very unusual and rapid catastrophic conditions. The vertical orientation of the whale is also reminiscent of observations of vertical tree trunks extending through several successive coal seams. Such phenomena cannot easily be explained by uniformitarian theories, but fit readily into an historical framework based upon the recent and dynamic universal flood described in Genesis, chapters 6-9.[10]

This was later followed by another letter.

SIR: Dr. Helmick, how dare you imply that our geology textbooks and uniformitarian theories could possibly be wrong! Everybody knows that diatomaceous earth beds are built up slowly over millions of years as diatom skeletons slowly settle out on the ocean floor. The baleen whale simply stood on its tail for 100,000 years, its skeleton undecomposing, while the diatomaceous snow covered its frame millimeter by millimeter. Certainly you wouldn't expect intelligent and informed establishment scientists of this modern age to revert to the outmoded views of our forefathers just to explain such finds!

> Why, even the people of Noah's own generation
> couldn't buy the idea of a universal cataclysmic
> flood. (Of course, they missed the boat.)[11]

Sometimes reading letters to the editor can be instructive as well as entertaining.

Biological Evidence

In addition to geological data regarding the flood, one would also expect biological evidences. One would expect to find evidence of a great killing off of animals all over the globe. Such evidence of biological catastrophe also exists and is referred to by various names in the literature. Sometimes it is called the "end of a universe." Sometimes it is referred to as "The Great Dying" or "The Great Extinction." Evolutionists go to great lengths to try to interpret the evidence of a great dying as separate events. They do this in order not to associate the event with the flood. The evidence is clearly there, however, and there are firm indications the events were not widely separated in time, as evolution would have us think. One author describing the "Pleistocene" extinction writes:

> It might at first appear that many of these great animals died natural deaths; that is, that the remains that we find in the Pleistocene strata over the continent represent the normal death that ends the ordinary life cycle. However, where we can study these animals in some detail, such as in the great bone deposits of Nebraska, we find literally thousands of these remains together. The young lie with the old, foal with dam and calf with cow. Whole herds of animals were apparently killed together, overcome by some common power. . . . Such piles of bodies of animals or men simply do not occur by any ordinary natural means.
>
> Neither the Pleistocene animals nor their untimely end are phenomena peculiar to the American continents.[12]

The earth was in turmoil during this great dying. Volcanic eruptions were taking place. There was also violence in the atmosphere.

> One of the most interesting of the theories of Pleistocene end is that which explains this ancient tragedy by world-wide, earth-shaking volcanic eruptions of catastrophic violence. This bizarre idea, queerly enough, has considerable support, especially in the Alaskan and Siberian regions. . . .
>
> Throughout the Alaskan mucks, too, there is evidence of atmospheric disturbances of unparalleled violence. Mammoth and bison alike were torn and twisted as though by a cosmic hand in godly rage.[13]

Evidence of catastrophe is clearly present. The atmospheric disturbances that must have taken place to cause such wholesale destruction are difficult for us to even imagine. They would fit nicely, however, with the events described in Genesis 7 and 8. The differences in temperature caused by the cold at the extreme north and south intermingling with the warmer currents from lower latitudes must have caused fierce winds. Perhaps this is what Genesis 8:1 refers to: "Then God remembered Noah, and every living thing, and all the animals that were with him in the ark. And God made a wind to pass over the earth, and the waters subsided" (Genesis 8:1, NKJV).

Gradual Catastrophe

The evidence of great catastrophe in the biosphere has been noted for many years. An interesting title and associated subtitle to an article commenting on the great dying of animals states: "Crises in the History of Life: How is it that whole groups of animals have simultaneously died out? Paleontologists are returning to an earlier answer: natural catastrophe. The catastrophes they visualize, however, are not sudden but gradual."[14] It is interesting that the author seems forced to admit catastrophism but tries desperately to avoid the idea of associating it with the flood. The catastrophes must be gradual rather than sudden. It is difficult to imagine how a catastrophe can be gradual.

A Watery Death

The great dying is also nearly always associated with a watery death. This has also been frequently noted in the literature. Most often those who try to avoid a flood explanation attempt to associate the clear evidence of involvement with water with a local event, such as a local flood or river overflow or animals falling into a lake. In some cases, however, there is admission that the extent of water damage was continent-wide or more.

One of the puzzles generated by evolutionary theory is what happened to the dinosaurs. Every few years, it seems someone suggests a new theory to account for their sudden extinction. Evidence for a watery death is so clear it has even been suggested that a giant wave caused by a meteor impact may have drowned the dinosaurs. In commenting on this possibility, one writer observes:

> This is the latest entry—or at least a new variation of an earlier entry—to try to explain one of the longest-running and most intriguing mysteries of science: what caused the Great Extinction that wiped out the dinosaurs and many other land and water species? . . .
>
> "One of the big effects that hadn't been talked about is the possibility that an impact would produce a huge tidal wave . . . five kilometers (three miles) high at the source and 500 feet high half-way around the world," Ahrens said. "We don't know if that killed the dinosaurs, but . . . we think there's a very good chance a tidal wave could have inundated much of dinosaur country."[15]

Avoiding the Real Issue

Most geologists before Darwin's day were catastrophists. They explained the geological features this way because of the strong evidence for it. Since then, however, there has been a shift away from the biblical explanation for origins and earth history. Studied attempts have been made to find other explanations for the evidence. Research since Darwin's day has uncovered much new evidence, but evidence that builds an even stronger case for catastrophism. I suspect that catastrophism would be adopted wholesale throughout the scientific community if it were not for the support that it lends to the biblical account of the flood. This is as much as admitted in some places. For example, in discussing the evidence for a watery cataclysm in the scabland area of the northwest United States, one scientist writes,

> Geology was not a science until the legendary Noachian flood and six-day creation were replaced by explanations derived from careful study of rocks. The doctrine that past events should be explainable through no more than reasonable extensions of observable processes has played a vital role in substituting the plausible for the preposterous and the feasible for the fanciful in geology. Many geologists, mindful of this important truth, have been reluctant to accept such a catastrophic mechanism to explain the scablands and have tried to find other explanations based on combinations of more ordinary processes. This has stimulated healthy controversy but does not seem to have seriously weakened the Spokane Flood hypothesis. The sheer magnitude of the whole scabland complex and the many ways in which it exceeds the bounds of normal stream erosion and deposition seem to justify, if indeed they do not demand, an outsize agent operating under extraordinary circumstances.[16]

This comment represents an attitude common in historical geology. There is a conscious and studied effort to avoid an obvious and biblical interpretation of the data. The biblical view of history is held up to ridicule. Strained logic is used to avoid the direct implications pointing to a worldwide flood. *Ad hominem* arguments are used in place of solid reasoning from the data. Those who hold to a biblical flood are said to be uneducated, unscientific, obscurantist, stubborn, or a combination of all of these. False statements are made which imply that no scientist believes in biblical history. In actual fact, many scientists believe in biblical history, but this is either ignored or passed over with the statement that only "fundamentalists" believe in biblical history. Thus the real issue is avoided.

The real issue is not who believes a particular view but whether or not that view is true. The question that should be asked is, Is biblical history true? There is a definite bias against interpreting geological data from a biblical viewpoint. Fallen man naturally assumes that nature is autonomous. He does not want to be accountable to a Creator. He does not want to admit that biblical history might be true. Geological uniformitarianism is closely associated with biological evolution. These two together have formed a smoke screen to hide the real issue: man's bias against having the natural world be dependent moment by moment on the Creator.

Chapter 11, Notes

1. Joseph C. Dillow, *The Waters Above* (Chicago: Moody Press, 1981), 98-100.

2. Dillow, *The Waters Above;* John C. Whitcomb Jr., *The World That Perished* (Grand Rapids: Baker Book House, 1973).

3. Everett H. Peterson, "Evidence for a World-Wide Flood?" *Creation Research Society Quarterly* (December 1983): 189.

4. Duane T. Gish, "Petroleum in Minutes, Coal in Hours," *Acts & Facts* vol. 1, no. 4, 1971, 1-5; A. Snelling, "The Recent Origin of Bass Strait Oil and Gas," *Ex Nihilo*, vol. 1, no. 2 (Int), 1982, 43-46; H. R. Appell, et. al., *Converting Organic Wastes to Oil*, Pittsburgh Energy Research Center, U.S. Department of the Interior, Bureau of Mines, 1971; Melvin A. Cook, *Prehistory and Earth Models* (London: Max Parrish, 1966), 209-53.

5. Joseph Haggin, "Argonne Scientists Make Artificial Coal," *Chemical & Engineering News*, 21 November 1983, 42-43; "Raking Theory Over the Coals," *Science News*, 6 August 1983, 93.

6. J. Eberhart, "Unveiling the Sahara's Hidden Face," *Science News*, 26 June 1982, 419-20.

7. Mayr, "Darwinian Revolution," 985.

8. W. A. Berggren and John A. Van Couvering, eds, *Catastrophes and Earth History* (Princeton, N.J.: Princeton University Press, 1984).

9. Kenneth M. Reese, "Newscripts," *Chemical & Engineering News*, 11 October 1976, 40.

10. Larry S. Helmick, "Letters," *Chemical & Engineering News*, 24 January 1977, 5.

11. Harvey O. Olney III, "Letters," *Chemical & Engineering News*, 21 March 1977, 4.

12. Frank C. Hibben, *The Lost Americans* (New York: Thomas Y. Crowell Co., 1946), 169-70.

13. Ibid., 176-77.

14. Norman D. Newell, "Crisis in the History of Life," *Scientific American* (February 1963): 77.

15. Robert Locke, "Did Giant Wave Drown Dinosaurs?" *Red Bluff Daily News*, 15 March 1982, 6.

16. Shelton, *Geology Illustrated*, 351.

Chapter 12

Age of the Earth

*F*or philosophical reasons evolution requires vast amounts of time. The hypothesis of geological uniformitarianism was embraced as a means of providing that time. Athough the term uniformitarianism is often used with different meanings,[1] its common usage implies the idea of slow gradual change for events in earth history. It is the assumption of infinite regression of natural cause and effect. Biblical creation and catastrophism are specifically excluded since they remove the necessity for great amounts of time. The duration of geologic time and the age of the earth are thus key discussion points between creation and evolution.

Looking for an Old Earth

The necessity for vast amounts of time was not only recognized by Darwin himself but by subsequent evolutionists.

> By this time [i.e., Pasteur's] the alternative to special creation, namely, the idea of continuity and historical succession, or EVOLUTION, had occurred to a number of thinkers. Some of these recognized that any concept of evolution demanded an earth of

sufficiently great age, and they set out to estimate this age.[2]

In Darwin's day, however, application of actual scientific principles and evidence did not allow the amount of time Darwin wished for. Darwin needed a great amount of time, because in his thinking evolution was the accumulation of a myriad of small changes. Great numbers of changes were needed to bring plants and animals to their present state of complexity and diversity by natural process alone. Each small change takes time; great numbers of changes require much time. Darwin eagerly accepted Charles Lyell's view known as uniformitarianism because it provided an opportunity to obtain the vast amount of time he wished for. Physical reasoning from actual scientific data, however, caused Darwin problems.

> The inflationary tendencies [regarding time] of Lyell and Darwin were rudely checked, only a few years after the publication of *The Origin of Species,* by a third giant of English science, the physicist William Thomson, Lord Kelvin (1824-1907). Applying physics to the study of the earth's age, Lord Kelvin calculated such items as mass, temperature, and heat loss, and came out with shattering results. At first he saw thirty million years as about the maximum. Then he reduced the figure to twenty million, or even fifteen.[3]

Darwin was greatly disturbed by Kelvin's work. It was based on firm principles in physics, and Darwin did not know how to respond.

> A few years after he published the *Origin of Species,* he was faced with convincing evidence that the Earth was too young for evolution to have worked its wonders. . . . No wonder Darwin called Kelvin "an odious spectre"—he had thrown all of evolutionary theory into question.[4]

Darwin died before an answer to Kelvin's criticism could be found. The discovery of radioactivity in 1896 by Henry Bequerel was the basis for evolutionary physicists' later attempted refutation of Kelvin's work. Radioactivity was claimed to be a basis for proving the great amounts of time necessary for evolution.

It is interesting to note that Darwin held firmly to his evolutionary views in spite of contrary evidence. The fossil record did not show the required transitional forms, and physical evidence indicated the earth was not as old as his theory would demand. This troubled Darwin, but he chose to disregard the physical evidence so that he could retain a philosophical viewpoint which allowed him to get around biblical history. Vast amounts of time are a philosophical necessity for those who reject biblical history.[5]

The Ultimate Escape Hatch

The thinking of evolutionists in this respect has not changed much since Darwin's day. Evolution of life from nonlife is a highly improbable process. This is acknowledged by evolutionists themselves. Time, however, is the escape hatch from the clear implications of the improbability of life arising by natural processes. George Wald, a well-known scientist and evolutionist, writes: "One has only to contemplate the magnitude of this task to concede that the spontaneous generation [life arising from nonlife] of a living organism is impossible. Yet here we are, as a result, I believe, of spontaneous generation."[6]

When a man says something is impossible and yet he believes it anyway, he had better dig himself out! I was interested, therefore, to read on and see what Wald was going to do in order to extricate himself from this "impossible" dilemma. I did not have to read far.

> Time is in fact the hero of the plot. The time with which we have to deal is of the order of two billion years. What we regard as impossible on the basis of

human experience is meaningless here. Given so much time, the "impossible" becomes possible, the possible probable, and the probable virtually certain. One has only to wait: time itself performs the miracles.[7]

It almost seems that for the evolutionist, time replaces God. The age of the earth is not just an academic question in the creation-evolution debate. Time is absolutely essential for the evolutionist. Thus an evolutionist cannot even consider any other possible interpretation of the evidence. Any evidence that indicates other than vast amounts of time must be explained away for philosophical reasons. Evidence that points to anything other than an old earth is, to use Darwin's term, "an odious spectre."

In discussing this point, one evolutionary writer notes that a number of major changes in thinking had to occur before Darwinism could be accepted. Heading his list of ideas which had to be changed was one regarding time. "The revolution began when it became obvious that the earth was very ancient rather than having been created only 6,000 years ago. This finding was the snowball that started the whole avalanche."[8] In Darwin's day there were scientists who would not agree that it was obvious that the earth was very ancient, just as there are scientists today who would also not agree. Nevertheless, the idea of vast amounts of time was essential for Darwinism to take hold.

Dating Systems

Many different geological systems and processes have been suggested for determining the age of the earth. However, in Darwin's day, only those methods Lord Kelvin used were based on solid physical principles. Kelvin's calculations, however, did not give an earth nearly as old as needed by the evolutionist.

Radioactive Dating

As already mentioned, in 1896 the phenomenon of radioactivity was discovered. Radioactivity involves the continuous breakdown of chemical elements during which process the elements give off radiations. The name *radioactivity* was selected because the breakdown gives off x rays, gamma rays, and other radiations and subatomic particles. The phenomenon of radioactivity was subsequently used in an attempt to date the earth. With appropriate evolutionary assumptions, it was possible to use data from radioactivity to calculate an age very much greater than that given by Kelvin's calculations. This dating technique could give the vast ages needed by evolutionists. As a consequence, Kelvin's conclusions were no longer considered valid. But the real question is, Are the assumptions true which are used for forcing radioactivity to give long ages? Other assumptions can be made for interpreting data from radioactivity and these do not lead to long ages. Certainly from a scientific point of view they should be considered also.

Evolutionists have considered radioactive dating (or radiodating) to be the most accurate method for measuring the age of the earth. In discussing the duration of geologic time, some geologists admit that geology is not of much help and explain why: "Unfortunately, most sediments do not contain reliable clues to how fast they were deposited—or to the durations of the intervals between layers."[9] While it is true that vast areas of the earth's surface are covered with sedimentary materials— materials settled out of water—these layers give little or no clue to how quickly they were laid down. Even if one were to know how long it took to lay down a particular layer, there is no indication of how much time elapsed between the layers. Thus geology is of little help in establishing a time scale for earth history.

Radioactivity was considered a most important dating tool:

> Radioactivity has provided geology with its first and only means of measuring the duration of long periods of geologic time in years. The techniques were all originated in the present century and are being continually refined, as new methods and

instruments are developed in the Atomic Age.[10]

Other scientists working in the area of geochronology and the age of the earth made similar claims. One well-known geochronologist writes in the preface of his book: "The principles of measuring long periods of elapsed time are outlined in this little book. As long as we stay on earth, these methods are all based on radioactive decay."[11]

Using certain assumptions, the phenomenon of radioactivity was used in an attempt to establish an evolutionary time scale for earth history. Since this method was considered to be more accurate than all other methods, let's examine it first in brief detail.

Principles of Clocking Systems

Radioactivity is indeed an interesting phenomenon. However, what do data from this branch of science show us? Is it true that data from the field of radioactivity establish a vast age for the earth? Before answering these questions, it will be helpful to examine a few principles applicable to clocking methods in general.

There are certain principles which any system used for telling time must obey. The system must have a known rate, and the system must also have a known calibration. If either of these is missing, it is not possible to use the system for telling time. These principles are general and apply to wristwatches and to astronomical methods, as well as to radioactivity.

Consider a wristwatch, for example. One may have a wristwatch which ticks off the seconds as accurately as desired. Even though the wristwatch progresses at a known rate, this is not sufficient for telling time. The wristwatch must also be set to a correct standard: it must be calibrated. The watch might be accurately ticking away and indicating a time of 3 P.M. But if it were dark outside, one would judge the wristwatch to be incorrect even though it was running at the correct rate. By checking with the radio or telephone, one finds it is 8 P.M. One would not be able to tell the time from the wristwatch alone unless it were also checked with a reliable standard. He must also have faith that the standard chosen is reliable. Both clocking principles must be met: a known rate and a known calibration against a trusted standard.

The Phenomenon of Radioactivity

In radioactivity, one chemical element spontaneously changes into a different chemical element. It will be remembered from a study of general science that chemical elements are composed of atoms. Not all atoms are alike, even for the same chemical element.

If we have a piece of iron, a chemical element, not all of the atoms in the sample will be exactly alike. They differ in their mass or "weight." Some of the atoms in the piece will have a weight of fifty-six units while others will have a weight of fifty-eight. Even though the atoms vary in weight, they are still iron atoms. Isotope is the term used to designate atoms of a particular weight. Isotopes are designated both verbally and symbolically. Iron atoms weighing fifty-six units are termed iron 56 and symbolized as ^{56}Fe. Likewise, the heavier isotope mentioned above is iron 58 and has the symbol ^{58}Fe. In general any sample of a chemical element is a mixture of isotopes.

Radioactive Dating and Isotope Ratios

Certain isotopes of some elements are radioactive. If we had a piece of charcoal (mostly carbon) from a wood fire and examined the type of carbon atoms it contained, we would find three isotopes, carbon 12, carbon 13, and carbon 14. Carbon isotopes ^{12}C and ^{13}C are not radioactive. However ^{14}C is radioactive and slowly changes spontaneously into the element nitrogen. As time passed, our sample of charcoal would have less and less of the ^{14}C isotope. While the number of ^{12}C atoms in the sample remained the same, the number of ^{14}C atoms would decrease. The proportion or ratio of ^{14}C to ^{12}C becomes smaller as time passes. This suggests that the ^{14}C to ^{12}C ratio might serve as a radioactive dating clock. Other radioactive dating systems also rely on the measurement of isotope ratios since these ratios change with time as one radioactive chemical element spontaneously changes into another chemical element. To be used as a clock, however, isotope ratio measurements must still obey the two fundamental clocking principles. We must have a known rate and a known calibration.

As I have pointed out elsewhere, the phenomenon of radioactive decay can be compared to a burning candle.[12] A burning candle is continuously becoming shorter and therefore could serve as a clock. This is similar to a radioactive element undergoing radioactive decay in an object we wished to date. For example, potassium is a component of many rocks, and one isotope, potassium 40, is radioactive and changes into argon 40, a gas. Most potassium atoms are ^{39}K and this isotope is not radioactive.

In the case of the burning candle, we observe by careful measurement that it is becoming shorter at the rate of one inch every hour. We know the exact *rate* at which the candle is decaying away. This is similar to knowing the decay rate for a radioactive element like potassium 40. Furthermore, we know the present condition of our candle clock or potassium-argon clock. We can measure the height of the candle and the potassium-argon isotope ratios as they exist at present. We note that the candle is exactly six inches high at present and we know the rate at which it is burning (one inch every hour).

Attempting to use the burning candle as a clocking system, we now ask the question, "When was the candle lighted? How much time has passed since the candle began burning?" Given only the information of the candle's present length and burning rate, you would probably respond by saying, "That's a foolish question! Tell me how tall the candle was to start with, and I will tell you how long it took, at one inch every hour, to get down to its present length of six inches." If the candle had been seven inches long to start with, at a burning rate of one inch per hour it would have taken one hour to burn down to its present length of six inches. If, on the other hand, the candle had been ten inches long to start with, it would have been burning for four hours.

Thus one must know the original length of the candle or its

starting condition (calibration of the clock) in order to tell how much time has passed. It is foolish to ask how much time has passed since the candle was lighted without a knowledge of initial conditions (original length) for the candle. You cannot use the candle as a time indicator without knowing both rate and initial conditions.

This is also true in the case of radioactive dating systems such as potassium-argon. We must know not only the rate at which the decay takes place (half-life) but we must also know the initial conditions, the original isotope ratios. Without a knowledge of initial conditions when a radioactive "clock" began, it is impossible to know how much time is measured by this "clock."

What were the initial conditions when the earth began? What were the initial isotope ratios? How much of a radioactive element was present in the beginning? No modern scientist was around to record those initial conditions. We simply do not know what they were. All a scientist can do is assume, estimate, or guess what the original composition of any radioactive system was originally. He can then make calculations based on these guesses to arrive at an age, but the age will only be as accurate as the assumptions about initial conditions.

One could calculate an age using the candle, for example, by estimating or guessing the original length of the candle. The accuracy of the time calculated, however, would only be as accurate as the guess about the original length.

In the case of radioactivity, we simply do not know what the initial conditions were. Some scientists have suggested that an approach known as the "isochron method" can give initial conditions for isotope ratios. However, it is now known that this method is also incapable of unambiguously providing initial conditions. The isochron method is also dependent on assumptions just as other methods are. The best evidence that isochrons do not provide a method of establishing true ages is that they give wrong answers when actually applied to rocks. Answers are either inconsistent or at variance with known data.[13]

The Uranium-Lead Clock

The uranium-lead clock is one of the clocks in the radioactive dating scheme considered to be most reliable by those who make old earth assumptions. It too, however, is dependent entirely on assumptions about original conditions and gives inconsistent answers. An expert on geochronology who believes in an old earth writes, "One can erect hypothetical systems, make whatever assumptions seem appropriate, and then calculate what would happen to such models with the passage of time."[14] He concludes that, "much geologic insight into the origin and history of ores can be gained from judicious interpretation of the isotopic composition of lead, but colossal misconceptions can arise from false assumptions."[15]

An additional problem for using radioactivity as a system of telling time is the fact that we cannot be sure radioactive decay rates have always remained constant. In fact, there is evidence that they may not have remained constant.[16]

The phenomenon of radioactivity was only discovered in 1896. Thus, rates of decay of radioactive systems (half-lives) have only been measured for less than a hundred years. Any statement about decay rates in the far distant past has to be extrapolated from present conditions. Extrapolations from a hundred years to millions or billions of years are suspect. It is scientifically unsound to make extrapolations of such magnitude.

Even the phenomenon of radioactivity itself is not yet well understood. It is not at all clear why an atom undergoes radioactive decay. All we know is that if we have a given sample of a substance which is radioactive, certain numbers of atoms will disintegrate in any given time. We do not know why one atom disintegrates and why another one right next to it does not. Even the laws that have been formulated to describe rates of radioactive decay are coming under scrutiny. They appear not to be entirely correct either.[17]

Thus, the radioactive dating system does not meet the fundamental requirements of a clocking system. We do not know the initial conditions, and even if we did, we cannot be certain that rates of radioactive decay have always remained constant.

Shaking the Fundamental Assumption

In addition to uncertainties about rates and initial conditions, there remains an additional question of even greater importance. This question concerns the primal assumption behind all radiometric dating: that isotope ratios are an indicator only of time. How can we be sure that isotope ratios are a time index? For example, in the potassium-argon dating system, the potassium 40/argon 40 isotope ratio is measured. In the carbon dating system, the carbon 14/carbon 12 isotope ratio is measured. How can we be sure that these ratios are a time index at all? Is the assumption that they are a time index the only assumption or even the best assumption that can be made? Obviously it is possible for a scientist to make other assumptions about isotope ratios. A more likely possibility is that isotope ratios are an indicator of geophysical processes which have occurred. Ratios could just as well be a process indicator as a time indicator. In fact, there is much evidence to support the former assumption. Likewise, there is much evidence to indicate that isotope ratios are not a time index as has been commonly assumed.

The assumption that isotope ratios are a time index can lead to some serious absurdities in light of actual scientific data. If the assumption that isotope ratios are a time index is correct, then different radiodating methods should give the same answer. But they don't. As an illustration, consider the problem of dating the moon. A scientist comments on moon dates: "If all the age-dating methods (rubidium-strontium, uranium-lead and potassium-argon) had yielded the same ages, the picture would be neat. But they haven't. The lead ages, for example, have been consistently older."[18] It is obvious that the moon has only one age. However, using different dating methods on samples obtained from different places on the moon, different ages were reported.

Isotopic ages have been obtained for material from five landing sites on the moon—those of Apollos 11, 12, 14, 15 and Luna 16; each site has a different age. But in a given site, the ages also vary, indicating that more than one event has occurred. Ideally, however, any one basaltic rock from a given site should yield the same isotopic age, regardless of the method used.[19]

Material first brought back from the moon, dated by radioactive dating methods, yielded the interesting result that the moon soil appeared to be older than the rocks it had come from, an obvious absurdity.

But the most puzzling data so far from the age dating by all three methods have been the apparent ages of the soil from all of the sites—ranging from 4.2 to 4.9 billion years—considerably older on the average than the ages for the rocks. How could the rocks be younger than the soil?[20]

The explanation given for these discrepancies is very interesting indeed. Instead of taking the ages at face value, the embarrassing discrepancies were explained away by saying that some *geophysical process* had adjusted the ratios. In order to save the assumption that isotope ratios indicate time, scientists speculated that heating of the rock, the evaporation of one chemical, or the addition of a second chemical had in some way adjusted the isotope ratios. These geophysical processes were postulated to have adjusted the ratios. "The findings are telling scientists as much about lunar processes and the behavior of volatiles in a vacuum as about the ages of the moon."[21] In other words, the isotope ratios might better be interpreted as indicators of geophysical processes instead of time indicators.

In another instance, earth rocks with a known historical age of about two hundred years were dated with the potassium-argon radiodating method. Ages were obtained which ranged all the way from near zero up to many millions of years. The isotope ratio age (radioactive dating age) did not agree with the known historical age. Again the explanation given for the discrepancy was that geophysical processes affected the isotope ratio. In this case the rate of cooling of the rock and the pressure under which the rock cooled were called on to explain the actual isotope ratio observed.

Time or Geophysical Process?

It is at least as reasonable to assume that isotope ratios are an indicator of geophysical processes as to assume they are a time index. Using the former assumption one could then determine the isotope ratios and from them determine what processes were involved in the formation of the rock, not how much time had elapsed.[22] In fact, there is a pattern in the literature on radiodating that whenever a sample does not agree with the expected evolutionary age, it is assumed that geophysical processes have somehow adjusted the isotope ratios. If this is the case, then one might well ask, "Given an isotope ratio, how do we know whether it is a true indicator of age or an indicator of some geophysical process? How do we select which samples have been altered and which have not? How do we know when to use the explanation that it is not a true age but has been altered some way by a geophysical process?"

It is also known that nonradioactive elements have variations in isotope ratios. Temperature of water affects the oxygen 16/oxygen 18 ratio, for example. This ratio is used to determine climates from the past. It is known that warm water has a different isotope ratio for oxygen 16/18 than does cooler water. The ratio is not affected by radioactivity because these isotopes are not radioactive. Yet their ratio value is adjusted by geophysical processes.

The answer one gets in looking at any particular set of physical data depends on the assumptions one uses to interpret that data. In the case of radioactive elements, it would seem just as reasonable to make the assumption that isotope ratios are an indicator of geophysical processes as to assume that they are a time index. However, if we admit that isotope ratios are not a time index, we eliminate radioactivity as a clock; we eliminate one of the main supports used for estimating evolutionary time.

Evolutionary assumptions with their attendant need of long periods of time do not agree with actual scientific data. Excuses must repeatedly be formulated to explain why actual evidence does not agree with that expected from evolutionary assumptions.

Radioactivity is an observed fact. But how much time has passed is an open question. There are even some indications, using radioactive data, that not many thousands of years have elapsed since radioactivity began.[23]

Dating by Geophysical Processes

Outside the area of radioactivity, a growing body of new scientific information also indicates that evolutionary assumptions have led to greatly exaggerated ages for events in earth history.

Geological Rates in the Laboratory

Let's consider the case of petrification. Movement of the mineral silica under earth-surface conditions is necessary for petrification to occur. Silica is a mineral which replaces organic matter during the process. Petrified wood is organic matter that has either been filled in or replaced with silica. The rate at which this process occurs depends on the rate at which silica can be moved. It had usually been assumed that this was a very slow process. One would not attempt, for example, to petrify a piece of wood in the laboratory if he assumed it took thousands of years. He would wish to get the experiment finished in his lifetime. For many years, therefore, no one really attempted such experiments because of the assumption that so much time was involved.

A few years ago, however, some scientists did attempt this work.

> Quartz has been considered to be chemically "inert" in most environments at or near the earth's surface. It has been assumed that, at temperatures below

100° C, the formation of quartz from supersaturated solutions or from amorphous silica requires thousands of years. . . . We have synthesized quartz crystals directly from aqueous solution at earth-surface conditions within 3 years. . . . Our experiment suggests that quartz growth in nature may occur in relatively short intervals of time, provided saturation is reached.[24]

Other similar experiments have also produced interesting results.[25] Such work has shown that the assumption of long periods of time is not valid when compared with actual experimental data.

It thus seems worthwhile to study in the laboratory other geophysical processes associated with earth history. Data on actually observed rates is much more convincing than hypothetically assumed rates. If rates for processes actually determined by experiments in the laboratory are much faster than the rates supposed by using evolutionary assumptions, this would have great bearing on the interpretation of earth history.

Geological Rates in Nature

In addition to studies simulating natural conditions in laboratories, observations of geological processes in the natural world are also being carried out. One such event was the formation of the new island known as Surtsey. In studying geological processes associated with this event, one scientist writes:

When the news of a volcanic eruption in the sea off the Vestmann Islands reached the ears of Icelandic geologists in the early morning of November 14, 1963, some of them had to have it repeated to them and received it with a grain of salt all the same. And when they in the spring and summer of 1964 wandered about the island which was being born then, they found it hard to believe that this was an island whose age was still measured in months, not years. An Icelander who has studied geology and geomorphology at foreign universities is later taught by experience in his own homeland that the time scale he had been trained to attach to geological developments is misleading when assessments are made of the forces—constructive and destructive—which have molded and are still molding the face of Iceland. What elsewhere may take thousands of years may be accomplished here in one century. All the same he is amazed whenever he comes to Surtsey, because the same development may take a few weeks or even a few days here.[26]

Many similar observations were made when Mount St. Helens erupted in May of 1980. It was assumed that following the eruption many of the subsequent geological processes would take many years. However, after the eruption had ceased, consolidation of dust and mud materials into hard, rock-like material was much more rapid than had been assumed. Material washed by tributaries into the Columbia River became hard so quickly it was difficult to dredge the Columbia to make room again for ships. Also plant life in the devastated area came back much more quickly than had been thought possible. Rivers that had been flooded with hot water and volcanic debris had fish life returning to them within a short while.

Many earth processes assumed by evolution to be extremely slow have thus been shown to be much more rapid when actually measured or when carried out under simulated conditions in the laboratory. Again, the answers one gets about how much time has passed during earth history are dependent upon one's assumptions. We need to ask, "What are the best assumptions for interpreting the data?"

If, for example, one were to assume a biblical time scale[27] for earth history, is it possible to make assumptions that interpret the data within this time scale? The answer is clearly *yes*. Some may not wish to interpret the data this way, but it is not because of scientific data: it is because of a philosophical bias. This point must be recognized! Time is something God created and He controls. He also tells us truth about earth history events.

The only absolute reference point is, therefore, the Word of God. It can be trusted even when it talks about earth history and associated events.

Signs of the End

Scripture makes some interesting predictions about attitudes and conditions in the last days just before the return of Messiah. One prediction is that scoffers will arise. Not only does it predict this, but it tells what they will scoff about.

> [K]nowing this first: that scoffers will come in the last days, walking according to their own lusts, and saying, "Where is the promise of His coming? For since the fathers fell asleep, all things continue as they were from the beginning of creation." For this they willfully forget: that by the word of God the heavens were of old, and the earth standing out of water and in the water, by which the world that then existed perished, being flooded with water. But the heavens and the earth which now exist are kept in store by the same word, reserved for fire until the day of judgment and perdition of ungodly men (2 Peter 3:3-7, NKJV).

Notice three things. First, scoffing will be aimed at creation. The idea that the heavens resulted from God's command will not be tolerated. Second, men will deny a worldwide flood in the days of Noah. And third, this denial will be in spite of vast amounts of evidence.

It is largely by ignoring the flood that geological uniformitarianism has so drastically missed the mark with respect to the age of the earth and other details. It has caused evolutionary thinking to miss the chemistry behind coal and oil formation.[28] It has also caused evolutionary thinking to make the highly questionable assumption that isotope ratios are a time index. Wrong assumptions about rate processes associated with earth history in geochemical events such as petrification or erosion are also directly traceable to evolutionary assumptions.

Disbelief in a worldwide flood is largely a modern-day phenomenon. Two hundred years ago most scientists accepted the biblical record of earth history, including the flood. It has only been in the last century or so that this event has become subject to such ridicule. To observe the ridicule, all one need do is enroll in a general science or geology course and then mention in the classroom that he believes in the worldwide flood.

The Days of Noah

When asked by the disciples what signs would be present when the time for his return was near, Jesus responded by reminding the disciples of the situation in Noah's day.

> But about that actual day and time no one knows— not even the angels of Heaven, nor the Son, only the Father. For just as life went on in the days of Noah so will it be at the coming of the Son of Man. In those days before the flood people were eating, drinking, marrying and being given in marriage until the very day that Noah went into the ark, and knew nothing about the flood until it came and destroyed them all. So will it be at the coming of the Son of Man (Matthew 24:36-39, Phillips).

Let us remember what Noah's day was like. Noah had an advance warning that the flood was coming, a warning that came more than a hundred years ahead of the event. And Noah was a preacher of righteousness. His generation knew about the coming event; they were warned. They also had a high level of science and technology as we have discussed earlier. However, they used this to fill the world with violence. Their only thought was for day-to-day living. They had no time for thoughts about God.

Jesus reminds the disciples that in the end times, there will be a situation very similar to Noah's. People will have been warned about coming events, about the return of Christ. There is a parallel to Noah's day in the violence and terrorism that fill our present world. And people have been warned that the return of Christ is near. Publications, books, radio programs, and talk shows all have been discussing these points.

Just as the truth of the Noachian flood will be ignored in the last days, Jesus' warning about the parallel social and religious conditions of Noah's day to our day will also be ignored. People tend not to take the Scriptures seriously. The event of Noah's day came, just as God said it would; and the events of the end time will also come, just as Christ said they would.

Jesus also said that the world would not always be here. "'Heaven and earth will pass away, but my words will never pass away'" (Matthew 24:35). Just as creation was sudden, so the end will be sudden. Just as creation did not involve millions of years of processes, so the end will not involve millions of years of processes. It will be just as sudden as was creation.

We mentioned earlier that the people of Noah's day were warned about the coming judgment of a worldwide flood. The warning was in the form of preaching: "He did not spare the ancient world when he brought the flood on its ungodly people, but protected Noah, a preacher of righteousness" (2 Peter 2:5). While Noah was building the ark, he was also preaching. Everyone on earth had a chance to hear Noah's message and be warned.

The Final Warning

There is another interesting Scripture regarding a warning from God. Just before the last judgment of this world, God will send a final warning to all mankind.

> Then I saw another angel flying in mid-heaven, holding the everlasting gospel to proclaim to the inhabitants of the earth—to every nation and tribe and language and people. He was crying in a loud voice,
>
> "Reverence God, and give glory to him; for the hour of his judgment has come! Worship him who made Heaven and earth, the sea and the springs of water" (Revelation 14:6-7, Phillips).

The message will be to everyone on earth and it will be

very clear: "Worship God because judgment is near." And the message is that God is the Creator. We are not here by chance; there is a God who created us.

It is interesting to note that the recent rise of interest in creation is a worldwide phenomenon. It is not peculiar to the United States. Creation organizations have recently been formed in Latin America, Asia, and other areas of the globe. Why this sudden rise of interest in creation science? I believe it is because we are being warned that God's judgment is near. The angel with the loud voice is getting his message and warning out.

Just as creation and the flood came suddenly, so the events of the final judgment will come, not as a slow, gradual process over millions of years, but suddenly.

> "Yet the day of the Lord will come as unexpectedly as a thief. In that day the heavens will vanish in a tearing blast, the very elements will disintegrate in heat and the earth and all its works will disappear" (2 Peter 3:10, Phillips).

But mankind has been warned.

> But you, my friends whom I love, are forewarned, and should therefore be very careful not to be carried away by the errors of unprincipled men and so lose your proper foothold. On the contrary, you should grow in grace and in knowledge of our Lord and saviour Jesus Christ—to him be glory now and until the day of eternity! (2 Peter 3:17-18, Phillips).

Even so come, Lord Jesus.

Chapter 12, Notes

1. Mayr, "Darwinian Revolution," 985; W. A. Berggren and John A. Van Couvering, editors, *Catastrophes and Earth History* (Princeton, N.J.: Princeton University Press, 1984), 9-15.

2. Weisz, *The Science of Biology,* 636.

3. Norman Macbeth, *Darwin Retried* (Boston: Gambit, Inc., 1971), 108-9.

4. John Gliedman, "Was Darwin Wrong?" *Science Digest* (Special Sept./ Oct. 1980), 56.

5. I have treated this point in "Dating the Earth and Fossils" in *Symposium on Creation II,* ed. Donald Patten (Grand Rapids: Baker Book House, 1970), 57-74.

6. Wald, "The Origin of Life," 46.

7. Ibid., 48.

8. Mayr, "Darwinian Revolution," 988.

9. Shelton, *Geology Illustrated,* 304.

10. Ibid., 305.

11. Henry Faul, *Ages of Rocks, Planets, and Stars* (New York: McGraw-Hill, 1966), vi.

12. Chittick, "Dating the Earth and Fossils," 66.

13. C. Brooks, D. E. James, S. R. Hart, "Ancient Lithosphere: Its Role in Young Continental Volcanism," *Science,* 17 September 1976, 1086-94; Felix Chayes, C. Brooks, M. Strobel, D. E. James, S. R. Hart, "Use of Correlation Statistics with Rubidium-Strontium Systematics," *Science,* 10 June 1977, 1234-35; Dr. Russell Akridge, "Radiometric Dating Using Isochrons," *Impact* 113 (November 1982): i-iv; S. R. Carter, N. M. Evensen, P. J. Hamilton, R. K. O'Nions, "Neodymium and Strontium Isotope Evidence for Crustal Contamination of Continental Volcanics," *Science,* 17 November 1978, 743-47; S. A. Morse, "Strontium Isotope Fractionation in the Kiglapait Intrusion," *Science,* 8 April 1983, 193-95.

14. Faul, *Ages of Rocks,* 63.

15. Ibid., 69.

16. Robert V. Gentry, "Cosmology and Earth's Invisible Realm," *Medical Opinion & Review* (October 1967): 79; Barry Setterfield, "The Velocity of Light and the Age of the Universe," *Ex Nihilo* 4, no. 1 and no. 3 (1981); George Aweig, "Quark Catalysis of Exothermal Nuclear Reaction," *Science,* 15 September 1978, 973-79; "Nonrandom Radioactivity," *Chemical & Engineering News,* 5 April 1971, 29.

17. H. C. Dudley, "Radioactivity Re-examined," *Chemical and Engineering News,* 7 April 1975, 2.

18. Everly Driscoll, "Dating of Moon Samples: Pitfalls and Paradoxes," *Science News,* 1 January 1972, 12.

19. Ibid.

20. Ibid., 13.

21. Ibid.

22. G. Brent Dalrymple and James G. Moore, "Argon-40; Excess in Submarine Pillow Basalts from Kilauea Volcano, Hawaii," *Science*, 13 September 1968, 1132-35; C. S. Noble and J. J. Naughton, "Deep Ocean Basalts: Inert Gas Content and Uncertainties in Age Dating," *Science*, 11 October 1968, 256-66.

23. Chittick, "Dating the Earth and Fossils," 69; Melvin A. Cook, "Where Is Earth's Radiogenic Helium?" *Nature*, 26 January 1957, 213; Thomas G. Barnes, "Evidence Points to a Recent Creation," *Christianity Today*, 8 October 1982, 34-36.

24. Fred T. Mackensie and Rudi Gees, "Quartz: Synthesis at Earth-Surface Conditions," *Science*, 6 August 1971, 533-34.

25. John H. Oehler and J. William Schopf, "Artificial Microfossils: Experimental Studies of Permineralization of Blue-Green Algae in Silica," *Science*, 17 December 1971, 1229-31.

26. Sigurdur Thorarinsson, *Surtsey* (Reykjavik: Almenna Bokafelagid, 1964), 39.

27. James B. Jordan, "The Biblical Chronology Question: An Analysis," *Creation Social Science and Humanities Quarterly* (Winter 1979): 9-15, (Spring 1980): 17-26; C. G. Ozanne, *The First 7000 Years* (New York: Exposition Press, 1970).

28. Haggin, "Argonne Scientists."

Chapter 13

A Christian Response

We are living in a culture which has become increasingly antagonistic to biblically based Christian faith. It is also unlearned about the Bible and Christian doctrine. This is evidenced in many ways. Young people in public schools and universities are bombarded with a value system and world view in opposition to Christian principles. At their work or in social interactions, Christians are often presented with questions and challenged about their faith. How then can we speak the "truth in love" to those in our culture?

All Christians need to be prepared to share their faith in current culture for several reasons. Some of these are to affirm the truth of the faith; to be obedient in carrying out the great commission of evangelizing those who have not yet become believers; and because we care for those who do not know the God who can forgive their sins and show them a victorious way of life. We want others to know the God who created them. Ultimately, however, we want to glorify God; this is the supreme reason we want to share our faith.

In this chapter, I would like to pass along some observations and suggestions for sharing one's faith in an antagonistic culture. Many of these hints are based on my years of personal experience. I have shared my faith with civic organizations, scientific meetings, universities, high schools, elementary schools, Christian camps and churches, as well as on a person-to-person level. In sharing my faith over the years, I have made many (sometimes painful) mistakes as well as experiencing some successes. It is from this background that I make the following comments in the hope they may prove useful to others.

Faith on the Battlefield

One who consistently lives for Christ and allows it to be known that he is following the Lord will sooner or later find his faith under attack. Young people especially need to know that attacks will occur. Yet the primary educational organ of the church, the Sunday school, seldom offers training to cope with these attacks. That situation must be remedied.

It is possible, of course, for a Christian to live an inconsistent life and hence come under attack. He might be belligerent or unkind in other ways and draw unbelievers' fire. This is not the type of situation we are discussing. We are talking about the natural fire that comes from those who are not yet in Christ's fold. There are only two drummers to march to: God or Satan. Jesus said, "'He who is not with Me is against Me, and he who does not gather with Me scatters abroad'" (Matthew 12:30, NKJV). Those who are not following Christ are under the control of the enemy, and he can use them to hurl attacks at believers.

The attacks can be vicious and intense. The word that Christ chose to describe them was *hate*. Jesus said, "'I have given them Your word; and the world has *hated* them because they are not of the world, just as I am not of the world'" (John 17:14, NKJV, emphasis mine).

Sharing Faith in an Unsympathetic Culture

How then does one present his faith in surroundings generally not sympathetic to historic, biblical Christianity? There are a number of items which can greatly assist one in doing this.

Be Prepared

First, be prepared. In being prepared, one needs to know the nature of the battle. An attack on one's faith, even though it may be phrased in intellectual terms, is really spiritual and moral in its source. Biblical truth is unpalatable to those who are hiding from God because of moral guilt. They are capable of using nearly any means to avoid facing truth, including even ridicule, lying, and false accusations.

It is important therefore for the believer to remember that the attack is coming. Even though the opposition may be expressed in intellectual terms, one should be aware of an additional important fact. The believer begins with a different presuppositional base. He interprets the world with a different viewpoint, and therefore interprets data in a different way.

When an unbeliever makes a factual statement which may seem contrary to biblical truth, the believer needs to remind himself to ask, What other interpretation of that fact is possible? What other interpretation of the data will lead to conclusions in agreement with biblical truth? He should get into the habit of thinking, That's interesting (the unbeliever's statement), but is it *true*?

Put on God's Armor

In addition to remembering that the unbeliever's attack is spiritual and moral in nature and that he interprets the data from a different presuppositional view, one additional help in being prepared is to use God's armor.

> In conclusion be strong—not in yourselves but in the Lord, in the power of his boundless strength. Put on God's complete armour so that you can successfully resist all the devil's craftiness. For our fight is not against any physical enemy: it is against organisations and powers that are spiritual. We are up against the unseen power that controls this dark world, and spiritual agents from the very headquarters of evil. Therefore you must wear the whole armour of God

that you may be able to resist evil in its day of power,
and that even when you have fought to a standstill
you may still stand your ground (Ephesians 6:10-13,
Phillips).

As well as stating the spiritual nature of our battle, this
passage of Scripture (and the verses that follow) describes
God's armor and how to use it. When attacks come, the believer
is to stand firm and not be swayed even by clever arguments
against the faith.

We need always to be in the habit of seeking truth and taking our stand on truth. If one is challenged about the historical
accuracy of the Bible, he can be prepared by noting that archaeology supports scriptural truth. History repeatedly has
shown that the skeptics were wrong and the Bible was right.
When we know things are true, we can stand firm because we
have checked them out. We know we are telling people the
truth.

Subtle Attacks

The attack on biblical truth may not always be direct or
frontal. Sometimes it comes in a more indirect or subtle way,
which may be even more dangerous than a frontal attack. In a
frontal attack, one is warned as to what is happening. In a subtle
attack, however, one's guard may be down.

One form of subtle attack is "managed news." We tend to
believe what the media present. However, events and situations
can be interpreted to us in such a way as to completely distort the
truth. School textbooks, for example, are rewritten to conform
to the prevailing paradigm or world view. Newspapers and
other news media often color the news in a way that gives an impression completely different from reality. All one has to do to
observe this problem is read an account in a major American
newspaper about an event of world significance and then read
about the same event in a newspaper from another country with
a different political philosophy. The accounts often are
markedly different.

A Christian Response   253

Another example appears in written accounts of a war. Accounts about the same event in the American Civil War found in history books written in the South are often quite different from those written in the North. Or one might consider an account of the Spanish-American War from a history book written in Mexico compared to one written in the United States. The accounts can give quite different impressions.

To cite a case in which I was personally involved, consider the distortions presented by the news media in the coverage of the creation-evolution trial in Arkansas in December 1981. The majority of the news media reports about that trial were extremely distorted. A fairly thorough documentation of this has been given by another witness at that trial, Dr. Norman Geisler, in his book, *The Creator in the Courtroom.*[1]

Christians are thus faced with the problem of obtaining the truth, as differentiated from that which is purported as true. Many statements made against the faith reveal more antagonism than can be accounted for by normal bias, and one must work to find out what is true. In some cases, this may take years of study, but one always needs to consider the veracity of sources of information.[2] "[W]e should no longer be children, tossed to and fro and carried about with every wind of doctrine, by the trickery of men, in the cunning craftiness by which they lie in wait to deceive" (Ephesians 4:14, NKJV).

Daniel in the Public Schools

Christian young people attending public schools face a particularly difficult situation. They are there to learn; they are the novices. Yet teachers and textbooks often take a philosophical position diametrically opposed to a biblical world view. Textbooks present evolution as fact, and teachers often ridicule belief in creation. Biblical views of origins, earth history, and world history are either ignored or relegated to outmoded or mythological or superstitious views.

My wife and I had children in public school who faced this problem, and we had to continually help them distinguish between truth and error. Many discussions around the dinner table centered on the conflict between the biblical world view and the contrary teachings of textbook and classroom. From talks with other parents and young people, I know they encounter a similar problem. What can we do to handle this problem using a biblical approach? Following are some suggestions.

Of first importance is a good home. Home is where the training must take place. Sunday school cannot do it all. Children are in Sunday school for less than one hour each week. But public schools have children many hours during the week. Television also presents a nonbiblical world view. The home, therefore, *must* be a place of Christian training. Children need to be warned that there is a conflict between biblical and nonbiblical world views. Parents can use specific examples from their own experience as a teaching tool to help their children work through the issues and gain experience in standing firm. Much pressure is placed on students to conform in all areas, including philosophical views. Yet in the area of moral absolutes and biblical truth, the young person may have to stand alone. We parents can help prepare a young person to do this. We can teach young people to "dare to be a Daniel," to be willing to stand against the tide and face ridicule and even ostracism from their peers. This is difficult and places tremendous stress on a young person.

Testing True

One of the questions I am frequently asked in seminars on creation is, How should students respond on school tests to questions about evolution? Often a test will ask a question and the expected answer is contrary to what a Christian child believes. What should that child do?

I believe there are several positive things that a young person can do and for which the Bible gives guidelines. Consider the case of Daniel and his colleagues. Daniel and his friends believed in God. While still a youth, Daniel was taken captive and moved from his home by a pagan nation, Babylon. Babylon had a high level of science and technology, one of the highest the world has ever known, but it was pagan. The Babylonians were worshipers in a religion totally opposed to Daniel's faith. As a young lad, Daniel and his friends were chosen to go to school in Babylon at King Nebuchadnezzar's expense.

> Then the king ordered Ashpenaz, chief of his court officials, to bring in some of the Israelites from the royal family and the nobility—young men without any physical defect, handsome, showing aptitude for every kind of learning, well informed, quick to understand, and qualified to serve in the king's palace. He was to teach them the language and literature of the Babylonians. The king assigned them a daily amount of food and wine from the king's table. They were to be trained for three years, and after that they were to enter the king's service (Daniel 1:3-5).

Daniel not only had to learn a foreign language, but he had to study intensely for three years. His studies included all the learning, knowledge, science, technology, philosophy, and religion of the Babylonians. The king was paying for his schooling and was going to give the final examination. Since the education was at the king's expense, he wanted results. The final examination was intense, and it was either pass or fail. King Nebuchadnezzar was a totalitarian ruler of immense power. It was said of him,

> "Because of the high position he [God] gave him, all the peoples and nations and men of every language dreaded and feared him. Those the king wanted to put to death, he put to death; those he wanted to spare, he spared; those he wanted to promote, he promoted; and those he wanted to humble, he humbled" (Daniel 5:19).

If Daniel and his friends passed, well and good; if they didn't, they were executed. There was indeed strong incentive to learn their lessons well during the three years they were being taught all the learning of the Babylonians.

Even though Daniel and his friends were in a pagan land, in a pagan school, being taught by pagan teachers, and no doubt asked to learn things contrary to what they believed about God and the Scriptures, they still worshiped God, and God aided them in their schooling. The first principle here is that God helps us in difficult situations when we continue to be faithful to him. "To these four young men God gave knowledge and understanding of all kinds of literature and learning. And Daniel could understand visions and dreams of all kinds" (Daniel 1:17).

At the end of three years, these young people stood before the king to take their final examination. It is said of them,

> In every matter of wisdom and understanding about which the king questioned them, he found them ten times better than all the magicians and enchanters in his whole kingdom. And Daniel remained there until the first year of King Cyrus (Daniel 1:20-21).

Daniel and his friends not only passed, they passed with honors. They were good students. They learned the things of pagan religion and pagan beliefs and could repeat these back even better than the pagans themselves.

Yet after learning all these things, Daniel still believed in his God. When asked about a pagan belief, he could give the correct answer regarding that pagan belief. This did not mean, however, that he personally subscribed to that belief. He showed himself to be a good scholar, yet he boldly retained his faith in God as the rest of the book of Daniel points out. He continued for many decades as a follower and a worshiper of God (Daniel 1:21).

It is possible to study non-Christian perspectives such as evolution in the public schools and repeat back what evolution says. The student, when asked a question from an evolutionary point of view, can answer, "According to the theory of evolution. . . ." This does not necessarily mean that the student believes evolution. It simply shows that he understands it, while he still believes the biblical account of history is better.

When a student knows pagan thought systems and still retains his belief in a Creator, it is a powerful witness to the non-Christian. The non-Christian cannot accuse the believer of retaining his faith only because he does not know the alternatives. A student can know the alternatives and still know that faith in Christ is better. He can personally witness and testify to the truthfulness of the passage, "You, dear children, are from God and have overcome them, because the one who is in you is greater than the one who is in the world" (1 John 4:4).

Having said this, however, I must caution that to fill one's mind with the wrong ideas can be devastating. While learning pagan ideas, it is *absolutely essential* that the child also be saturated with God's Word. It is only by studying and being filled with and meditating on truth from God's Word that it is safe to study pagan ideas. From evidence in the book of Daniel, it is clear that Daniel meditated and prayed to God daily. That was his custom. He continually purged his mind by talking to God and studying Scripture. A knowledge of Scripture and Scripture memory is absolutely essential to balance out pagan teaching. "How can a young man keep his way pure? By living according to your word" (Psalm 119:9).

Moses

Moses is another example from Scripture of a person who was educated in secular surroundings yet retained his faith in God. Moses was brought up to believe in the one true God. Because he was adopted by Pharaoh's daughter, he was also trained in all the learning of the Egyptians. Pharaoh's daughter hired an Israelite woman (Moses' mother) to nurse and train Moses in his early years. This provided the opportunity to teach Moses about the culture of Israel and about the one true God. When Moses became of age, he had been schooled in all the training and learning of the Egyptians but he still believed in God.

So it is possible for a young person to be a good student and still retain his faith. It will not always be easy. There will be pressure and there will probably be ridicule. But it is possible for a student to come through this experience in a positive way. "Dear friends, do not be surprised at the painful trial you are suffering, as though something strange were happening to you. But rejoice that you participate in the sufferings of Christ, so that you may be overjoyed when his glory is revealed" (1 Peter 4:12-13).

A student often has an opportunity to present essays or term papers. In these cases, by doing a thorough job and presenting a good paper, a student can give a positive witness to his faith and also cause others to think. He might present a paper on dinosaurs, for example, or another issue associated with origins and earth history. Many students have done this boldly, and if done well, it is a positive witness.

It is also very important for the student to exhibit a positive attitude toward a teacher who presents views that disagree with biblical teachings. A student is still under the teacher's authority and must have a proper attitude toward that authority. This does not mean, however, that the student needs to subscribe to pagan ideas. He can dare to be a Daniel. Sunday schools and churches need to support students who are taking these stands. The home is absolutely essential in augmenting what is taught in Sunday school so as to balance the pressure from the public schools placed on Bible-believing Christians.

Responding to Questions

We have offered several suggestions about standing firm for the faith against inevitable attacks. Now let us consider the question from a positive approach. Often those around us learn that we believe the Bible to be a true account of origins, earth history, and of man and his relationship to God. When they learn these things, they will often ask questions that show they have genuine interest. The manner in which we respond is important.

It is also essential to know why a question is asked. There are generally three reasons a nonbeliever asks a question. First, the question may only be bait to generate an argument. The questioner is not really interested in the answer; he just wants to have some fun. He wants to play intellectual games or have a debate or just hold the believer up to ridicule. In this case, the believer need not be particularly concerned about wasting time trying to answer the question. He should recognize the question as bait for an argument. We are instructed in Scripture to avoid arguments. "Don't have anything to do with foolish and stupid arguments, because you know they produce quarrels. And the Lord's servant must not quarrel; instead, he must be kind to everyone, able to teach, not resentful" (2 Timothy 2:23-24).

A second reason for questions is idle curiosity. The questioner does not really care about the answer. He just wants to find out if you have an answer. "Where did Cain get his wife?" Questions such as these, voiced simply out of idle curiosity, are what the Bible terms foolish. No time should be wasted on them. (In another context, however, the question of where Cain got his wife may be an appropriate question. In such a case an appropriate answer can be given.)

Finally, the questioner may have a genuine interest in finding an answer to his question. He may ask, "Are the early chapters of Genesis real history or are they only myth?" And he may really want to know the answer. Thus there is generally one of three reasons a person will ask a question: to argue, idle curiosity, or genuine interest.

As general rule, it is best initially to make the assumption that the question is genuine. If, after interacting for a few minutes, it becomes apparent that the question was in the first or second category, then one can quickly draw the discussion to a close. If we are not certain exactly why the question is being asked, it is possible to ask some test questions. This is a useful device used by Jesus Himself.

Test Questions

An interesting account in which Jesus used this technique is recorded for us in Matthew 21:23-27:

> Jesus entered the temple courts, and, while he was teaching, the chief priests and the elders of the

people came to him. "By what authority are you
doing these things?" they asked. "And who gave you
this authority?"

Jesus replied, "I will also ask you one question. If
you answer me, I will tell you by what authority I am
doing these things. John's baptism—where did it
come from? Was it from heaven, or from men?"

They discussed it among themselves and said, "If
we say, 'From heaven,' he will ask, 'Then why
didn't you believe him?' But if we say, 'From
men'—we are afraid of the people, for they all hold
that John was a prophet."

So they answered Jesus, "We don't know."

Then he said, "Neither will I tell you by what authority I am doing these things."

Jesus had been giving much evidence by the miracles He
did and the teachings He gave, that His authority was from God.
The religious leaders, however, did not wish to accept this.
They then came to Jesus and asked Him to tell them by what authority He was doing these things. That their question was not
really honest, however, is revealed by their response to Jesus'
test question. After Jesus asked them whether John the Baptist's
authority was from heaven or from men, the religious leaders
went aside into a little huddle. They considered only the two
possibilities: either John had his authority from heaven or it was
of men.

It was like an intellectual chess game. They figured out
what their move would be and then what Jesus' return move
would be for each of the options. First they considered the possibility of answering that John was from heaven. With this option
they figured that Jesus' response would be, "Why didn't you believe him?" If John spoke for God, then the religious leaders
should have obeyed what John said, and they hadn't. Thus they
rejected the first option.

Then they considered the alternative, that John was just a
man and didn't have any divine authority for what he was doing.

John's divine authority was so obvious, however, that the common people would have stoned the religious leaders.

Thus they considered both options with their attendant consequences, and rejected both. They went back to Jesus and lied. Their response was "We don't know." Then Jesus said, "Neither will I tell you by what authority I am doing these things." He was saying in effect, "If you don't play by the rules of the game, if your question is not really honest, then I'm not going to give you an answer."

Jesus' test question revealed the true motives of these religious leaders. They weren't interested in the answer to their question; they were just baiting Jesus.

Occasionally, while answering a series of questions from an individual, one may encounter a response pattern from the questioner that indicates further responses or questions are not really honest or genuine. Sometimes individuals ask questions not because of genuine interest but only to keep a Christian from getting too close with the gospel or other biblical truth. The question is simply an avoidance mechanism. In this case a special type of test question—motive disclosure inquiry—can be used. An example is: "If I answer that question for you, will you change your beliefs?"

One must be very gentle and discerning in these situations and take care to avoid offending individuals, but it is essential to find out why a questioner is asking the question.

Speaking Truth in Love

We must be gentle with questioners. Our instructions are, "speaking the truth in love, we will in all things grow up into him who is the Head, that is, Christ" (Ephesians 4:15). How do we speak the truth in love? I'm not sure I always know the answer to that. However, one of the ingredients is that we try to speak the truth in such a way that we allow a nonbeliever to change his mind and not be embarrassed. As the Oriental wisely says, we try to do it in such a way that the other person can change his mind and still "save face."

It is a compliment to be asked a question. In effect, the

non-Christian is admitting that he knows less about the subject than the one he is asking. He is putting his ego out on a limb. That is why we need to be gentle in our answers and do our best not to offend the questioner.

It is also helpful to try to learn something about the questioner. We want to discern truth-readiness. Give only as much answer as the individual is ready for. We do not usually need to give an extensive discourse. A simple answer is better, even if it is too short. If the answer is too short, the questioner can continue to ask questions, getting additional details until he is satisfied. If we present too much information in response to a question, we can bore or even harm the individual receiving the information.

Jesus had lots of information He wanted to tell His disciples. It would have been profitable for them, but only as they were able to bear it. He knew that they had a certain truth-readiness. " 'I have much more to say to you, more than you can now bear' " (John 16:12). Jesus knew His disciples were not yet ready for the additional things He wanted to tell them. They were not yet ready to receive certain truths.

Likewise a questioner may not be ready for all the details we might give in answer to a particular question. We have a tendency to be impatient. We want to give all the details we have learned over many years of time. We want to bring a questioner up to our level of expertise in just a few minutes. But God is not in a hurry. We need to be patient and not expect a questioner to grasp everything at once. Seeds sown take time to sprout and grow. An individual encountering new truths may require considerable time to assimilate them and integrate them with the rest of his knowledge. Only then will more information be appropriate and useful to the questioner.

Some Will Not Believe

We must also be aware that some will not believe no matter how much evidence we present or how good our answers. We should not be too disappointed when this happens. Even though our answer may be good and complete with much supporting evidence, someone may not accept that answer. We must be prepared for this and not be discouraged by it. *Our* responsibility is to present the truth. *Their* responsibility is to accept it. Recall the account in which the wealthy young man asked Jesus, "Good teacher, what must I do to inherit eternal life?" (Luke 18:18). Jesus gave him a good answer, but the young man went away sorrowful. He rejected the answer Jesus gave.

Stay on the Offensive

It is usually not wise to be on the defensive in presenting our faith. We want to be careful here, of course, because there are certain instances in which it may be wisest to take a defensive posture. It may be less offensive to the questioner. In general, however, we should not be apologetic or defensive concerning our faith. It seems to help people think through a matter much more quickly if we are not.

I remember a young man who claimed to be an atheist but nevertheless asked me for evidence for the existence of God. Rather than list a series of evidences on the possibility that one would be acceptable to him, I asked what kind of evidence he would accept. He answered that if God would come and sit in the chair next to him in response to my prayer at that moment, he would believe in God.

From previous similar encounters I knew that such an approach tended to end up in long philosophical discussions of side issues. That would be of no benefit to him, so I responded with a question designed to aid him to think through the nature of his question. "How do you know God is not sitting there now?"

He responded, "Because I can't see him sitting there." He was still missing the point and to help him I asked one further question.

"What does God look like?"

Still missing the point, he responded, "I don't know."

"If you don't know what God looks like, how can you be so certain He's not sitting there now?"

Questions are often phrased to put the believer on the defensive. We need to take a moment to think through what is being asked so that we do not respond by being on the defensive. Our goal is to help people think through the issues. Our goal is to speak the truth in love. We are not out to win arguments. We can win arguments and lose people. Our purpose is to win people to faith in the Lord Jesus Christ.

Must We Be Perfect?

Sometimes an additional hindrance to sharing our faith comes in the form of an accusation from the Evil One. He will remind us of some sins in our life and that we are less than perfect. The thought will come to our mind that we have to be perfect before we can share our faith and tell others about becoming acquainted with the Savior. We need to recognize this for what it actually is—a trick to silence the believer.

I have found when we are honest with people, they do not expect us to be perfect. They know we are aiming toward a more mature faith. They know our goals are high. However, they are also aware we have not yet reached them. We do not want to try to fool people into thinking we are perfect. Nor do we need to wait until we are "perfect" before we share our faith. In this life we will never reach perfection.

The apostle Paul compared this life to running a race. He himself said that he was still in the race; he had not yet reached the goal. As long as we are in this life, we will have areas that need improvement.

> Not that I claim to have achieved all this, nor to have reached perfection already. But I keep going on, trying to grasp that purpose for which Christ Jesus grasped me. My brothers, I do not consider myself to have grasped it fully even now. But I do concentrate on this: I forget all that lies behind me and with hands outstretched to whatever lies ahead I go straight for the goal—my reward the honour of my high calling by God in Christ Jesus (Philippians 3:12-14, Phillips).

Truth Is Not Democratic

For those who believe the early chapters of Genesis are literally and historically true, the accusation will sometimes be framed, "But your view is not shared by the majority of educated people or scientists or even theologians. The majority of scientists believe that it was by evolution, not creation." Statements to this effect often appear in print, as well as being encountered in personal discourse.

It is well to remember that truth is not democratic. One does not take a majority vote to find out what is true. Truth is what God says it is.

There are many examples in science where the overwhelming majority opinion was later shown to be wrong. To cite a specific case, let's look at the research on the scientific description of the human liver. For a hundred years and more, scientists described the human liver as a series of interconnected crooked cylinders. Great authorities on human anatomy taught this. Textbooks, even recent ones, used this description. Drawings of these organs were in agreement with verbal descriptions, as crooked cylinders.

However, when one scientist attempted to make photomicrographs of cross sections of the liver, it was impossible to document or verify this classical description. Instead, he learned that the liver was a series of plates rather than interconnected cylinders. On making this discovery, this scientist wrote:

> For me, this was one of the most devastating, shocking experiences in my life. How could it be possible that the greatest anatomists of the 19th century and contemporary authorities whom I venerated could have made such a blunder? They had "documented" their erroneous statements with correct pictures which, when examined objectively, showed a structure quite different and exactly the reverse of what the text affirmed.[3]

In discussing the reason for the propagation of this error, the author explains that even when laboratory students examining the liver would come across evidence contradicting the accepted opinion of the textbook, they would reject the evidence in favor of the printed word. The printed word and the majority opinion led the students to unconsciously reject new evidence. Thus, for more than a hundred years, a majority scientific opinion was held which was contrary to reality. The majority can be wrong. Majority opinion is not a suitable test of truth.

In the case of the creation-evolution discussion, we are reminded of instances similar to this. The Piltdown Man popularized by evolutionists was later shown to be a hoax. A majority accepted it as valid, and it took many years for the error to be discovered. The fact that one holds a minority view does not mean it is wrong. Creation and the associated world view in which nature is dependent on the Creator is unpalatable to the majority of the world's population. Jesus said:

> "Enter through the narrow gate. For wide is the gate and broad is the road that leads to destruction, and many enter through it. But small is the gate and narrow the road that leads to life, and only a few find it" (Matthew 7:13-14).

Fact or Interpretation?

Perhaps the biggest problem of all, however, is the problem of distinguishing in the scientific literature what is being presented as fact and what is merely an interpretation of the facts. This is especially true in reading about creation and evolution. When interpretations of facts are presented as facts, great confusion results. It is extremely difficult, especially for a student, to make the distinction. To cite a specific example, evolutionists often state that evolution is a fact. This is a gross abuse of scientific theory. Evolution is merely an interpretation of factual evidence; it is a world view. It is not in itself a fact.

It is even more confusing for students when interpretations of the facts are presented in visual form, as in cases of fossil man. Fossil man is often represented with a hairy animal-like body and animal-like features. This, however, is merely a reconstruction in an artist's mind. It is misrepresentation to present this reconstruction as if it were fact.

In taking the biblical world view, which disagrees diametrically with the evolutionary world view, one should always remember that our disagreement is not with the facts but with the *interpretation* of the facts. Students are often pressured by being told that if they disagree with evolution, they are disagreeing with scientific fact. This is not the case; they are disagreeing with an interpretation of the facts, not the facts themselves. This is a significant distinction.

If We Don't Know

What should we do when we are asked a question to which we do not know the answer? All we have to do is simply admit that we do not know. None of us knows it all. The fact that we do not know the answer to a particular question does not mean there is no answer. It does not weaken our case to admit we do not know. We can be honest because we are still learning.

The Christian also has the privilege of asking God for guidance.

> And if, in the process, any of you does not know how to meet any particular problem he has only to ask God—who gives generously to all men without making them feel guilty—and he may be quite sure that the necessary wisdom will be given him (James 1:5, Phillips).

Also, when we are held up to ridicule for our belief in creation, it is well to remember that ultimately we are responsible to God. We want to please him, not men. We must speak the truth even though it may not be well received.

SUMMARY

Creation and evolution are differing world views. They are philosophies in conflict. It is not a matter of science versus religion; one may be "religious" and hold either world view. It is a matter of one belief system in conflict with another because they come from different starting assumptions. They are different faiths. They are antithetical; if one is true, the other is false. To try to harmonize the two is logically impossible.

Creation is the idea that the natural world is dependent moment by moment on the Creator. Evolution is the idea that nature is autonomous; it is not dependent moment by moment on the Creator. One cannot harmonize these two opposite views. It is a conflict between rebellious man's ideas arising from his desire to be autonomous and independent of the Creator, versus truth which God has revealed.

In order to help fallen man consider his need of a Savior, we noted that creation and the fall are essential to presenting the gospel. This means we need to begin from a framework of a healthy theology of science. A biblical approach gives answers to big questions. Why do we have a universe? Why is there being or mind? Why is the universe capable of being described by scientific laws? As we have discussed, creation *ex nihilo*, as an act of the Creator using pure spiritual power, gives big answers to these big questions.

In our day we are seeing a rise of interest in creation and in a scientific interpretation of data from the creationist point of view. The Bible suggests that in the last days before God's final judgment, creation will be presented on a worldwide basis. There is a prophetic message associated with the rise of interest in creation (Revelation 14:6-7).

Lastly, we presented suggestions for sharing one's faith and for answering questions relating not only to science and the Bible but to presenting the Christian faith in today's culture. Hints were given for handling questions and for presenting truth.

It is my prayer that this book will be helpful to those struggling with the issues of creation and evolution. Although it is not intended to be an exhaustive treatment of the issues, I sincerely hope it will direct people's attention to God, our loving Creator, and to His Word which is His revealed truth.

Chapter 13, Notes

1. Norman L. Geisler, *The Creator in the Courtroom: "Scopes II"* (Milford, Mich.: Mott Media, 1982); Bill Keith, *Scopes II, the Great Debate,* (Shreveport, La.: Huntington House, 1982).

2. Ashley Montagu, ed., *Science and Creationism,* (New York: Oxford University Press, 1984); Niles Eldridge, *The Monkey Business: A Scientist Looks at Creationism* (New York: Washington Square Press, 1982); Philip Kitcher, *Abusing Science: The Case Against Creationism* (Cambridge, Mass.: MIT Press, 1982).

3. Hans Elias, "Three-Dimensional Structure Identified from Single Sections," *Science,* 3 December 1971, 993.

Select Bibliography

Many students and parents have asked me for a list of materials which could help them in their study of creation-evolution issues, especially as related to various classes in schools and universities. Many adults as well would like to be better prepared to intelligently defend and present their faith and convictions. To that end, the following bibliography lists representative materials which in my experience have proved to be helpful.

BOOKS

Andrews, E. H., *God, Science & Evolution*. Welwyn, Herts., England: Evangelical Press, 1980. Good treatment of basic issues.

_____. *Is Evolution Scientific?* Welwyn, Herts., England: Evangelical Press, 1977. Good treatment of basic issues.

Barnes, Thomas G. *Origin and Destiny of the Earth's Magnetic Field*. El Cajon, Calif.: Institute for Creation Research, 1983. Presents evidence for a recent creation.

Beddoe, Everett E. and Frances Sorensen. *Let's Talk About Giants*. Mountain View, Calif.: Pacific Press, 1966. Children.

Bowden, M. *Ape-Men: Fact or Fallacy?* Bromley, Kent, England: Sovereign Publications, 1977. Excellent exposure of "missing links."

Custance, Arthur C. *The Mysterious Matter of Mind*. Grand Rapids: Zondervan Publishing House, 1980.

Dillow, Joseph C. *The Waters Above*. Chicago: Moody Press, 1981. College-level—preflood conditions.

Geisler, Norman L. *The Creator in the Courtroom*. Milford, Mich.: Mott Media, 1982. Report on Arkansas trial.

——————————. *Miracles and Modern Thought*. Grand Rapids: Zondervan Publishing House, 1982. Good discussion refuting objections to biblical supernaturalism.

Gish, Duane T. *Dinosaurs: Those Terrible Lizards*. San Diego: C.L.P. Publishers, 1977. Children.

Hooykaas, R. *Religion and the Rise of Modern Science*. Grand Rapids: Wm. B. Eerdmans Publishing Co., 1972. College level—demonstrates Christian roots of modern science.

McDowell, Josh and Don Stewart. *Reasons Skeptics Should Consider Christianity*. San Bernardino: Here's Life Publishers, 1981. Good summary with answers to typical questions.

Parker, Gary E. *Creation: The Facts of Life*. San Diego: C.L.P. Publishers, 1980. High school level—good list of evidences for creation.

Rehwinkel, Alfred M. *The Flood*. St. Louis: Concordia Publishing House, 1951. High school level—good summary of evidence.

Schaeffer, Francis A. *The God Who Is There*. Downers Grove, Ill.: InterVarsity Press, 1968. College level—basic issues and apologetic base.

Steidl, Paul M. *The Earth, the Stars, and the Bible*. Phillipsburg, N.J.: Presbyterian & Reformed Publishing Co., 1979. Good summary of issues.

Wheeler, Ruth and Harold G. Coffin. *Dinosaurs*. Mountain View, Calif.: Pacific Press, 1978. Children.

Whitcomb, John C. and Donald B. DeYoung. *The Moon: Its Creation, Form and Significance*. Winona Lake, Ind.: BMH Books, 1979. High school—good comparison of various origin theories.

Wilder-Smith, A. E. *Man's Origin, Man's Destiny*. Minneapolis: Bethany Fellowship, 1966. College level— well documented.

Wysong, R. L. *The Creation-Evolution Controversy*. Midland, Mich.: Inquiry Press, 1976. College level—excellent balance, fair; shows what each side says about the facts.

PERIODICALS

Acts & Facts. Institute for Creation Research, 2100 Greenfield Dr., El Cajon, CA 92021. Popular style.

Creation Research Society Quarterly, 2717 Cranbrook Rd., Ann Arbor, MI 48104. For scientists, but readable.

Bible-Science Newsletter, 2911 East 42nd Street, Minneapolis, MN 55406. Popular style.

Students for Origins Research, P.O. Box 203, Goleta, CA 93116. College level.

Ex Nihilo, Eric Fellman, P.O. Box 281, Glen Ellyn, IL 60137. Contains popular as well as technical articles.

FILMS

Footprints in Stone; The Great Dinosaur Mystery; The World That Perished. Well documented, popular style. *Origins*. Six part series; good scholarship; college level. Films for Christ Assoc., 2432 W. Peoria Avenue, Suite 1327, Phoenix, AZ 85029.

FILMSTRIPS

Creation Filmstrip Center, Inc., Rt. 1, Haviland, KS 67059. High school level, variety of topics.

The Creation Concern, 9445 S.W. 62nd Drive, Portland, OR 97219. Excellent filmstrip on the Grand Canyon.

MAGAZINE ARTICLES

Ancil, Ralph E. "The Limits of Human Thought and the Creation Model." *Creation Research Society Quarterly* (June 1983): 30-39.

Beckwith, John and Larry Miller. "Behind the Mask of Objective Science." *The Sciences* (November/December 1976): 16-17.

Broad, William J. "Fraud and the Structure of Science." *Science,* 10 April 1981, 137.

Bush, Vannevar. "Science Pauses." *Fortune,* May 1965, 116-67.

Calbreath, Donald F. "The Challenge of Creationism: Another Point of View." *American Laboratory,* November 1980, 9-10.

Davies, P. C. W. "The Tailor-Made Universe." *The Sciences* (May/June 1978): 6-10.

Engel, A. E. J. "Time and the Earth." *American Scientist* (Winter 1969): 459.

Gentry, Robert V. "Cosmology and Earth's Invisible Realm." *Medical Opinion and Review,* October 1967, 65-79. Evidence for sudden creation.

Gould, Stephen Jay. "Evolution's Erratic Pace." *Natural History,* May 1977, 12-14.

Hitching, Francis. "Was Darwin Wrong?" *Life,* April 1982, 48-52.

Holden, Constance. "The Politics of Paleoanthropology." *Science*, 14 August 1981, 737-40.

Hoyle, Sir Fred. "The Big Bang in Astronomy." *New Scientist*, 19 November 1981, 521-27.

Hull, David L., Peter D. Tessner, and Arthur M. Diamond. "Planck's Principle." *Science*, 17 November 1978, 719.

Jastrow, Robert. "Evolution: Selection for Perfection." *Science Digest*, December 1981, 87.

————————. "God's Creation." *Science Digest*, Special, Spring 1980, 66-71.

Kaufmann, William, III. "The Most Feared Astronomer on the Earth: Halton C. Arp." *Science Digest*, July 1981, 76-81, 117-18.

"Letters." *Chemical and Engineering News*, 24 January 1977, 21 March 1977, 25 April 1977. Referring to "Newscripts" by Kenneth M. Reese, 11 October 1976. Must reading about a whale found in dolomite.

Mayr, Ernest. "The Nature of the Darwinian Revolution." *Science*, 2 June 1972, 981-89.

Polanyi, Michael. "Life's Irreducible Structure." *Science*, 21 June 1968, 1308-12.

————————. "Life Transcending Physics and Chemistry." *Chemical and Engineering News*, 21 August 1967, 54-66.

Rensberger, Boyce. "Facing the Past." *Science* 81, October, 41-51.

Wald, George. "The Origin of Life." *Scientific American*, August 1954, 46-49.

Subject Index

Abraham, 93
Absolutes, 33, 35, 111
Academic institutions, 186-87
Academicians, 93
Adam, 187, 198
American Association for the Advancement of Science, 98
Angel, 246
Antarctica, 193
Archaeology, 252
Argument, circular, 84
Arkansas trial, 253
Assumptions, 24-27, 29, 31, 33
Atheists, 164, 263-64
Atmospheric collapse, 208
Automobile analogy, 162-63
Autonomous science, 97. *See also* Science

Babylonians, 254-56
Baptism, John's, 260
Bible
  accuracy of, 99, 122
  as data, 162
  and facts, 251
  and reality, 174-76
  relation to science, 126, 129, 130, 135
Big Bang, 61-62, 99, 144
Biological catastrophe, 220
Biological Sciences Curriculum Study, 189
Black holes, 151
Bonneville Salt Flats, 217
Boyle, 15
Bush, Vannevar, 24

Carbon dating, 233, 237. *See also* Radioactive dating
Catastrophe, 217-18, 220, 221, 222
Catastrophism, 217-23

Cause and effect, 78
Chance and life's origin, 84
Chemistry, physics, and evolution, 28
Children, 104-5
Christ Jesus, 35
Christian schools, 105
Christian students, 97-98, 111
Climate change, 215
Coal and oil, 214
Colleges. *See* Universities
Columbia River 216-17
Continental drift, 195
Conversion, intellectual, 125
Cooling earth, 208
Cosmologists, 46-47
Creation
  absolute, 148
  beautiful, 89, 163-64
  days of, 156, 165-67
  doctrine of, 17, 28, 113, 135-43, 163, 184
  as final message, 245-46
  and gospel, 89-90, 142
  illustrations, 138, 161
  implications of, 20, 88-89, 142, 173
  importance of, 106, 113, 116, 137-38
  interpretation in media, 186
  and miracle, 104, 152, 162
  and new creation, 143
  opposition to, 44, 58, 87, 98
  and philosophy, 17, 89
  as "religion," 59
  research, 191, 192
  science, 71
  scientific? 59, 134-35, 139-40, 161
  uniquely biblical, 137

276